ABINGDON
THEOLOGICAL
COMPANION
TO THE
LECTIONARY

PREACHING
YEAR C

ABINGDON THEOLOGICAL COMPANION TO THE LECTIONARY

PREACHING YEAR C

PAUL SCOTT WILSON
EDITOR

Abingdon Press

Nashville

Library of Congress Cataloging-in-Publication Data

Abingdon theological companion to the lectionary : preaching year C / Paul Scott Wilson, editor.
    p. cm.
  ISBN 978-1-4267-2977-5 (book - pbk. / trade pbk. : alk. paper)
  1. Common lectionary (1992)—Handbooks, manuals, etc. 2. Lectionaries—Handbooks, manuals, etc. 3. Public worship—Handbooks, manuals, etc. I. Wilson, Paul Scott, 1949-
  BV199.L42A25 2012
  251'.6—dc23

                                  2011053023

CONTENTS

SEASON AFTER PENTECOST

SERIES PREFACE

Preaching Sunday after Sunday, month by month, is an amazing privilege, opportunity, and trust. It is also a remarkable challenge. Preachers struggle to speak God's word in a fresh way each week that will nurture and sustain the congregation, and in the process they also need to be nurtured by that same word. The steps of preparing a sermon—studying the biblical texts, praying, researching, and writing—are traditional spiritual exercises of preachers. Preachers' lives today are often so demanding that their spirituality gets shortchanged. They desire to climb to the spiritual mountaintop to proclaim God's word, but they may often feel they get only partway up that mountain each week. Of course the Spirit can make a rich treasure out of even a small offering, but how much better are preachers served if the resources they use provide them with clear paths and theological guiderails that help them to reach the inspired summits for which they aim.

Welcome to a unique and exciting ecumenical preaching resource, an offering to the church at large for the enrichment of both preachers and their congregations. It provides important tools not found in other lectionary-based resources. Here preachers will find vital help in specific theological areas where sermons commonly fail or falter. These include: focusing on one key thought that arises from the biblical text/s that can give unity to the sermon, discussing a related theological question that congregational members are likely to ask, connecting the particular reading/s to actual pastoral needs in the congregation, identifying practical things people may do in their lives by way of ethical living and social justice, and linking specific texts to the larger gospel story in the sermon for the purpose of fostering faith.

These various theological matters provide particular lenses with which to think about God and human beings in relationship to God. The demands of faith are explored here, and also the help God graciously gives by way of empowerment in meeting those demands. This essential emphasis on grace, too often missing from preaching resources, is built into each of the theological lenses provided here. The effect of these various lenses can be to radically transform and enhance the sermon-making process. It can mean the difference between creating adequate sermons and creating strong sermons that foster growth and nurture congregational life. These lenses also nurture the preacher, daily providing more ways to see and think about God's gracious love and empowerment.

What further sets this resource apart is that in writing for each worship day, top theologians are paired with top teachers of preaching. The theologians are responsible for addressing a key theological question in clear and simple ways, while the homileticians address the other matters; thus each scholar writes half of the total length. Other lectionary resources typically bypass the systematic or constructive theologians of the church in favor of biblical scholars, even though biblical studies these days are generally less interested in matters of theology, the church, and faith than in history. Here theologians share their important voice with good reason. Throughout history they have been concerned with matters of faith and life, and can provide a key bridge between the Bible and the sermon. This project does not supplant but rather supplements biblical commentaries. It assumes that preachers have already engaged in basic exegetical work. In other words, this volume starts where other resources may leave off, and arguably it takes preachers much further along the journey to sermons that meet deep needs of congregations at several interrelated levels: personal, communal, intellectual, spiritual, pastoral, emotional, missional, and ethical, to name a few.

A final distinctive feature of this project is the help it gives in fostering sermon unity. Some preaching resources offer an array of independent offerings each week that can make the sermon process confusing. They stimulate many thoughts and possible directions, but they offer little help in developing one, and the result can be evident in preached sermons. By contrast here, a natural flow connects the components for each Sunday entry: the assigned Bible readings from the lectionary lead to a theme sentence, and the theme sentence leads to each of the other elements. Because this unity and coherence were built into the process, preachers will find that the various elements readily connect with each other. They support a unified focus from the beginning of the preaching task, and they contribute to the final unity of the sermon.

The weekly entries begin with a précis of each of the assigned lectionary readings (Old Testament, Psalm, Epistle, and Gospel). This provides an overview of the lessons and identifies possible links between them. Nearly every book on homiletics worth its salt speaks to the importance of each sermon having one focus—whether a sermon is inductive or deductive, the listener needs to be able to say in a sentence what the sermon is about. An inductive sermon needs to lead somewhere specific, just as a three-point sermon needs to have a single overarching thrust. This kind of clarity requires discipline on the part of the preacher to do more than identify a single topic (like love or justice), and more than just ask a question about the topic (like what is love?), rather a complete sentence is needed that makes a strong claim about the topic (e.g. God loves without end). A **theme sentence** is required, a complete thought with subject, predicate, and object. For preachers who are imagistic thinkers, finding this kind of clear focus each week can be particularly challenging—they might rather compose the sermon, see where it goes, and then figure out what it is about; but by then it might be too late. Yet all preachers can struggle here, and all may benefit from having a clear direction right from the beginning of their weekly sermon labors.

An additional feature maximizes the potential helpfulness of the theme sentence. It focuses on a key action of God in or implied by the biblical text/s, thus God, in one of the persons of the Trinity, is its subject. This helps to ensure that God has a key role in the sermon and points the preacher and the congregation toward the help that God gives in meeting the challenges of postmodern living. The writers here identify an action of God that focuses on grace and empowerment, in order that the sermon may get to good news. In order for the theme sentence to be memorable, it is generally under six or seven words. The theme sentences are based on one or more of the biblical texts for a Sunday, normally the text/s that seem most in line with the liturgical season. No attempt is made here to harmonize all the lessons for a Sunday to make them say the same thing. A brief explanation connects the theme sentence to the details of a particular text/s.

Concerning **the key theological question**, the systematic theologians identify an issue that arises out of the theme sentence and the text/s. Anselm defined theology as "faith seeking understanding," and that applies no less today when there is so much that engenders puzzlement and confusion in our diverse world with its pluralistic cultures. Where helpful, our theologians identify a traditional theological loci or doctrine to which the theme sentence closely relates. For example, eschatology or teaching about the end times tends to dominate in early Advent. These theologians deal with key ideas in ways that the preacher can easily connect to the experience of the congregation—eschatology provides answers to the anxious question, "What's going to happen?" The theologians refer to the biblical text/s, but they do not write a detailed commentary, per se. Instead, they provide a theological reflection that goes beyond what many biblical commentators might say by engaging matters of faith, God's actions, and faithful life.

Local preachers are in the best position to make connections to pastoral needs, so in identifying **a pastoral need** we make a suggestion for preachers to consider. Who might need to hear a sermon on this theme sentence, and why? If a sermon speaks to one person's need, it is likely to speak to many. By contrast, if a sermon speaks to no one's need, it may not need to be preached. By imagining a person in need during the composition of the sermon, and including in the sermon someone in a similar kind of situation, the preacher can be concrete about what pastoral care to offer—what the biblical text says to such a situation. The pastoral need is a felt need, one that a hearer might identify for himself or herself. It is not one that the writer assigns, as when a preacher decides that on Trinity Sunday the people need to know about the Trinity—the felt need may actually be, "How can I know God?"[1]

God's actions towards humanity have implications for our actions towards God and neighbor. The **ethical implications** of a text are identified out of the theme sentence, inviting faithful discipleship and social justice as part of the mission of the congregation. What difference might this sermon make in individual or congregational living? What outcome or behavioral purpose does the preacher imagine this sermon to have in the lives of the hearers? Ethical considerations normally put a burden upon listeners, setting forth tasks they might do, and one danger is that they can have the effect of reverse miracles: they can turn the wine of the good news in the sermon back into water. In such instances the ethical demands become a new law about what must be done on one's own resources. Thus our writers also speak of God's help and empowerment. The ethical implications thus become invitations to new ways of living in the power of the gospel. They can even become expressions of the good news when connected to God in this manner. They are descriptive of the new creation that through the Spirit is already begun in Christ and will be fulfilled at the end of time. They are concrete examples of the kinds of action that individuals and communities might undertake in their specific contexts, yet they are typically more descriptive than prescriptive.

Finally, our writers address **the gospel implications** of the sermon, namely the specific links between a biblical preaching text and the larger Christian story. Some lectionary texts do this themselves, but they are fewer in number than we might think. This process involves looking for images, ideas, or echoes of God's saving action anywhere in the Bible, like the Exodus, and in particular to the central message of good news as it is found in Jesus Christ. The approach is akin to the ancient practice of typology, but in preaching on Jonah, instead of saying, "Jonah is a type of Jesus," a preacher today might say, "The truth that we find in Jonah's rescue after three days in the belly of the whale is the same that we encounter in Jesus Christ, who on the third day rose to set us free from our bondage." This can help remind listeners of the way in which Jonah's story is their own. Other parts of the worship service, like the hymns and prayers, can make clear the fullness of the gospel of God's saving love. Still, there is value in the sermon doing this.

The issue here is being as clear as possible about who is this God in whom we may trust. One can testify to the power of Jesus by preaching a text like Jesus healing the bleeding woman, but one can also stop short and not clarify for the congregation what that has to do with us. How is Jesus any different from a superhero in a comic book? Our basis for affirming that power lies in the resurrection that each Sunday celebrates: it is not the dead Jesus but the living Christ who encounters worshippers. In other words, the gospel implications clarify how a particular biblical text is a panel in a larger quilt, and they show how it links to the bigger pattern through image, idea, or echo. The gospel implications in the sermon itself might lead to a kind of joy or excitement that testifies to the hope God offers and where it is rooted. Since Jesus' life, death, resurrection, ascension, and Second Coming are central, what does this text lead preachers to say about any one of them?

The tools offered in this resource promise strong help for preachers and their congregations. Preachers able to nurture congregations through theologically grounded sermons are likely to be nurtured by that same Word they proclaim. By the same token, congregations hearing such sermons will find their lives transformed in the Spirit.

The theologians and homileticians who have contributed here have worked hard to establish excellence, drawing upon insights from recent scholarship in various disciplines with a view to enriching the theological contribution of sermons for many years to come. This is their volume and their gift to the church in the hope that preachers will consult it each week. I am very grateful to these writers who have brought not only their skill and knowledge to bear on their tasks, but also their patience and good humor in carrying them out. So much of my joy in working on this project has been interactions with them.

Readers may recognize that the various components structuring each entry have their roots in my homiletical theory, for example, *The Four Pages of the Sermon* (Abingdon Press, 1998). There, for purposes of sermon unity, preachers were encouraged to focus on one text, one theme, one doctrine, one need, one image, and one mission. I have treasured the friendship and guidance of editors Robert Ratcliff, Paul Franklyn, and Michael Stephens at Abingdon Press. They recognized the value of developing a theological companion to the lectionary that built upon those instruments with a view to feed the spirituality of the preacher and to deepen sermons. Their editorial work is a ministry that has been enriching to me and essential in bringing these volumes to completion. As always, I am deeply thankful to my wife, Deanna Wilson, for the patience, advice, and nurture she lovingly provides that helps projects such as this in so many ways. To Derek and Katherine Knoke go many thanks for much hard work in setting up the early stages of this project, sending the invitations, and coordinating the initial submissions. I am also grateful to Principals Peter Wyatt and Mark Toulouse of Emmanuel College, and to President Gooch and the Board of Regents of Victoria University in the University of Toronto for the kind support they have given in this endeavor.

PAUL SCOTT WILSON

GENERAL EDITOR

1. Excellent examples of identifying felt needs in relation to theological doctrines may be found in Shirley C. Guthrie, *Christian Doctrine*, revised edition (Louisville:Westminster John Knox Press, 1994), where each doctrinal issue in the table of contents is introduced by a question (e.g. for the Holy Spirit, "What's new?").

First Sunday
of Advent

The Lessons in Précis

Jeremiah 33:14-16. After years of trouble, God will raise a righteous Branch (leader) from David's line and the people will be saved.

Psalm 25:1-10. The psalmist cries out for rescue and forgiveness for his youthful sins and testifies to God's steadfast, reliable love.

1 Thessalonians 3:9-13. Paul gives thanks for the joy he receives from knowing the Thessalonians, and prays that they may be blessed in all ways and be blameless at the coming of the Lord. Note: the troubles that are present in the other texts can be found in verses 6-8.

Luke 21:25-36. Jesus warns his disciples of the terrifying signs that will precede the coming of the Human One. He urges his disciples to watch for signs of his coming, to be alert, and not to allow self-indulgence or worldly worries to keep them off guard.

Theme Sentence

Christ is coming so be ready! The context of all the day's texts is trouble. Amidst that trouble the biblical writers have hope that God will act. The Gospel foretells the decisive act, the coming of Christ. So remain faithful and be ready.

1

A KEY THEOLOGICAL QUESTION

Paying Attention

Advent is the season when we pay close attention to the phrase "from thence he shall come to judge the quick and the dead." These texts draw our attention to the doctrines of the end time (eschatology), sin and salvation, Christology, and end-time Christian living.

The lessons for the day draw a tight link between the coming decisive action of God and the present life of the individual believer and the community of faith. Present hope and joy are generated in light of what God is about to do in spite of current troubles. The coming action of God is not anticipated by the surface of world events, nor is it a logical deduction from historical processes. The coming near of the kingdom of God is not a natural, immanent possibility; only God can and will do it. Joy and hope are the character yield in the life of a community that invests in the promise of the coming of God, despite ominous current conditions. These virtues are nurtured through worship and reading the word in the light of God's promises, not the promises in the light of the world. As with so many of the texts that will be read in the season of Advent, the appropriate posture is sitting on the edge of our seat, looking up and around in watchfulness. People who hope in God look up toward the coming rule of God in the Human One's return.

Leaning and looking forward to the coming of God is not generally a posture of the Church, individually or corporately. The sort of doomsday scenario presented, particularly by Luke's Gospel, is at odds with much of mainline Christianity. The idea of God coming near and shaking down the powers in a cosmic work of rebirth isn't often within the imaginations of what is left of establishment Christianity. Our imaginations are stoked not with eschatological promise or stories of apocalyptic change, but rather with natural probabilities. Church architecture often bespeaks, for example, permanent and settled arrangements; our forward planning for church life may involve one-dimensional models that anticipate our action, not God's. Our church investments in community, government, military, and economy are based on things as they are rather than what they will be. We struggle with these biblical texts both at the level of imaginative comprehensibility and possibly at the level of their threat to our long-term investments in the current status quo. It's hard to be joyful and hopeful about the shaking down of Wall Street or the Pentagon, or "the powers of the heavens" (Luke 21:26, NRSV), when they are the guarantors of current fragile prosperity and safety. Proclamation of these texts can feel more like, "Put your head down—your damnation is drawing near."

Reinhold Niebuhr (1964) divided his treatment of sin into two parts: pride and sensuality. The second of these categories is particularly rich for conversation with our Advent texts. Sensuality is actually the sin of putting our heads down and settling in, chameleon-like, in the world as it is. Among other things, sensuality, says Niebuhr, is "an escape [into unconsciousness] from the tension of life" (237). Our Gospel text, together with other Advent readings (Rom 13:11-14; 1 Pet 4:1-6, Eph 5:15-18), singles out sins of dissipation as particularly alluring when waiting for regime change. When trouble is served in the form of exile, displacement, crises of conscience, or marginalization, the temptation is to sink into sensuality rather than to hold out for what God will do. Debauchery and revelry are anesthetizing schemes, ways of losing our faithful selves and relieving the tension between the not yet and the already by not paying attention, even doping down the attention we can pay. This is a sinful move because it is a form of unbelief and lovelessness. It is distrust in God's promise and denies the neighbor the church's joyful, hopeful witness to a new order that God is already bringing. Cynical and doped-up-sleeping-on-your-feet living does not correspond to the promise of his coming again.

What a joy it is for the church to be instructed by these readings. An apocalyptic wake-up call gets issued on the first Sunday of Advent. It is about to shake things up. For people who pay attention, a positive reordering of the world is hopeful, encouraging the people of God not to settle too soon for too little. To hope for the salvation that the rule of God brings is to live already with more hope and joy in the world. This is the Sunday the preacher might point to the watch tower that holds the church bell as a symbol of the current moment. The preacher needs to be careful not to lessen the tension between the world on the way and the world as it is now. We need to avoid transposing what is obviously a text about the transformation of the public visible cosmos into simply a matter of the heart or into an ethical or political program of our own clever devising. The joy- and hope-generating news is that Christ is coming; that's the riveting, tiptoe event. Reality will undergo a radical renovation. Paying attention, head uplifted, on the lookout, tensive; that's the posture for the community which believes the promise, "Your redemption is near" (Luke 21:28).

A PASTORAL NEED

The texts for the day say, "Christ is coming so be ready," but we may hear that as, "Christmas is coming, so get ready." There is a difference between those statements! The cultural celebration of Christmas can immerse us in life as it is in the present, a fondue of acquisition and anxiety. Advent lifts our eyes to a broader horizon and invites us to hope.

On this day the candle of hope is lit in many of our churches. It is sometimes said that where there is life, there is hope. It may be that the opposite is also true: where there is hope, there is life. Many Christians have been influenced by *Man's Search for Meaning* by Viktor Frankl. Frankl was a psychiatrist practicing in Vienna, Austria, before World War II. As a Jew, he was arrested and sent to a concentration camp. In that dreadful place, he noticed that while there was ample reason for any prisoner to die, those who had a faith which provided a sense of meaning were more likely to survive. These included practicing Jews, believing Christians, and dedicated Communists. These people were more likely to be able to hope. If they lost hope, they would die almost immediately thereafter. Hope may be almost as necessary to life as food and drink.

Any congregation will have individuals with varying pastoral needs. Among all Christians, however, one key need is always having a reason to hope. Our texts point to that hope.

ETHICAL IMPLICATIONS

No one knows the date of Jesus' birth. It is sometimes claimed that the church placed the celebration at December 25 as a counterweight to a pagan celebration, *Dies Natalis Solis Invicti* (birthday of the unconquered sun). According to this theory, church leaders were dismayed by the eating, drinking, and loose sex of that celebration and wanted to give Christians an alternative. Perhaps the pagans won! There remains much of what our Gospel reading calls drinking parties and drunkenness (Luke 21:34) in this season. We may avoid such practices, but what about the third quality warned against in the Gospel reading, namely, anxiety? In this connection, one might contrast the official church year with the year as observed in wider society. In the former, the early days of December are part of Advent. In the latter, it is Christmas. If you doubt this, simply listen to the music played in the shopping malls at this time of year. This implies that the celebration of Advent is at least mildly countercultural.

There is a particular Christian ethical posture fit for the Advent season: a readiness to see the world differently from the way the world sees itself, preparation for God's future rather than our own present, self-discipline rather than self-indulgence. This is more than merely avoiding the obvious sins of the season. It is also leaning forward into God's future. How to do that is worthy of explanation in a sermon.

GOSPEL IMPLICATIONS

It is sometimes possible to hear the gospel, even in shopping malls. Amidst the easy sentimentality of seasonal favorites, you will sometimes hear some of the most profound theology of the Christian faith. Someone will sing, "Word of the Father now in flesh appearing," or "Veiled in flesh the Godhead see," or "O holy child of Bethlehem, descend to us we pray. Cast out our sin and enter in; be born in us today." Few will notice. Stores play such music to put us in a spending mood. But for those with ears to hear, the Good News is there: Christ is coming.

There is an amazing video that can be found at www.youtube.com, "Christmas Food Court Flash Mob, Hallelujah Chorus." The video shows a scene in a crowded food court of an ordinary shopping mall. Shoppers are resting and eating. Then suddenly, an organ breaks into the opening bars of the *Hallelujah Chorus*. A young woman stands, cell phone still to her ear and in a spectacular soprano voice, begins to sing. A young man ceases chatting with his girlfriend and joins his tenor voice. More and more shoppers rise and join the chorus. When you least expect it, in the most ordinary place imaginable, the kingdoms of this world become the kingdom of our God and of his Christ! When you least expect it . . .

Notes

Victor Frankl, *Man's Search for Meaning*, 1959.
Reinhold Niebuhr, *The Nature and Destiny of Man*, vol. 1, 1964.

STEPHEN FARRIS

RICHARD TOPPING

SECOND SUNDAY
OF ADVENT

THE LESSONS IN PRÉCIS

Malachi 3:1-4. Malachi prophesies the coming of a messenger to prepare the way before the Lord. But his coming will be hard to endure, as he will purify Israel as a refiner's fire.

Luke 1:68-79. Zechariah, father of John, praises God who has acted to fulfill the ancient promises to Israel. He prophesies the coming work of John who will go before the "dawn from heaven" (vs. 78).

Philippians 1:3-11. Paul thanks God for the Philippians who have supported him in proclaiming the gospel and now in prison. He prays that their love may overflow so they may be blameless on the day of Christ.

Luke 3:1-6. Luke sets the coming of John in the world context. John preaches a baptism of repentance for the forgiveness of sins in fulfillment of the prophecy of Isaiah 40. Note: this text is a précis of the work of John.

THEME SENTENCE

God sends a messenger to prepare the way of the Lord. Preparation is necessary before the day of the Lord. That preparation will be difficult and demands repentance, but forgiveness will result. John prepared the way for the coming of Jesus, but preparation remains necessary today.

A KEY THEOLOGICAL QUESTION
Putting the Crisis Back into Christmas

On this second Sunday of Advent, we greet John the Baptist, whose preaching provokes a crisis. The teachings of the church that intersect in these passages are the doctrines of God, redemption and the kingdom coming in Christ. The prospect of judgment/salvation is raised at the impending arrival of "God's deep compassion" (Luke 1:78). Repentance and forgiveness signified in ritual baptism are practices that anticipate the "dawn from heaven" (Luke 1:78).

John the Baptist summons up recollections of First Testament prophets. Like Jeremiah (1:4, 11), Hosea (1:1) and Joel (1:1) his prophetic career is kicked off with "God's word came to John." His unusual attire, described in Mark 1:6 and Matt 3:4, reminds the reader of the hairy mantle and leather belt of Elijah (2 Kgs 1:8). His coming again was expected to precede the coming of the Lord and to signal the end of the age (Mal 3:1; 4:5-6). Like other prophetic ministries (Hos 1:1; Jer 1:1; Isa 1:1), the Gospel writer identifies the political and religious powers in place at the time of John's prophetic call to speak the word of the Lord. Readers familiar with biblical calls, the prophetic office, and messages entrusted to prophets by the Lord rightly anticipate disruption, crisis, and conflict with the powers. Ordinarily, God does not requisition the life of the prophet to deliver a status quo, everything-is-just-fine message.

Will Willimon says John the Baptist gets introduced into the story of Christmas to keep it from becoming a Hallmark occasion. In a church where I served, we tried for a number of years to introduce the figure of John the Baptist into the Christmas pageant. His trail traced by a spotlight, he bounded into the church sanctuary yelling, "Repent, repent, for the kingdom of heaven is at hand!" What a contrast to serene, youthful Mary, awkward-adolescent Joseph, cute shepherds, and regal wise men parading into church in costume. Every year this "innovation" was greeted with some chagrin. At first, we toned down our efforts. Eventually, we dropped John from the cast. John the Baptist comes to provoke personal and collective crisis (Mal 3:1-4) at the coming near of God. He is not an "I'm ok, you're ok" prophet. This last of the Old Testament prophets straddles the BCE/CE divide. He signals upheaval just around the corner in the midst of settled political and religious arrangements. In the days of emperors, rulers, and high priestly appointments, the word of the Lord came to John in the wilderness.

If postmoderns are right about the importance of social location, then we ought to take note that John works not the tall-steeple circuit but the outback. He's the kind of preacher who names what is crooked and rough, and so provokes crises. John spends time in prison and is murdered for calling a king to repent (Matt 14:1-12; Luke 9:7-9). If a prophet wants to provide critical commentary on current moral and power arrangements, it may be best to rent space where contact sports and tractor pulls ordinarily take place. John does not come to the established centers of power to deliver his word from the Lord. He gives it where he gets it—in the wilderness. People come to him to hear the word of the Lord. God is about to shake up the current arrangements—mountains and hills made flat, crooked places made straight, rough ways smoothed out. Salvation is announced as leveling, upset, and overturning. The announcement takes place at a distance from the bricks and mortar of concrete society. The act of coming out to the wilderness may in itself render pliable hearers of John's message of repentance.

Crisis as a theological theme in the prophets is not meant to leave us with a reigning sense of catastrophe. Wherever a sense of crisis looms as though judgment and doom were the last and final words, the word is not from the Lord. Karl Barth's early theology, a theology of crisis, has much to teach us here. Crisis, God's "no" to the current arrangements, is always and only the other side of the definitive "yes" God speaks in the Gospel. The "no" to crooked ways, rough arrangements, and mountainous hubris, is for the sake of making the divine "yes" heard. "The divine Yes is the background of the radical crisis which is suspended over the whole of life" (Berkhouwer, 1956, 33).

In the preaching of John the Baptist, crisis is evoked by the coming of salvation. A sense of crisis—economic, military, and political—is a part of life in the Western world these days. The work of the preacher on this second Sunday of Advent will be to direct our attention to the central crisis, the theological crisis, the one generated by the coming near of God. It may be that this Sunday our work is to give people trouble they did not realize they had; but this is trouble worth having. We are not the sort of people who are ready. We're comfortable in ambient arrangements. We are not the sort of people who can by our own provision make ourselves ready. The coming of salvation from outside of us exposes our need. We can only accept the crisis in penitence and sorrow, and receive baptism for the forgiveness of sins. We can only turn toward the covenant-keeping God whose provision, mercy from on high, comes.

A Pastoral Need

Verses in Luke 1:76-79 of the *Benedictus* interconnect the concepts of forgiveness and peace. In many churches the candle of peace is lit this Sunday. But peace remains elusive. There was supposed to be a "peace dividend" after the end of the Cold War in 1991, but as this entry is written two decades later, there are "wars and rumors of wars" all around. What may be the situation of any who read these words cannot be predicted but, failing the parousia, world peace is unlikely. If there is peace within nations, it is unlikely there will be social peace. If there is social peace, there may be little peace in our souls. An old evening hymn prays, "Forgive me, Lord, for thy dear Son/ the ill that I this day have done/ that with the world, myself and thee/ I ere I sleep at peace may be." We long for such peace though we scarcely know how to achieve it. We think peace is something we achieve through negotiations with our enemies. But peace cannot be gained apart from God and apart from that uncomfortably theological word, forgiveness.

Ethical Implications

While Zechariah's song words to the infant John connect peace and forgiveness of sins, the preaching of the adult John adds a third concept, repentance. He proclaimed "a baptism of repentance for the forgiveness of sins" (Luke 3:3, nrsv). "Repentance" sounds like "penance" and "penitence" so we sometimes think it is either a liturgical act we perform to make things better or feeling sorry for our sins. While liturgical acts can heal, and feeling sorry often accompanies repentance, neither gets at its meaning. In Greek, repentance means to "change one's mind," a change not of an opinion but one's whole way of thinking, a change in the fundamental orientation of life. That takes us to the Hebrew verb behind "repent," which means "to turn." If one is driving in the wrong direction, the key is not to feel sorry, nor to engage in a liturgical act, but to turn around. To speak about repentance is to recognize that there are indeed ethical implications to our texts!

But there is a practical difficulty here. There is no such thing as generic repentance. Repentance is always specific, and always has to be worked out in practice. The specific outworking of what repentance means comes immediately *after* our reading, however, in what is read on the following Sunday. One could simply leave the content of repentance for the following Sunday, but many of our listeners will not be back the following week. It may be necessary, therefore, to anticipate in part what may be said again the following week.

GOSPEL IMPLICATIONS

Preaching repentance is like walking a tightrope; it is possible to fall off on either side. One tumble would be not to take seriously God's demand for change, not to realize that the choices we make matter deeply. The other, more common, fall would be to suggest that it is all up to us, that we can please God only by our efforts at moral reform, whether personal or social. That would be to forget the gospel. Long before the adult John cries, "Repent," in the desert, the grace of God is proclaimed over his cradle. John will preach repentance for forgiveness of sins but the knowledge of forgiveness of sins comes only by "God's deep compassion." "The dawn from heaven" is not created by our efforts. Rather it will break upon us. ("It suddenly dawns on us" may be a good summary of Advent hope.) It will "give light to those who are sitting in darkness and in the shadow of death, to guide us on the path of peace" (Luke 1:79). Darkness and the shadow of death are all around us; we cannot find light on our own. We ache for peace but cannot find it unless our feet are guided in its ways. Think of a toddler child, scarcely able to walk. Out of great love, the parent or grandparent holds the child's hands and enables her to walk in safety.

Repentance is always a necessary response to the gospel, not a precondition of the gospel. If we are faithful to our texts we cry, "Repent," but only if we also point to the tender mercy that alone will guide our feet into the longed-for ways of peace.

Notes

G.C. Berkhouwer, *The Triumph of Grace in the Theology of Karl Barth*, 1956.

STEPHEN FARRIS

RICHARD TOPPING

THIRD SUNDAY
OF ADVENT

THE LESSONS IN PRÉCIS

Zephaniah 3:14-20. The prophet summons Israel to praise God. The day will come when the people need fear no disaster, for God is in their midst. The passage concludes with a series of promises from God, who will bring the exiles home.

Isaiah 12:2-6. The prophet anticipates the joy and praise of the people on the promised day of salvation. The grounds for this joy are the mighty deeds that God, who is in the midst of the people, will do.

Philippians 4:4-7. Paul urges the church to rejoice in the Lord. The Lord is near, so we need not worry but can make our needs known to God. God's peace will keep us in Christ Jesus.

Luke 3:7-18. This passage reports the teaching of John. So fervent and strong is his teaching that some think he is the Messiah, but John points to the one greater than he.

THEME SENTENCE

Rejoice and do not worry, for God is near. We can rejoice in God even amidst present troubles because God is present. This certainty takes away anxiety and allows us to pray with confidence. Our hearts and minds can be at peace in Jesus.

A KEY THEOLOGICAL QUESTION
The Joy of Divestment

The third Sunday of Advent, with the pink candle, is traditionally called *Gaudete* Sunday, from the first word in the Latin Mass—rejoice. These texts teach us about the proximity of God, salvation in Christ, eschatological expectation, and the character of the Christian life as one of joy and repentance, repentance and joy. The balance between the already and not yet of salvation in Christ tilts toward the already in these texts. Joy is realized in the lives of those who grasp *and* practice the truth: "the Lord is near" (Phil 4:5).

The mood change from last Sunday's texts to those we now consider is palpable. Both this week and last, we concern ourselves with the appropriate response to the promise and proximity of God. With God just about to keep promises and arrive in our midst, there is crisis. The way it is will be shaken down. With the coming of the God who keeps the covenant, there is joy. God will reorder the world. The Gospel lesson this Sunday gives the response of the crowd, in whom John's preaching provokes a troubled response; "What then should we do?" (Luke 3:10). John provides the application. No one leaves the service wondering about the practical implications of his sermon. No one asked, "What does that have to do with us?" The practical applications John doles out to the gathering involve giving up property and privilege. The coming of salvation means fewer coats for the rank and file and divestment of ill-gotten gain for those tight with the Empire. Repentance in the form of letting go of both possessions and perverse advantage is the fitting response to salvation on the horizon. Paths are made straight and rough places are made smooth, by generosity and justice. What a contrast with the other lections: God is coming, God "will do" (9 times in Zephaniah), the Lord is near and so rejoice, and again, rejoice. Can there be both joy and penitent scaling back at the coming of salvation? Is less more in the light of the dawning of redemption?

The liturgical context this Sunday encourages the reformation principal of allowing scripture to interpret scripture. Paul Ricoeur spoke of bringing different genres of biblical literature into contact with each other and letting the sparks of meaning fly up. What if we thought about the practice of repentance as a joyful affair? What if divestment of property and immoral gain actually frees us up for joy? Divestment—radical giving instead of taking, justice instead of extortion—could be conceived as release from a burden for a new existence conjured up by the dawn of redemption. Interestingly, one church where I served held white gift Sunday on this Sunday—congregants brought wrapped, token gifts of food to church for distribution to food banks. Joy was linked historically to giving away the stuff we usually store for our own consumption.

There would be no need for a prophet like John if what he speaks against was not a powerful temptation. In the tension between the already and the not yet, the temptation is to settle into the current arrangements and work them to our benefit. On this *Gaudete* Sunday a little bit more of the not yet seeps into the life of the community that repents by way of divestment. Our longing, or anxiety, for comfort and security leads to practices of accumulation that both in their means and ends are forgetful of the coming of the Lord. We live in an exhausted, depleted, polluted world, largely rooted in our efforts to accumulate wealth and security for ourselves. We compete for coats and good returns on investments, about which we don't want to ask too many questions.

We might connect John the Baptist's sermon to the visions of John of the Apocalypse. The latter John contrasts Babylon with the New Jerusalem. Toxic Babylon "with its ecological imperialism, violence, unfettered commerce, idolatry and injustice" (Rossing, 212) is the settled arrangement that is forgetful of the coming rule of God. Babylon has become "a home for demons and a lair for every unclean spirit . . . a lair for every unclean and disgusting beast . . . and the merchants of the earth became rich from the power of her loose and extravagant ways" (Rev 18: 2,3). The New Jerusalem, on the other hand, is a city where all is shared, where even those without money get the essentials given to them. The political economy of the world that is on its way is founded in the generosity of God. Borrowing from Isaiah, John of the Apocalypse (Rev 21:1-4) envisions a restored New Jerusalem.

> I'm creating
> a new heaven and a new earth:
> past events won't be remembered;
> they won't come to mind.
> Be glad and rejoice forever
> in what I'm creating,
> because I'm creating Jerusalem as a joy
> and her people as a source of gladness. (Isa 65: 17-18)

Joy is the present dividend paid out by the hope that the nearness of God will be God's palpable, life-giving, and world-transforming presence. Repentance is the practice of those who have settled into the current arrangements but are now turned to the future that is about to get traction in our world. We confess that God will bring God's kingdom. Redemption will be made complete at the coming of the Lord. God will do it. However, we anticipate the world on the way in our generosity and just actions. We point to generosity and justice that will one day be at home in the world by divestment now. The Lord is near. A new world is about to touch down. Joyfully, we relax our grip on foreclosed futures.

A PASTORAL NEED

Is happiness the same as joy? If so, there can be a problem, for many people are profoundly unhappy at this time of year, something made harder to bear by the seasonal expectations of happiness fostered by the culture. For many, it's a not so wonderful life. Consequently, some churches hold a "Blue Christmas" service to acknowledge grief. To such folk, a command to rejoice may seem bitter irony. To the rest of us, the command may merely seem unreasonable. We are happy or we are not. Feelings cannot be commanded or demanded, even by prophets or apostles.

The preacher must note two points. First, there is trouble and sorrow in the background of all our texts. Zephaniah anticipates the appalling judgment of God rendered upon Israel in the exile. Isaiah 12:1, strangely excluded by the lectionary, speaks of the "anger" of God. Philippians is written from a jail cell. John preaches to an occupied and oppressed people. These texts are written by people whose condition resembles more the Blue Christmas congregation than the smiling families in advertisements. A command to rejoice is, after all, necessary only when sorrow is present. Second, happiness and joy certainly overlap, and happiness of any sort is a gift to be treasured. Nevertheless, they may not be the same. Happiness may be a feeling, but joy is an orientation of the person. Joy comes from trust in the good promises of God, repeated so often in our texts and summarized by "The Lord is near." An orientation *can* be commanded. It may be that in God's time, the feeling will follow the orientation.

ETHICAL IMPLICATIONS

John's sermon provides the specific content of the repentance demanded in the readings for last Sunday. It is homiletically harsh. "You children of snakes!" (Luke 3:7). Perhaps some "snakes" have come to observe the religious spectacle, as some of us might watch with amusement the antics of a disreputable evangelist, secure in their/our own special relationship with

God, as children of Abraham. But repentance is never a spectator sport. "You can be replaced!" warns John. But give credit to the snakes. They listen to John's word. "Simplify your life," he says, which is not an easy message in the run-up to Christmas. Some of John's specific words have to do with not going along with the Empire. He warns soldiers and tax collectors not to take advantage of the roles they have within the social system. Repentance has a social as well as an individual element. Those of us who live in Western society may live in the closest contemporary analogy to the Roman Empire and may need a similar warning. To give one example, remembering the gospel even in our purchasing might be a relevant equivalent at this time of year. If getting every gift as cheaply as possible is our only concern, we may be patronizing companies that cheat or shake down the poor as thoroughly as first century tax collectors or soldiers.

Gospel Implications

Good preaching depends on getting the indicative/imperative relationship right. Perhaps we move too early to the imperative, telling people what to do and what not to do, a reason why the word *sermon* has so many negative connotations. We fail to declare the indicative, to announce what our gracious God has done. We cannot simply preach the equivalent of John's word to the crowds, even without harshness, if the demand for repentance does not rest on a promise. To fail to preach the demand or "law" in our Gospel text would be homiletical disobedience. To preach demand without promise, or law without gospel, would be legalism from the pulpit. Fortunately, the promise of God is clear, "The Lord is near." Joy is a primary response to the presence and activity of God in the world. The first message of our texts is not demand but promise. The sting of unhappiness in the season may be the feeling of being alone, like a child wandering from a mother in a grocery store and suddenly awakening to her aloneness. We are not alone; soon we will see this, for God is near! Because of the promise, joy is freed from the tyranny of present circumstances.

Notes

Barbara R. Rossing, *Christianity and Ecology: Seeking the Well Being of Earth and Humans*, 2000.

Stephen Farris

Richard Topping

Fourth Sunday
of Advent

The Lessons in Précis

Micah 5:2-5a. The prophet declares that the one who will rule Israel will come from little Bethlehem. All will live secure, for he is great to the ends of the earth and is the "one of peace" (vs. 5).

Luke 1:46b-55. Mary praises God who has done great things for her and who has acted for Israel, in fulfillment of ancient promises. God acts for the poor and powerless and against the rich and powerful.

Hebrews 10:5-10. Christ ends the sacrifice of animals by doing God's will and offering himself as sacrifice. As a consequence, we are made holy before God.

Luke 1:39-45, (46-55). In obedience to the angel's word, pregnant Mary visits the aged and also pregnant Elizabeth. Elizabeth's baby, John, jumps for joy in the womb to greet the mother of the Lord. Elizabeth declares that Mary and her baby are indeed blessed.

Theme Sentence

God keeps his promises and acts for us. God has promised one who rules righteously and in peace, particularly for the poor and those without strength. Jesus is this ruler, and some have recognized that this is so from the beginning.

A KEY THEOLOGICAL QUESTION
God's Revolutionary Fulfillment

God makes good on historic covenant promises in our lessons. The surprising and reorienting faithfulness, mercy, and grace of God loom large. Incarnation has begun, and it sets two women singing.

Divine faithfulness is rooted in divine election and calling. God purposes from the first pages of the Bible not to be God without a human partner. God creates and seeks fellowship with people because that's the kind of God we have. This divine choosing is an act of overflowing love. God ties up God's own name with the flourishing of the people and the world he has created. While people defect from faithfulness to God, God draws close for the salvation of the world.

The *Magnificat* repeats—seven times—"He has" as it details the reversals God works in the world through the Son Mary bears. The ground for all the covenant-keeping actions of God is singular and named in the last verse: "according to the promises God made . . ." (Luke 1:55, author's trans), God is true to himself, and Mary and Elizabeth are favored. The good-news is that God's faithfulness, while it does not derive from human potential, is for human flourishing. God keeps promises; and Mary, Elizabeth, the lowly, the hungry, his servant Israel, and the whole world are blessed. Divine glory and human good are not set in a zero-sum game. God moves to keep faith, to keep his *Word*, and people are blessed. When God is most true to his Word, we are most fully alive.

As the creed tells the story, we are between "conceived by the Holy Spirit" and "born of the Virgin Mary." This is about the time of the year that explanations of the meaning of incarnation will be offered in various newspapers and periodicals. One year I read something like "the virginal conception and birth of Jesus is the birth of human potential." While there is a wide range of interpretation concerning the incarnation, it is certainly not about human potential. The story of the meeting of Elizabeth and Mary focuses on the blessing that accrues to these women because of God's action. Elizabeth's Holy-Spirit-inspired cry of blessing upon Mary is incited not by Mary's potential for motherhood but by God's fulfillment and favor in the child Mary bears. Mary's being is "lit up in a new way by the Kingdom of God which has come near . . . in Jesus," and she is blessed "in spite of all appearances to the contrary" (Barth, 1958, 189).

Mary's *Magnificat* blesses God for the victory won over the proud, powerful, and rich for the sake of the lowly and the hungry. It is a song that celebrates favor and faithfulness from God in the form of revolutionary upset. It is too easy to hear this song from Mary as an innocuous soprano solo. And yet the words she sings are revolutionary. Like Union boss Mrs. Flynn from an Updike (1996) novel: "When she calls up the world that might be, instead of the one that is, you can hardly keep from crying at the beauty of it. Women equal, not slaves in the kitchen, and children not having to go to the mills at eight or nine, and there being no workers and owners, because the workers are the owners . . ." (99).

Remember: Mary is related to John the Baptist, that wild, wilderness preacher of repentance. Her praise and rejoicing to God draws on the revolutionary repertoire of Israel. This is more like Janis Joplin protest at Woodstock than it is Charlotte Church sweetness at the Metropolitan Opera. It is John Mellencamp cranking out: "When the walls come tumbling, tumbling, down . . ."

God moves, and the powerful—the guardians of the way it's "got to be," the people on top who have organized reality in their favor to the detriment of others—come under siege. God keeps covenant, and a teenager testifies to wealth redistribution for the sake of the hungry. Redemption draws nigh, and the bullies and power-brokers of this world come under threat. Mary reads the Emancipation Proclamation, and slave holders are brought down and slaves freed for flourishing in the new reality which, like creation, comes *ex nihilo* by the Word of God. It isn't about her power and potential to enact salvation. It is God's power and not human potential; but Mary is caught up in it. The fact that she sings means that God does exalt the lowly; that this has happened to her means that the overturning of inhumane order has begun. She is lowly, and she is lifted up. She is hungry, and God has filled her with good news. Mary is exalted by the Word of God become flesh, which she is the first to serve.

Theologically speaking, the *Magnificat* focuses unwaveringly on the action of God. People sing, but it is God's topsy-turvy work of redemption that is both the content and the inspiration of the song. God is faithful for the sake of the world. The world and its arrangements are acted upon, and Mary sings. God moves toward us in a child, Jesus, and reorders the world. As Canadian songwriter Bruce Cockburn sings, "redemption rips through the surface of time in the cry of a tiny babe." That's a good, bad news prospect. It all depends on whether we're willing to inhabit a gospel renovated world.

A Pastoral Need

Many churches light a candle of love on the fourth Sunday of Advent. It makes liturgical sense to do so on the climactic Sunday of the season, because love is "the greatest of these" (1 Cor 13:13). But this emphasis is scarcely drawn from the day's texts that never mention the word love. With these texts, it might be better to light the candle of justice or the candle of God's sovereignty. It would be no bad thing to identify as the chief pastoral need for the day something that is not pressing upon our particular listeners. We preachers and most of our listeners are, by world standards at least, comfortable. But there are millions starving, and the "proud in the imagination of their hearts" (Luke 1:51, KJV) run rough-shod over the humble of the world. Our needs look small in comparison. Perhaps it is a good thing on this Sunday before Christmas, when our chief dietary concern may be to avoid gaining weight, to remember the poor and the hungry. We ought to be able to lift our eyes above our own needs, at least today.

It may be, however, that the candle of love still sheds a worthy light on the texts of the day. It is easy to let preaching about justice become a self-righteous harangue. The people to whom we preach may not be desperately poor by world standards, but some of them are still hurting. It does no honor to the one who would not break a bruised reed to add to their hurt. Justice without love may even be cruel and is not the work of Christ. That work, from incarnation, through cross and resurrection is "love to the loveless shown that they might lovely be" (Crossman). Besides, they will hear better if justice is preached with love.

Ethical Implications

It is easy to see ethical implications in Mary's song. The difficulty is finding the courage and the right words to say what needs to be said. Tony Campolo has the courage. He is reported to have said to a staid Christian audience: "First, while you were sleeping last night, 30,000 kids died of starvation or diseases related to malnutrition. Second, most of you don't give a shit. What's worse is that you're more upset with the fact that I said shit than the fact that 30,000 kids died last night" (Campolo).

That is a powerful critique of our conventional priorities, which may never be so strong or even warped as at Christmas, Mary's *Magnificat* is an even more devastating critique: "[God] has scattered those with arrogant thoughts and proud inclinations. He has pulled the powerful down from their thrones and lifted up the lowly. He has filled the hungry with good things and sent the rich away empty-handed" (Luke 1:51-53).

All this is neither to make light of starvation nor to advocate the use of barnyard language in our sermons. (Though the Bethlehem story reminds us Jesus was born in a barnyard. Christmas cards are far too tidy.) In more standard English, Campolo's phrase denotes caring (or rather, not caring) about something. Here is the good news: God does care . . . profoundly. Our job is to line up our lives with the God who cares. A preacher with the right kind of relationship with the congregation might be able to say that in Campolo-style language. The rest of us will probably need to find more conventional ways to say the same

Gospel Implications

Here is the really good news how much God cares: God actually gives a . . . son. God does that to put right with Godself even those with such skewed priorities that they worry more about crude language than about starvation. That too is the Christmas story. We hear the challenge of the texts as those who have been put right with God by the willing sacrifice of Jesus. "Live with others, especially the poor, as if that were really true," might be another way of stating the ethical challenge of the text. But the challenge must not drown out the good news.

Here is another thought, gained from disastrous experience: it is easy to forget that Mary's song is a hymn. It is not a dissertation on the importance of social justice and still less is it a harangue. It is an outburst of joy in a gracious, active God who simply will not let injustice reign forever. There is an old gospel song, "How can I keep from singing?" Mary cannot, and perhaps, if we speak aright of the goodness of God, neither will our listeners.

Notes

Karl Barth, *Church Dogmatics*, IV.2, 1958.

Tony Campolo, www.christianitytoday.com/ct/2003/january/1.32.html

Bruce Cockburn, "Cry of a Tiny Babe," 1990.

Samuel Crossman, "My Song Is Love Unknown," 1664.

John Mellencamp, "Crumblin' Down," 1983.

John Updike, *In the Beauty of the Lilies*, 1996.

Stephen Farris

Richard Topping

CHRISTMAS EVE/DAY, THIRD PROPER

THE LESSONS IN PRÉCIS

The time of watching and longing is finally ended. Where there had been only darkness and discouragement, God has burst into our lives, bringing light and new life.

> *Isaiah 52:7-10.* After much waiting, God has come at last, restoring life where there had been destruction. How beautiful are the feet of those who bring this good news.

> *Psalm 98.* The psalmist announces that "every corner of the earth has seen our God's salvation" (vs. 3). All people and even all creation are invited to shout in joy at what has been seen.

> *Hebrews 1:1-4 (5-12).* God chose to partially unfold his great plan to our fathers and mothers in the faith. But now in our own time God has chosen to reveal the fullness of life in Jesus.

> *John 1:1-14.* "In the beginning was the Word" (vs. 1). When the time was right, the eternal God entered our world in Jesus, bringing light where there had been darkness.

THEME SENTENCE

God is the light shining in our darkness. The scriptures proclaim God doing wonders in a world that longs for deliverance. Jesus as the light of the world is especially welcome in these days near the winter solstice. In the spirit of Isaiah's text, preachers name the grace of light present in their communities.

A Key Theological Question

Silent Night! Holy Night!
Son of God love's pure Light
Radiant beams from thy Holy Face
With the dawn of redeeming grace
Jesus, Lord at thy birth
Jesus, Lord at thy birth

Sometime today the church will sing these words, the third verse of "Silent Night," as the congregation gathers to worship and celebrate the mystery of the Holy Night. At Christmas we feast on word and sacrament and find ourselves inundated by images and symbols of God's unfathomable Mercy made Flesh: starlight dawning, manger glowing, mother/father loving, shepherds adoring, radiant angel choruses singing.

If our hearts are so disposed, we may find ourselves truly caught up in the Light of a Love beyond our power to comprehend, beyond our power to speak of. Such an extravagant love is forever beyond our capacity to contain. Yet, once again, we experience on this Christmas Day the "dawn of redeeming grace" that comes to claim each and every one of us. This universal, redeeming Love is the mystery we bow before in awe and wonder—the mystery of a God who comes to us in the most "un-god-like" of ways. Sundered of all the marks of power, achievement, fame, and prestige, the light of the world, "the reflection of the God's glory and exact imprint of God's very being" (Heb 1:3, NRSV) is enthroned on a manger bed, born into a hostile world that has no room for him. The paradox that will mark Jesus' future life, ministry and fate confronts us in this lowly birth, revealing more than we might comfortably take in.

Who is this God? The reading from Isaiah exults in a restoring and redeeming God, whose return in power is "right before their eyes" (52:8). This in-breaking God does more than assuage grief and discomfort; God delivers Israel in a blissful act of return and reunion. Ruins ring with the joy of this deliverance; the re-creating power of this God cannot be contained. There is healing in this restoration; joy jumps from these verses.

The reading from Hebrews manifests the dawn of right relationship in the God who speaks "to us through a Son" (1:2); a Son whom God appointed "heir of everything and created the world through him" (1:2). God's Word-made-Son accomplishes through his obedience the messianic restoration that is possible only through the humility of a manger and the surrender to the cross.

The reading from the beginning of John's Gospel invites us to draw near to the God of Life who has first drawn near to us. Creating all things through the gift of the all-powerful Word, the Living God is revealed as the indwelling God: source and completion of right relationships in all creation. To know and love this God is to accept the invitation to live in the light revealed in "the glory like that of a father's only son, full of grace and truth" (1:14).

The message is quite clear. This God is serious about us. Our healing and our full restoration into right relationship is the good news, the light to the nations, and the power revealed to become children of God. Conforming our lives to the demands of relationship lived in the Light of the Living God will stretch us into the limits of our selfishness and distorted understandings. In the ruins of hurt and broken relationships, this God longs to meet us and teach us the ways of restoration, healing, and ultimately joy. If we truly allow the mystery of this Holy Night to enlighten us, we cannot but radically alter our vision of the God revealed in Jesus. The glory of a God who does not act like one enters our world of darkness and lights the way for those so disposed to find the Love at the center of all reality. Our tradition teaches us that more often than not, it is the poor, the dispossessed, and the marginalized who are particularly disposed to be open to the Mystery of Love. Dietrich Bonhoeffer (1996) writes, "For the mighty ones, for the great ones of this world, there are two places where their courage deserts them, which they fear in the depths of their souls, which they dodge and avoid: the manger and the cross of Jesus Christ" (p. 16).

Approaching the crèche as a child of this God surely makes demands upon us. If we have the courage to really enter into the mystery of the Holy Night, we will recognize that just like Mary and Joseph, the angels, and the shepherds, we each have an indispensible part to play in the unfolding of the Christmas proclamation. Adoration must find its proper fulfillment in relationships of loving care and forgiveness. Power and prestige must bend the knee and acknowledge any misappropriation of gifts entrusted for the common good. Our mutual need to be found and restored by the God of Life must be celebrated with humble joy.

A Pastoral Need

Some people experience seasonal affective disorder (SAD) in these dark and cold winter months. They feel a special kind of depression brought on by lack of exposure to bright light. This lack of light seems to affect the brain in ways that are not entirely clear to researchers. Darkness brings on a feeling of gloom for these individuals; bright light helps restore a sense of well being.

Although the precise number of people who suffer from SAD is not known, an Internet search at this writing shows that there are over 75,000 sites that discuss or sell the bright, therapeutic lights designed to bring relief to those who suffer from this disorder.

Those who struggle with mood disorders in the winter months might remind us that it is no accident the church, situated mostly as it was in the northern hemisphere, chose late December as the date to celebrate Christmas. The pagans of the fourth century knew the importance of light and darkness in the rhythm of their lives. Rather than try to suppress something so deeply ingrained in people's spirits, the church wisely adapted the pagan's practice of lighting candles and bonfires to dispel the darkness. As a church we began to celebrate the birth of Christ as the light of the world. We Christians also know that we need the light of Christ to dispel our darkness. Some in our congregations may be struggling with economic hardships or chemical dependency. Perhaps some are experiencing the darkness of broken relationships. Perhaps most are doing well enough, but are still aware that some light in their lives would be very refreshing right now.

These Christmas scriptures announce the light of Christ who has come to dispel the darkness. The true light is again coming into our world!

ETHICAL IMPLICATIONS

When Christ entered our world as light, he commissioned us to spread his light everywhere. However, too much darkness still prevails. Television news broadcasts are filled with darkness. We hear about the darkness of terrorism, physical violence, dishonest financial practices, poverty, and on and on. In addition to that darkness out there in the world, we know darkness in our own souls. Christ is the light, but he calls us to continue bringing his light to those who still wander in darkness. How are we to carry out that mission?

The Chinese have an ancient saying, "It is better to light one candle than to curse the darkness." Politicians and community organizers have repeated this aphorism ever since the first person in China uttered those famous words. But in the 1940s James Keller, a Catholic priest, made the saying the motto of the Christophers, an organization still going strong. The Christophers have the mission of encouraging people to realize they have the ability to make the world a better place. We Christians have the choice of living our own version of SAD, or the choice of being missionaries who carry the light of Christ to others.

Isaiah tells us how beautiful are the feet of those who run with this light. Those same television news programs that report so much darkness are also more frequently including an uplifting story, usually at the end of the broadcast, that describes persons who make a difference. A child might organize a fund-raising program for children in Haiti. A mother of a soldier might gather folks to collect and send gifts to men and women serving in distant conflicts. More than one story describes an individual who donated a kidney to a stranger. Folks are carrying the light all around us. How might Christ be calling us to shed a bit of light in our own corner of the world?

Gospel Implications

Our Christmas sermon might warn folks about the temptation to grab the light out of Jesus' hand and sprint away from Bethlehem as we try to dispel all the darkness in the world. Although Jesus calls each of us to be the light of the world, ultimately, it is his light that shines through our actions. Any light we may extend to others has first been a light that we have received from Christ. When I was a very young preacher, I struggled to find just the right phrase or the perfect image that would make people outstanding believers. It has taken many years of ministry to gradually realize my call is to let Christ use my words so that he can be the light shining in the darkness of those who seek him.

Dietrich Bonhoeffer was certainly right in observing that the great ones of this world fear the manger and the cross of Jesus Christ. But for the little ones, for the ones who know where real life and light can be found, both the manger and the cross are wonderful events that help us realize once again how blessed we are to celebrate this great light of Christ.

Notes

Dietrich Bonhoeffer as quoted in *Dietrich Bonhoeffer, The Mystery of the Holy Night*, ed. by Manfred Weber, trans. by Peter Heinegg, 1996.

Daniel E. Harris

Colleen Mary Mallon

First Sunday after Christmas Day

The Lessons in Précis

1 Samuel 2:18-20, 26. Samuel, like the boy Jesus in today's Gospel, remained in the temple as his parents returned home. Unlike Mary and Joseph, Samuel's parents had agreed to allow their son to remain in temple service. Like Jesus, young Samuel grew in the estimation of God and people.

Psalm 148. The psalmist calls all creation, including young men and women along with the old, to praise the Lord.

Colossians 3:12-17. Paul encourages his listeners to put on Christ and live with one another in peace. Related to the first reading and the Gospel, he asks us to teach and admonish one another in the spirit of true wisdom.

Luke 2:41-52. The boy Jesus remains behind in the temple as his parents return home. When they return to find him conversing with the wise teachers, Jesus expresses surprise that his parents would not realize he needed to be in his Father's house.

Theme Sentence

God calls us from our youth to seek true wisdom. Young Samuel and young Jesus were drawn to God's house to grow in true wisdom. Today's youth have access to more information than the ancients ever dreamed would exist. But true wisdom is far more than a world of information.

A Key Theological Question

The readings for the Sunday after Christmas are rich with theological themes that come close to home and invite reflection on the extraordinary Mystery that approaches us in our ordinary lives. Today's readings affirm that growing in wisdom is a family affair. We are invited to notice how Holy Wisdom walks with us, disguised and undistinguished in routine. The Gospel, in particular, calls us to note how a predictable journey can end up turning us upside down. Paying attention to the Holy Family's sojourn to Jerusalem, we might also recognize several other journeys being mapped in this story.

There is the pilgrimage of a devout family. We are told that this was a familiar journey for Mary, Joseph, and Jesus. They traveled every Passover to Jerusalem. Yet no matter how familiar, think of all the preparations needed to make such a trip: food, resources for shelter, care of the household left behind. Consider as well the mindset of pilgrims: anticipation for what lies ahead, sharing the journey with fellow pilgrims, awareness of the dangers that might intervene. And still, religious devotion and trust animate these faithful hearts, casting out fear. The pilgrim journey is itself an act of worship, a setting of the heart towards the things of God in the most embodied manner a human being can manifest. "I myself will go to the house of the Lord and offer praise for all God's blessings and tender mercies." Pilgrims move outside their comfort zone. They willingly encounter contingencies and unexpected delays. And their reward is often the companionship of fellow sojourners and the shared confidence that the journey is as important as the destination.

There is the terrified journey/search of forlorn parents for a missing child. How could Mary and Joseph have anticipated the drama of a missing son and all the terror such an experience unleashes in the hearts of parents? How did a predictable Passover journey come to this? What did that moment do to them? How did they manage the emotional upheaval of those three days, searching throughout Jerusalem? What did they say to each other? How did they comfort each other? When the mystery of loss interrupts a couple's life, sustaining their own relationship can be one of the greatest challenges. Grief, guilt, and fear are heavy burdens and pose a difficult life lesson: how do we carry pain together? What depths of generosity does such suffering carve out of two human hearts, made one by marriage? Truly, this suffering foreshadows a future Passover in Jerusalem; a journey that will culminate in the complete disaster of the cross and, yes, three days of waiting. In Luke's Gospel, Jerusalem is not simply one destination among others. This is the destination for Jesus; all journeys lead ultimately to his fate in Jerusalem. And it is in Jerusalem that grief-stricken disciples will birth a faith and initiate apostolic journeys of mission and gospel transformation.

There is the coming-of-age journey of the adolescent Jesus. This story is the only place in the Bible where we are given some hint of the boy Jesus and his maturing years. Consider for a moment the momentous changes that every child endures on the road into maturity. This is a difficult and awesome human journey, trekking the heights of uncovered powers, affections, and potentials, as well as the depths of doubt, uncertainty, and insecurity. The journey into self-knowledge is a trying wisdom-journey; it demands courage to face our light and our darkness, our gifts and our limits. Imitating the faith and values caught from our parents cannot fully sustain us. Something more beckons our attention and response: the mystery of our own life, its true purpose and potentials. Theologically, we understand this dawning consciousness as an invitation into the "journey of the soul." Few among us comprehend the approach of wisdom in our adolescent years. However, if we take time to consider the journey faith has mapped in our lives, we might recognize love's persistent approach. We can only imagine how the persistent approach of love within the heart of the child Jesus shaped his self-understanding. Today, with Mary and Joseph, we witness love's claim on the young Jesus of Nazareth. He knows and loves a Father beyond all telling. In the embrace of that love, he entrusts himself to a father and a mother who still have much to teach him.

There is the pilgrims' return journey. There are moments that simply change everything. There are journeys that transform us, whether it is the transition into young adulthood or the ongoing transformation that is the journey of parenting. How do we welcome each other back home after these moments of transformation? Change can be disruptive of relationships, threatening our sense of security and belonging to each other. Yet we know that growth requires that we risk change and humbly embrace the ups and the downs of our learning curves . . . together. In the domestic church that is the Christian family, learning how to create "home" together is an ongoing work-in-progress. Here it is that the Christian (parent and child alike) learns the primacy of love and its wise and holy expression in relationships marked by mutual respect, care, tenderness, and fidelity.

May wisdom truly find a home in our families, today and always.

A PASTORAL NEED

Many people today need to know that they are taking the right path, that they are following the right wisdom. Plato has Socrates reminding us that the unexamined life is not worth living. It is less clear who first rejoined that the unlived life is not worth examining. On this Sunday when we hear about young Samuel and young Jesus growing in wisdom as they explore their faith, it is interesting to recall that Socrates uttered those famous words when he was on trial partly for encouraging youth to question and challenge the accepted norms and discover for themselves the wise way to live. Young people gain the confidence to begin their journey toward wisdom from families that support and nourish them toward maturity. But the moment of maturity nearly always means that a young person must leave the family to fully become the man or woman he or she was created to be. Some fear to begin this journey; others refuse ever to end the journey, preferring to be life-long seekers of wisdom.

Our scriptures invite us today to examine our lives as a journey toward spiritual wisdom. One does not need to be young nor in full-time temple service to be on this journey. God expects each of us to be on the journey according to where we are in life. This Sunday's sermon might invite folks to ask whether they have settled into a comfortable routine of day-to-day living in which they seldom think about their relationship with God or God's people outside of Sunday worship.

ETHICAL IMPLICATIONS

A few days after I was ordained a priest in the Roman Catholic Church, I was walking with my brother through his neighborhood. He introduced me to one of his neighbors, telling him that I had just been ordained. Thirty-seven years later I can still hear the neighbor saying, "Well, I hope you stick to preaching about God and stay out of politics." Was he saying that religion is about church matters, spiritual things? We preachers dare not delve into the real world that must run by its own worldly wisdom? We ministers can appreciate the need to separate partisan political discourse from authentic Gospel preaching, but that does not mean that the Christian life is separate from "real life."

As Jesus spoke with the wisdom teachers in the temple, did they perhaps discuss the Roman occupation of Jerusalem? While we can only speculate on what Jesus spoke about, the scriptures are filled with stories about the Jewish people dealing with the political realities of their world. They certainly believed that God was very much invested in this aspect

of their "real lives." The gospel demands that we do not compartmental-
ize our lives into matters of faith and matters of everyday life. Jesus calls
us to live our relationship with him at work, at school, at home, and
everywhere else. As we mature, we come to the difficult moment when
it is time to leave our parents and our families to set out on our journey
as adults. In the same way, believers need to step out of the familiar setting of the Sunday worship community to live their faith in the public
square. The difference of course, is that we can return to the faith community each Sunday so that we may find the encouragement we need to
continue living our faith openly in all aspects of our lives.

GOSPEL IMPLICATIONS

"Meanwhile, the boy Samuel kept growing up and was more and more
liked by both the LORD and the people" (1 Sam 2:26).

"Jesus matured in wisdom and years, and in favor with God and with
people" (Luke 2:52).

The Lectionary editors hope that we preachers will notice these final
verses of the first reading and the Gospel. God's word speaks of growth
pleasing to both God and the community. But how does this growth take
place? Where is the power to grow? Many years ago as a college student,
I assisted in a Bible study class for children from a very poor area of Chi-
cago. Our team agreed that the lesson for next week would be the mystery
of God producing growth in the disciple. The team leader decided that we
would give each child a little cup of dirt and one wheat seed. We would
show them how to plant the seed, water it, and then step back. Their
work was finished; they did not have the power to give the growth. They
could only enjoy the wonder. As we planned this lesson, I suddenly had a
frightening thought. "What happens if some of the seeds fail to grow?" I
asked. The team leader said confidently, "Don't worry about that. I took
the seeds to a friend who is an atomic scientist. He treated them with
radiation. Those seeds will grow!" Who produces the growth in us as we
mature in wisdom in the sight of God and the community? While we
teachers told the children that God produces the growth in us; we kept a
bit of control just in case God did not come through. Jesus, who entrusted
himself to Mary and Joseph and his heavenly Father, asks that we entrust
our whole selves to a God who will produce a mature faith in us.

DANIEL E. HARRIS

COLLEEN MARY MALLON

EPIPHANY OF THE LORD

THE LESSONS IN PRÉCIS

A new era has dawned for God's people, who have waited for deliverance. The one promised long ago to God's chosen people is revealed today as the savior for all peoples and nations.

> *Isaiah 60:1-6.* Isaiah calls to mind the days of chaos before creation when darkness covered the earth. But God called for light, and the world burst into creation. This passage suggests a new creation for God's land when all nations will see the glory of God's people.

> *Psalm 72:1-7, 10-14.* This psalm is a hymn in honor of Solomon, asking that the Lord bless him with all wisdom. Foreign kings and nations will pay him tribute.

> *Ephesians 3:1-12.* Paul reflects on his call to bring the good news of the savior to the Gentiles. The Spirit reveals this plan that has been hidden in times past but is now made known to all.

> *Matthew 2:1-12.* The magi evade crafty Herod and are led by the star to the house where they find the child with his parents. They offer gifts of gold, frankincense, and myrrh.

THEME SENTENCE

God reveals the long-hidden mystery of salvation to all peoples and nations. Most people enjoy a good secret; God seems to be no exception. From eternity God has planned to embrace our world as savior. But only now is the mystery made known for all peoples. This Sunday, Christians celebrate the news that the secret is out!

31

A KEY THEOLOGICAL QUESTION

What does it mean to have an "epiphany"? There are some interesting answers that come from a Google search of that very question: from the sublime ("manifestation of God" and "a divine showing") to the not so sublime ("I had an epiphany about my ex-husband. He's an idiot!"). Be that as it may, the notion that there are things we presently do not know that eventually become known to us stretches across the spectrum of human experience. In that sense, the experience of coming into awareness and the dawning of a realization are the conditions for contemplating the Feast of the Epiphany. Moreover, if the dynamics of disclosure are our door into "epiphany," we cannot go too far without exploring our theological understandings of both the experience of epiphany and the Mystery revealed or disclosed in the experience.

The experience of epiphany. If today's readings truly celebrate "the mystery hidden for ages in God who created all things" (Eph 3:9, NRSV), then we must ponder the theological significance associated with the process by which this mystery is "made known." Today we feast on rich and diverse images: God's glory dawning in darkness (Isa 60:3), a king whose righteousness showers a tired and thirsty earth as rain (Ps 72: 6), Gentiles invited into "the immeasurable riches of Christ" (Eph 3:8), and foreigners who discover under a dawning star the child born to be a different kind of king (Matt 2:2). The experience of epiphany discloses. In the "aha" moments of epiphany new knowledge comes to light. Reality is seen and known as "what truly is," and even the potential upheaval of new insight can be most welcomed. "Then you will see and be radiant; your heart will tremble and open wide "(Isa 60:5). But there is more. True epiphanies are transformative experiences. Not limited to mere intellectual conversion or insight, epiphanies of the divine Mystery embrace and empower us at the core of our being. These are redemptive moments when, touched by grace, we recognize that God does indeed deliver the needy and poor who have no helper (Ps 72:12). The fullness of the redemptive disclosure emanates beyond the individual, impacting whole communities. To borrow from Asian Christian interreligious dialogue, this is true "enlightenment," where new knowledge is transformative of new beings and new relationships.

The Mystery disclosed. Reflecting on the dynamics of disclosure requires that we honor the tensive interplay between that which is revealed and that which remains concealed. This is a critical theological point, because at the heart of the Christian understanding of revelation is the Mystery of the Living God, a God revealed and concealed in our scriptures, our creeds and sacraments . . . indeed, in the very midst of all that is. This limit (concealment) that we place on revelation is on our side of the equation, so to speak. The God revealed in Jesus the Christ is Limitless Love who is always and at all times immediately present to all. Our capacity, however, to take in and recognize this "immediacy of presence" is limited by our sinfulness and also our human finitude. All knowledge and experience of God, therefore, is "mediated." The Dominican theologian Edward Schillebeeckx (1981) spoke of this as "mediated immediacy."

> What we have here is not an intersubjective relationship between two persons—but a mutual relationship between a finite person and his absolute origin, the infinite God. . . Between God and our awareness of God looms the insuperable barrier of the historical, human and natural world of creation, the constitutive symbol of the real presence of God for us. The fact that in this case an unmistakable mediation produces immediacy, instead of destroying it, is connected with the absolute or divine manner of the real presence of God: he makes himself directly and creatively present in the medium, that is, in ourselves, our neighbours, the world and history. (p. 809)

Even in concealment, God is with us, God is turned toward us, and God is for us. This is the fullness of the mystery that we celebrate today. Even as light dawns and God is revealed, the One revealed remains forever Mystery, forever Other, and forever beyond our capacity to name and to comprehend. Theologically, it is never the case that we have the most adequate words for God. Rather, we aspire to speak of God in the *least inadequate* manner.

Today, God discloses the divine intention for communion with all of creation. We are told by Paul that this is the mystery that belongs to the church in a profound manner: "God's purpose is now to show the rulers and powers in the heavens the many different varieties of his wisdom through the church " (Eph 3:10). As a church we must apprentice ourselves to the dynamism of disclosure. Treasuring the Light that claims us, we humbly acknowledge the impossible reach of our own grasping. *We will never exhaust the mystery of God revealed in Christ.* Epiphany is more than a feast; it is a way of being a pilgrim people entrusted with a divine gift for the life of the world.

A PASTORAL NEED

"The Lord has a plan to bring good out of this tragedy." When news reporters interview the parents of a child who has died in a senseless act of violence, the grieving mother or father will sometimes say that God has some mysterious plan in all of this. When good people suddenly face confusing and inexplicable difficulties in their everyday lives, they tell us, "God is in control. God has a plan to bring forth good from this situation." On the one hand it is refreshing to see such faith and confidence when good people suddenly face their share in the cross. But one might wonder if there is not also an attempt to keep some level of control by saying, "God knows what God is doing; we must simply trust. Someday we will understand the reason why such terrible things happen. God always brings good out of evil." Case closed. All is normal once again, life goes on.

Is it really honest to explain God's ways with such certitude? Once God has been squeezed into our version of salvation history, is there any mystery left to be revealed to the nations? The Epiphany not only celebrates the good news being revealed to all peoples, but it also celebrates that some aspects of our God are not revealed. Can we embrace the mystery, or do we demand control? Our preaching is less about explaining God and much more about helping believers encounter a loving God who is with us every moment of life.

ETHICAL IMPLICATIONS

A television documentary on homelessness featured a brief but moving few seconds that I vividly recall many years later. A man who lived on the streets stood in the doorway of an abandoned building in a large city. He looked at the camera and said, "I cannot figure out why we people are here in the world. I would give anything to the person who could tell me the reason we are here." I still feel myself wanting to shout back to the television, "Ask me! I know. I can tell you why we are here." We believers have been let in on a great revelation that others long to hear and believe. Perhaps they were not raised in stable, believing families; perhaps they once believed but lost faith. Whatever the reason, we are entrusted with a great Mystery that must not be taken to our private corner of the world to enjoy all by ourselves.

The Epiphany is not buried in the past. It is far more than a story about three wise seekers who one day visited the Holy Family. We do not simply look back to that great event and recall it each year the way we might gather in the community cemetery on Memorial Day to praise the heroism of days long gone. The Epiphany is about here and now. God continues to reveal God's life in our hearts and asks that we share the secret to all those in our daily lives.

For most of us, the challenge is to live our faith openly enough that others will see that Christ has made a difference to us. Recall the famous insight of Saint Francis who told his followers to preach always, and to use words if necessary. The three magi recognized the hand of God in an ordinary, Jewish family living in temporary housing. What might modern seekers see as they look at the way we live our faith?

Gospel Implications

Epiphany is about the manifestation of God in Christ and of Christ to the whole world. The first disciples carried on or continued the Epiphany by witnessing to the Christ they personally knew through his preaching and miracles. Some shared his day-to-day life. But all spoke less about what other believers ought to do and much more about the Christ they knew personally. Contemporary preachers are also witnesses to the Christ they know personally. This raises anxiety in many new preachers. When I have encouraged seminary students to tell us about the God they know personally, they usually respond, "I don't ever want my preaching to be about me." Good for them for not wanting to be an obstacle to the Word.

And yet, can we really preach Christ if we do not let others in on the great revelation we have received? In our second reading, Paul reflects on the ministry of preaching by observing, "God gave his grace to me, the least of all God's people, to preach the good news about the immeasurable riches of Christ to the Gentiles" (Eph 3:8). It is hardly surprising that Paul's preaching was permeated with personal witness. He would remember the old days when he poured so much energy into trying to suppress the young church. But God had other plans for Paul. We preachers are called to let our people know what God has done in our lives so that the mystery will live on.

Notes

Edward Schillebeeckx, *Christ: The Experience of Jesus as Lord*, 1981.

Daniel E. Harris

Colleen Mary Mallon

BAPTISM OF THE LORD (FIRST SUNDAY AFTER THE EPIPHANY) [1]

THE LESSONS IN PRÉCIS

Throughout Epiphany we continue to mark the manifestation to the world of God in Jesus Christ, in whom God rejoices.

> *Isaiah 43:1-7.* God brings the people back from Babylonian exile in the trappings of a new exodus. God promises to be with the people as they pass through fire and water because the people are precious in God's eyes.

> *Psalm 29.* The heavenly court cries out praise to the one God to whom all honor is due. God's might echoes through the thunder of the storm.

> *Acts 8:14-17.* As the young church grows, God's love extends even to the people of Samaria. Peter and John go there and lay hands on the people, who receive the Holy Spirit.

> *Luke 3:15-17, 21-22.* After Jesus was baptized and at prayer, the Holy Spirit descended on him and a voice from heaven proclaimed him to be the beloved son.

THEME SENTENCE

God Sends the Spirit to enliven the church. The scriptures for this Feast of the Baptism of the Lord show God embracing our human world in amazing ways. God brings the chosen people out of Babylonian exile in what is clearly meant to be a new exodus; the Holy Spirit descends on new believers in Samaria; and the Holy Spirit descends on Jesus, solemnly declared the beloved Son of God.

36

A KEY THEOLOGICAL QUESTION

"When you pass through the waters, I will be with you; when through the rivers, they won't sweep over you. When you walk through the fire, you won't be scorched and flame won't burn you" (Isa 43:2).

Could the prophet Isaiah make the God of Israel's intention anymore explicit? *I will be with you*—through trials, tribulations, suffering, and struggle—*I am with you*. I will restore you, I will gather you.

These readings of cycle C for the Feast of the Baptism of the Lord call us to ponder the intention and the action of God in the midst of God's people. God has a plan for all creation, and make no mistake, God *is acting* to bring all "whom I created for my glory" into lasting communion (Isa 43:7). Only God's own Spirit can effect this divine intention. Theologically, then, we want to consider the Holy Spirit, the animating power expressed through all the readings of the Feast.

Pneumatology is not a forte of the Western church, and the thinness of its reflection impacts the theologies as well as the ecumenical relationships between Eastern and Western Christianity. Robust Christologies and ecclesiologies dominate Western Christian systematic theology; however, the Holy Spirit simply has not received the same kind of attention. In contrast, the Eastern Churches make pneumatology foundational to their ecclesial self-understandings. Roman Catholic theologian Yves Congar understood this difficulty quite well and lamented the poverty of Western theology in the area of pneumatology. In Congar's (1986) reflection on the significance of the Baptism of the Lord, we glimpse how pneumatology deepens Christological reflection. We can affirm heartily Congar's maxim: "No Christology without pneumatology and no pneumatology without Christology" (introduction).

Specifically, when Western theologians locate the Incarnation as the beginning of Christ's mission on earth, they inadvertently reduce the significance of his baptism in the Jordan, making it "no more than a manifestation pointing . . . to the truth of Christian baptism" (Congar, p. 87). What happens to the richness of our reflection when we relocate the inauguration of Christ's mission at his baptism? Yes, it is the Spirit who makes the Word flesh in the womb of Mary, but it is only at the waters of the Jordan that others publicly recognize Jesus as One filled with the Spirit. This public baptismal anointing is a new declaration of his sonship because in it he becomes *Son-for-us*.

A new communication or mission was initiated in the event of his baptism, when he was declared the Messiah, the one on whom the Spirit rests, who will act through the Spirit and who, once he has become the glorified Lord, will give the Spirit. If he was consecrated at the time of his baptism to carry out his prophetic ministry, then he was able to pour out the Spirit when he was 'exalted at the right hand of God' (Acts 2:33) (Congar, 1997, 16.)

In his baptism, Christ is anointed for his prophetic mission. The words and deeds of Jesus from this moment forward reveal his unique sharing in the Spirit of God. From his baptism, through his public ministry, to his death and resurrection, the messianic actions of Christ witness to his nature as Son of God. In his death and resurrection the saving revelation of his identity is complete. As glorified Lord, he is the Son who does not simply possess the Spirit; he gives the Spirit.

Three events in the life of Christ hold special meaning for our understanding of how God desires to be with us in all circumstances and at all times: Christ's conception in the womb of Mary, his baptism in the Jordan, and his resurrection/exaltation. As moments in the economy of salvation, each event manifests Jesus as *Son-of-God-for-us.* The Spirit of God is uniquely present in each of these events, revealing the breadth and depth of God's intention and action to *be with us.* The theophany of Christ's baptism empowers and affirms his saving mission, just as it foreshadows another Spirit-descending, mission-empowering moment. Pentecost will be for the church what this baptism is for Christ. Thus at every Christian baptism we celebrate the power of the Holy Spirit making and revealing the children of God. For it is the work of the Spirit to effect in us the same quality of filial life that is Christ's own; the very same Spirit *is making us sons and daughters of God,* the God who calls us precious, honored, and beloved.

A PASTORAL NEED

Many people today feel alone. Social networking technologies allow people to be connected as never before. When the British monarch has her own Twitter page, it is obvious that we are experiencing a major shift in the way people communicate with one another. And yet, while technology allows multiple conversations with people in many parts of the world, many people still feel alone. Some may wonder if they are far down on God's list of email contacts. A recent study reported by the American Association of Retired People concluded that 43 percent of respondents between the ages of 45 and 49 reported being lonely. People in the study who reported being lonely were likely to avoid social contact, including church attendance. Even if the vast majority of lonely people may not attend church, we may safely assume that many in our congregations likely feel lonely. This Feast of the Baptism of the Lord can be a time for folks to hear that God knows each of them by name. No one is unknown or alone in relationship to God.

Jude Siciliano, the Dominican priest who writes the online *Preachers' Exchange*, tells us there is an old saying in the South that goes, "God has no grandchildren." The saying means that our faith is not handed on the way family heirlooms or family stories are handed on from one generation to the next. Although we honor our ancestors in the faith from Adam and Eve, through Abraham, Moses, and the apostles, our faith is not handed down from them. God has no grandchildren; God has only children. The Lord entered our lives directly through our baptism. Our parents and godparents certainly want to see us have the gift of faith they have received, but they cannot give that gift; it is from the Lord.

ETHICAL IMPLICATIONS

The comedy team of Bob and Ray created a variety of interviews with "average persons on the street." In one of their routines, they mentioned that radio listeners have an endless fascination with the opinions of the person on the street. They added wryly that they were not sure why anyone should really *care* about the opinions of the average person on the street. But so many people do care. Call-in programs still permeate talk radio. As this article is written, the Nielson Company reports there are over 161 million blogs on the Internet (www.blogpulse.com). A great many people long to be heard, and many others are obviously willing to listen. Radio programs and Internet blogs are very safe places to be in touch with the ideas of others because they put no real demands on listeners to interact. The listeners can be passive.

Since we are church, we need to be in communication with others on a much more interpersonal level. However, once someone has been burned in a relationship, they may well fear ever to be vulnerable again. This fear of rejection can cause wounded people to avoid the risks of establishing deep, personal relationships. This fear may even lead to eventual isolation. If someone stops risking rejection, they cannot be hurt ever again; neither can they be fully alive.

To all those who fear the risk of loving another, God shouts out through Isaiah, "Don't fear, I am with you" (Isa 43:5). A fellow preacher once confessed that after he had delivered a powerful message about the gospel, he sat for a moment of silent prayer and asked, "Do I really believe what I just told the congregation?" Perhaps our preaching this week might offer an opportunity to share with the congregation our own journey of allowing the Lord to assure us that we are never alone.

Gospel Implications

At his baptism, Jesus heard his heavenly Father say, "You are my Son, whom I dearly love; in you I find happiness" (Luke 3:22). These words must have continued to strengthen Jesus throughout his years of challenging ministry. Most of us tend to invest ourselves more deeply in our ministry when we know that others appreciate our efforts. Jesus went forth from his baptism bolstered by that heavenly pronouncement. He spent the next three years telling others about the Father who spoke those important words. He opened eyes and ears so that others could see and hear the one he had experienced at his baptism. We preachers continue that mission.

In today's psalm we ask, "Let the LORD give strength to his people! Let the LORD bless his people with peace!" (Ps 29:11). This prayer reminds us that God gives us what we need to live our own discipleship as well as offer this good news to others in our preaching. This week, as we pour over our concordances and favorite hermeneutical resources in preparation to preach, let us allow the tone of confidence from these scriptures to sink in so that we may echo them in what we say to our people.

Notes

Yves Congar, *I Believe in the Holy Spirit*, 1997.
Yves Congar, *The Word and the Spirit*, 1986.

Daniel E. Harris

Colleen Mary Mallon

SECOND SUNDAY
AFTER THE EPIPHANY [2]

THE LESSONS IN PRÉCIS

The plan of God for God's people gradually unfolds in a marvelous way as Jesus begins his public ministry with a wondrous sign: water is changed into fine wine.

> *Isaiah 62:1-5.* Isaiah invites the listener to imagine the joy and hope that fills the hearts of a young couple on their wedding day. This is the joyful spirit that describes a forgiving God who once again takes a wayward Israel as a beloved bride.

> *Psalm 36:5-10.* This psalm in praise of God's steadfast love provides a fitting response to Isaiah's message that God takes his people in marriage.

> *1 Corinthians 12:1-11.* Paul reminds the Corinthians that the one Spirit of God has given many gifts to individuals but that all the gifts are for the good of the community.

> *John 2:1-11.* Jesus turns water into wine at the wedding in Cana. The waiters and the chief steward are no doubt astonished, but the disciples see this first wonder as a sign that the kingdom is in their midst; and they believe.

THEME SENTENCE

God reveals to all nations what was once hidden. Isaiah tells us that just as spouses publicly declare their once hidden love in a joyful wedding ceremony, so God takes the chosen people in a covenant. It is at a marriage celebration that Jesus publicly shows God's wonder by turning ordinary water into very fine wine.

A KEY THEOLOGICAL QUESTION

What is it that we celebrate at a wedding feast? I remember the day my sister got married in the mission church at Santa Clara University. She had met her husband-to-be in that very church at the "10 a.m. community" two years earlier. I remember, too, the phone call I got after that first meeting. There was something different about this guy. Two years later we gathered in the place where it all started to celebrate what a single chance meeting had blossomed into—a love willing to risk "forever, together."

It is no surprise that when theologians try to speak adequately (or more truly, *least inadequately*) about the gift of faith, they often point to the human experience of the marriage covenant. There are few examples in human life of entrusting that come close to the leap of faith a couple makes together when they commit to a lifelong love without the certainty of knowing who they or their partner will become in the years ahead. The sacred unfolding of relationship happens to rhythms a couple can only partially anticipate. The mystery of "us" seeded in the early years of knowing and growing in union, with time and fidelity, comes to fruition as a *third reality*, a transcendent gift that is so much more than a conjugation of "you and me." Robert Bly's poem "The Third Body" captures something of this emergent "us." The poet deftly limns a contemplative moment between a man and a woman. We see a couple sitting together, and we witness the simple gesture of one handing a book to the other, Bly focuses us on their faithful shared presence and invites us to testify with the poet to what we have seen: these two manifest in their togetherness a "third body," an entity realized by their uniquely obedient and loving attending to their union.

> A man and a woman sit near each other;
> As they breathe they feed someone we do not know,
> Someone we know of, whom we have never seen.

We touch on the reality of this "third body" when we consciously come to awareness of what the absence of the other would do to the worlds of meaning we have created together. Death interrupts the mystery of "us," reminding all that the beauty and goodness we know in our most intimate relationships is a foretaste of a heavenly wedding banquet where "He will wipe away every tear from their eyes. Death will be no more" (Rev 21:4).

Today's readings use the imagery of a wedding feast to tell us some-thing of the steadfast love of God. There is an "us" created at baptism that binds us to the God of Jesus in an irrevocable way. God will not undo this covenantal love. Only we are capable of that. When we know and celebrate the love of God animating our being, we are ready to be a gift to others. We are initiated into the larger "us," readied by the Spirit to be church. Covenantal love is always about bringing the best wine to the table. As our God is, so we are invited to become. Alive in the Spirit, we can respond to the call into Christian community with generous and gracious hearts. Yet, we have all been tempted otherwise. Whether stalled by laziness, gripped by jealousy, or simply moving too fast to be careful with others, we all know moments when we have arrived at the table with less than steadfast love for our neighbor and our God. Today we are encouraged to come to the feast, desiring hearts transformed by cov-enantal love so that "as the bridegroom rejoices over the bride, so shall your God rejoice over you" (Isa 62:5, NRSV).

A PASTORAL NEED

In the horrors of the concentration camps pious Jews and other prisoners must have asked, "Is God still with us?" When a young child is killed in the crossfire of a gang dispute, the family certainly must wonder, "Is God still with us?" And perhaps when you and I have a very difficult day, we may ask this same question. We need to know that our God is with us; that our God cares about us.

Several creative authors have written science fiction novels in which humans discover that we and our world exist within a complex computer program. Our creators have developed this program that has evolved far beyond their original design. As I listened to one of these authors spin his intriguing plot on a radio talk show, I found myself yelling, "Yes, but your problem stems from starting with your own world and then fabricating a god! What about the Bible, in which God is revealed as a loving creator?" But after I chided the author for being so shortsighted, it occurred to me that perhaps he and others have not heard the genu-ine story of our creation from preachers who are called to carry on the Epiphany message.

The folks who faithfully attend church and hear our preaching cer-tainly have heard the message that we have a loving creator. They have heard that God has taken each of us in the same way that a husband and wife vow their fidelity to one another. But perhaps we have not preached the mission that believers have to continue the Epiphany message outside the church walls.

ETHICAL IMPLICATIONS

The prophet Isaiah tells us today, "With the joy of a bridegroom because of his bride, so your God will rejoice because of you" (Isa 62:5). Do we really believe that? I am sure if we asked our congregations if they believe these words of the prophet, most everyone would nod their affirmation. However, if we asked them, "What is it like for you to have God as your spouse?" we might get a few blank looks. What is it like for you and me, the preachers, to have God as our spouse? The section above dealing with the Key Theological Question explores the mystery involved in our relationship with God. It is mysterious that our God chooses to speak of his love for us in terms of the marriage bond. It also helps us to understand why our relationship with God can sometimes seem like the moments of conflict that all healthy marriages must deal with. Spouses need to learn how to disagree but never to give up on one another.

In his book *Living Faith*, former President Jimmy Carter speaks about how he and Roslyn are both strong-willed and do not like to admit they are wrong. One evening, after a rather strong argument, Mr. Carter went to his woodworking shop and cut a piece of walnut about the size of a blank check. He carved these words into it, "Each evening forever this is good for an apology or forgiveness, as you desire." He said that so far he has been able to honor that pledge each time his wife presented it to him.

If we are going to take to heart God's word that God sees us as a spouse, how might our image of God need to change? How might our prayer change?

GOSPEL IMPLICATIONS

The Epiphany celebrates that what was once hidden is now brought out into the open. Jaws must have dropped at the wedding feast when Jesus turned water into wine—the kind that was suitable to be served for the opening wedding toast. It is significant that Jesus did not produce wine that was just good enough. This is not the wine we buy for the office gift exchange. This is the wine we buy when our most cherished friends are coming to dinner. God does all things well. The implication, of course, is that God in Christ through the resurrection and gift of the Spirit has turned the water of our own lives into rich wine that gives glory to God.

Our psalm for today declares, "Your righteousness is like the strongest mountains; your justice is like the deepest sea. LORD, you save both humans and animals" (Ps 36:6). Have you ever walked among the mighty mountains? Creation is such a powerful glimpse into the love God has for us. Nearly every summer evening, I take time to admire the sunset. I often pray, "Very nice work, God. You did well on that one." Whether it is fine wine, or mighty mountains and sunsets, or a spouse's tender love, God has lavished sacramental moments on us to let us know how deeply he cherishes each of us. We are always loved.

Notes

Robert Bly, "The Third Body" in *Eating the Honey of Words,* HarperCollins Publishers, Inc., 1999.

Jimmy Carter, *Living Faith*, 1998. Accessed via audio file on: being.publicradio.org.

Daniel E. Harris

Colleen Mary Mallon

THIRD SUNDAY
AFTER THE EPIPHANY [3]

THE LESSONS IN PRÉCIS
The lessons invite us to rejoice in God's word, fulfilled in Jesus the Christ.

Nehemiah 8:1-3, 5-6, 8-10. Ezra the priest/scribe presides at a solemn service of the word that lasts from early morning until midday. He adds words of interpretation so that those gathered can understand the word. The leaders of the service urge the faithful to depart in a spirit of celebration.

Psalm 19. Verses 7 and 8 of the psalm announce joy in hearing God's word as they proclaim the perfection of God's law and its salutary effects on the faithful. They echo today's Gospel and the word from Nehemiah.

1 Corinthians 12:12-31a. Paul reminds the Corinthians that they are the very body of Christ. As such they share diverse gifts, but all gifts are to be used to build up the one body. There is no room for dissention.

Luke 4:14-21. As Jesus continues his early public ministry he enters the synagogue and preaches his first public sermon. After reading the prophet Isaiah, Jesus declares that the Spirit is upon him and the scripture is fulfilled in his speaking.

THEME SENTENCE
God's word has power. God's word had the power to enthrall Ezra's people all morning long. Jesus began his preaching ministry by proclaiming that this word, treasured through the centuries, is at last fulfilled in him.

A Key Theological Question

Theologically, today's readings point towards the unrelenting, divine initiative to gather all people into living, faith-filled friendship. The unfolding of particular friendship with all creation took a specific historical embodiment with the Mosaic covenant and the gift of the Law. Recall even further the sacred promises made to Abraham for descendants and land. Remember, too, that these covenantal gifts were indissolvably bound to Abraham and his descendants becoming a blessing to all people. The scholar Paula Fredriksen emphasizes this point. The apparent "exclusivity" of the Abrahamic covenant is really a divine ploy to manifest the sacred desire to bring all people into covenant relationship. Ultimately, all covenant election is fueled by *missio Dei*, the living God's own outpouring of life and love on all.

The law, too, is a manifestation of this divine outpouring of life and love. God's word has power. From exodus to exile this gift governed the relationship of Israel to the God of Abraham, Isaac, and Jacob, bestowing identity and a recognizable form of life that gave witness to the nations of the reality of YHWH. Tender and terrible, as Israel's prophets' witness, the gift of God's holy law became the one magnificent thread of life-giving relationship that sustained an uprooted people. With the fall of the temple in Jerusalem and the Babylonian exile, there was no reason to believe that this ancient people could survive the powerful forces of cultural assimilation. This people should have been swallowed up by the reigning cultures of Babylon and, then, Persia.

But God acted once again for Israel, and today's first reading tells us how the law, newly received, moves the people to their depths. God's word has power. Ezra, the priest who interprets and proclaims the ways of God to the people, understands the power that is being unleashed once again. The life-bestowing law of God instructs the soul and gladdens the heart, just as it did in David's time. Exiles and sojourners are once again transformed into a holy people.

The Spirit that stirs the hearts of Ezra's people is the same Spirit that sets upon Jesus, making him the new translator and proclaimer of God's desire for God's people. Fulfilled in their hearing, the people are both amazed and incredulous. The seed of a believing people is planted, but this will take time; for who could seriously believe that the son of Joseph has been both anointed and sent as the prophet Isaiah foretold?

The seed planted, the word of God made flesh among us, bears its ultimate fruit on the wood of the cross. Raised to a transformed existence on the third day, Jesus the Christ manifested this Easter reality in the very being of those disciples who came to believe that such a transformation had indeed taken hold of them. Resurrection faith, the gift and task of receiving the good news of salvation into our own existence is the ongoing unfolding of the Spirit's claim on us. We become what we proclaim, a gospel people, a holy temple, the very body of Christ.

Paul's words to the Corinthians illuminate the Christian belief that this living body of Christ is no mere metaphor. We belong to each other because we belong to Christ, and we manifest our belonging to Christ in and through our belonging to each other. In and through this body, we participate in the *missio Dei*. We are indissolubly bound to each other as God's promise revealed to all, even as we await the fullness: all creation anticipating the revelation of the daughters and sons of God. As members of his body, we are given to the world as Christ is given: salt, leaven, light, healing, instruction, nurture. Like the people gathered around Ezra, shaken to their core at the reading of the law, the revelation of our own identity in the body of Christ should shake awake our consciousness. We are called to respond and cooperate with the Spirit that continuously anoints and sends us as Christ's own presence to a broken and waiting world.

A PASTORAL NEED

Nehemiah tells us, "They read aloud from the scroll, the Instruction from God, explaining and interpreting it so the people could understand what they heard " (Neh 8:8). Does that job description sound familiar? We preachers continue the tradition of opening the word of God for those who hope to hear from us a word that will enthrall them as the word enthralled those who listened to Ezra all morning. A student of mine from Nigeria told me that in their village the people walk long distances to attend Sunday Eucharist. Priests traditionally talk for forty-five minutes or longer since a large part of the day is given to worship and fellowship. A young priest trained in a United States seminary preached a brief homily at his first Mass in the village. Later, some of the elders explained to him that his preaching was far too brief. He told them he was trained "the correct way" in the United States. Knowing that they would not change his mind, the elders spoke to the priest's mother. That solved the problem.

Does our preaching leave our congregations hungry for more? I would not suggest that we try preaching all morning as Ezra did. Good preaching is less about length and far more about feeding the hungry with a word that nourishes and enlivens. Paul tells us today that the Spirit has entrusted many gifts to the church. This weekend, the scriptures invite preachers to renew their commitment to exercise this gift.

Ethical Implications

Today's psalm offers a fitting prayer for preachers: "Let the words of my mouth and the meditations of my heart be pleasing to you, Lord, my rock and my redeemer" (Ps 19:14). Our three scriptures tell us that Ezra, Paul, and Jesus all fed God's people with a word that both refreshed and challenged. All three preachers believed that the word had the power to enliven God's people.

This section of reflection on the scriptures usually explores the ethical implications that the scriptures have for our congregations. I would suggest instead that we preachers consider the ethical implications for our ministry. I team-taught a course in which my teaching partner asked the class to list the elements of ethical preaching. The students discussed this issue in great depth. Among their many insights, several stand out strongly as an examination of conscience for preachers.

The students said that preachers owe their congregations a well-prepared message. Preachers need to be persons of prayer. We need to preach the whole gospel, not just those sections that appeal to us. We respect the freedom of the listeners to reject the gospel; if they are not free to reject the word, are they free enough to accept the word? We respect other denominations and faiths, never demeaning them from the pulpit. We have a relationship with the assembly; preaching among them and not down to them.

Most of us preachers typically begin our weekly sermon or homily preparation by asking what we will say to our congregation this Sunday. In light of today's scriptures, perhaps we might begin by asking ourselves, "Who has God called me to be for these people today? What is my responsibility toward these faithful who rely on me to break open the word in a way that truly nourishes their spirit?"

GOSPEL IMPLICATIONS

"He began to explain to them, 'Today, this scripture has been fulfilled just as you heard it'" (Luke 4:21). Most historians of preaching usually consider this event to be the first "Christian" sermon. It also offers insight into what takes place when the word of God is preached. Jesus stands before the assembly and announces that he is the fulfillment of the ancient prophecies. The preached word is therefore not simply a message about Christ; it is an encounter with Christ.

This sacramental nature of preaching offers both challenge and consolation for preachers. The challenge is that we faithfully pray and study the scriptures, that we prepare carefully, and that we know our congregations and our culture. The consolation lies in the fact that our human rhetoric is not what changes hearts; it is Christ working in us who changes hearts. All communication theories eventually conclude that if the messenger shapes the message well enough, and if he or she can control the variables just right, the communication will be a success. Preaching is far more mysterious. The word of God fortunately resists our control. While the Spirit nearly always works through our best human efforts, God can do as God wishes. May the word use us well this Sunday.

DANIEL E. HARRIS

COLLEEN MARY MALLON

FOURTH SUNDAY AFTER THE EPIPHANY [4]

THE LESSONS IN PRÉCIS

Jeremiah 1:4-10. Jeremiah receives the word of the Lord appointing him as a prophet to the nations. Though he is young, he has the words of God and is sent to the nations.

Psalm 71:1-6. God is strength and refuge, protection from danger. The psalmist recalls God's protection from birth and declares hope in God the rock.

1 Corinthians 13:1-13. All of the Corinthians' spiritual gifts are held accountable to the one gift of love. We are not to value spiritual gifts that bring about division between people. And we are in error if we think such gifts bring us complete transcendence or transformation in the present. There is future fulfillment to come.

Luke 4:21-30. Jesus reads the scroll of the prophesy of Isaiah on the Sabbath in the Nazareth synagogue and declares that this scripture is now fulfilled. The hearers are amazed, leading Jesus to predict that they will shun him and outsiders will receive him.

THEME SENTENCE

God gathers the nations. Both insiders and outsiders are gathered into life of God. Insiders may eschew the announcement of God's ongoing work of salvation. But God continues to call us to life that is release to the captives and freedom to the oppressed; even as it means inclusion of those whom insiders consider to be outsiders.

A KEY THEOLOGICAL QUESTION
God Gathers the Nations

One of the most worthy challenges precipitated by the gospel is negotiating the tension between God's claims on particular people and God's all-encompassing love for the world. This tension is named in biblical stories about God's pursuit of those who are chosen, and God's inclusion of those whom we thought were *not* chosen (e.g., Melchizedek, Rahab, the Syro-Phonecian woman, the thief on the cross). It is also consistent with the character of the triune God. That is, the God who is three particular persons is at the same time the one God who is all-in-all. While particularities and unity are both true to the Trinity, they are not (as they are in the world) in conflict with one another. Looking to the harmony between the "3" and the "1" in the life of God should therefore deepen our determination to participate as individuals in community with others created in God's image.

What is at stake in negotiating the tension between "individualization" and "participation" (Paul Tillich's terms)? If we emphasize the selective character of God's claims at the expense of God's expansive reach, then we risk perceiving the Kingdom of God as an exclusive club rather than a welcoming community. Such distorted emphasis too often leads to the justification of empires that have oppressed those perceived as peripheral to God's realm. On the other hand, if we emphasize God's love for all at the expense of remembering God's habit of calling distinct people in distinctive ways, then we risk compromising on the truth that God claims each beloved one, and not simply all in general. Such distorted emphasis inevitably breeds a watered-down sense of purpose, a superficial identity that lays aside any hope of ever seeing itself clearly because it has eschewed the face to face (1 Cor 13:12).

Theologians argue that *eros* is a kind of love that is necessarily exclusive, closing itself off to the world for the sake of commitment to lovers, family, or friends. But the love of God celebrated in 1 Corinthians 13—*agape* love—is not *eros*. Rather, it is love that extends always beyond itself to meet and include those beyond one's immediate circle. It feeds lambs; it tends sheep (John 21:17). It fills and enlivens us even as we acknowledge we do not always know, exactly, what God is up to in the world (1 Cor 13:9).

But it would be a mistake to think of *agape* as therefore abstract and diffuse, touching people's lives in random and almost accidental ways. As the psalmist bears witness, God's hold on us is intentional, tenacious, and specific: God, who "cut the cord when I came from my mother's womb," is our continuously delivering "strong refuge" (Ps 71:6, 7). The *agape* love of God always extends outward to the world, but only after it has looked the particular, beloved one directly in the eye and vulnerably asked, "Do you love me?" (John 21:16).

As Christians seek to honor both the reality of God's particular claims and the truth of God's desire to include all, they look to the example of Jesus. Joining Jeremiah in the work of God, Jesus gathers the nations by decentering those who err toward exclusivity and by reaching out to the captives one-by-one. He tells parables in which insiders discover they are outsiders, as outsiders are invited in. He reminds us of the particular character of God's calling by entering the womb of not-just-any woman but of Mary (Luke 1). By calling, specifically, Peter, Andrew, James, and John (Luke 5). By engaging a particular seeker, drawing water from a particular well, at a particular time of day (John 4).

The story of what happens following Jesus' reading of the prophet Isaiah highlights the challenges we face when we risk participating in God's inclusive vision while ministering in our own specific communities. At first, those who hear Jesus reading in his home synagogue in Nazareth rave about him—"so impressed were they by the gracious words flowing from his lips" (Luke 4: 22). As long as they think he is praising them as "one of them," they receive what he has to say. But when Jesus prophesizes that they will come to reject him, hinting that outsiders will ultimately accept his message, they become enraged and try to kill him. The idea that Elijah seeks help from Zarephath and not from an Israeli widow, the fact that Elisha heals Naaman the Syrian and not Israeli lepers, the suggestion Jesus comes to "set free" those who are not members of the community is clearly threatening to the folks back home. Sadly, we learn that the life-sharing work of gathering the nations can be a life-threatening enterprise.

Theologians discuss the gathering of the nations not only in relation to the doctrine of eschatology (reflecting on the coming of the Kingdom of God), but also in relation to ecclesiology. Calvin reminds us that God's church is not only "visible," but also "invisible." There are those who have simply not yet recognized that God has claimed them! Similarly, contemporary Latin American liberation theologian Gustavo Gutiérrez differentiates between the *ekklesia* (the church where worshippers confess Jesus as Lord) and the *koinonia* (the church that extends beyond the ekklesia to wherever the Holy Spirit is at work). The influence of the

Holy Spirit in the koininia reminds us of the provisional character of all our efforts, as members of the ekklesia. In this world, we know only in part (1 Cor 13). It is not simply the case, then, that we spread the good news *to* the nations who are being gathered; we also learn *from* them about who God is, and what God is doing.

A PASTORAL NEED

Growing in the life of the triune God is neither easy nor painless. Growing in the life of God means that we grow alongside all whom God has called: we grow in God with people who are different from ourselves. Growing with others in God points to a need to trust that God's ways are bigger than our ways. For instance, tensions around koinonia and ekklesia exist in many churches. Countless churches exist in the midst of changing neighborhoods and, often, members find ways to reach out to newer neighbors, perhaps offering different education classes that might fold them in. But change is hard. We hear stories about how a congregation tried one or another type of educational or service outreach program and was able to fold in some newcomers. Yet a folding in can be the extent of it, and this is not the same thing as honoring both individualization and participation. Are the newcomers really participating, or are they submitting to the status quo? And are long-time members really participating, or are they merely making a little space in the pew as long as not much else changes? Often this scenario is the case, and nothing much changes. The other scenario, of course, is that newcomers come and begin to ask for different ways of being church; they in themselves are different ways of being church. God fiercely loves us all, not abstractly but with particularity, and the gospel that confronts us is that we are gathered together by God.

ETHICAL IMPLICATIONS

In some circles there is discussion about congregations as centers of conversation, places of public discourse. We may already be accustomed to this. For instance many of us are familiar with contemporary models of large-membership congregations that work to organize every member into a small-group commitment, facilitating a sense of belonging, accountability, and communication. Another old model is that of the small-membership church functioning like small-town meetings, where every person's character is predictable and even though members might be in escalated disagreement with each other, they somehow continue to share a commitment to that group. But these days there are additional factors that weigh in on the quality of our communal conversations: we live increasingly fragmented livelihoods, patterned by the way we get our news in small portions, communicate in snippets of texts and email, and have less disposable time on our hands. However, the ethics of an ecclesiology that sees God's work as gathering the nations demands that we make time to do work together: time to meet, hear, learn, truly listen, negotiate conflict, and find ways to live as one, even as we live in our differences that come from our particularity. It is a good thing to create ways that members and newcomers alike can work side by side, engage in common interests, and learn about each other through common tasks.

Gospel Implications

By biblical accounts the Gentiles are outsiders. Again and again we hear language about God's covenant people and accounts of God reaching beyond the covenant people to include others. Yet Christian history recounts ways in which the followers of Jesus Christ have been grafted into the covenant, extending the language of covenant people to the disciples of Christ. It is important to keep this mixed heritage in mind when considering a gospel implication for this day because we might too easily identify ourselves (Christians) as the insiders, thereby taking on the mantle of dominance, centrality, and superiority. The history of Christianity shows centuries of missionary work in which the church behaved in a superior fashion. And one might take the theme of the day—God gathers the nations—as an injunction to consider ourselves as the center of God's universe and go forth and act on God's behalf. But a gospel implication means that we do not put ourselves at the center, rather we look to what God is doing in our midst. The texts witness to God's ongoing activity to gather together both insiders and outsiders in the work of salvation; it is an unpredictable ecclesiology. It is the ongoing work of the Spirit at the day of Pentecost, gathering everyone into God's unity. No matter what congregation we belong to or what our station in life is, we will do well to see our mixed heritage—outsiders brought in by the grace and mercy of God.

JENNIFER L. LORD
CYNTHIA L. RIGBY

FIFTH SUNDAY
AFTER THE EPIPHANY [5]

THE LESSONS IN PRÉCIS

Isaiah 6:1-8 (9-13). In the midst of a visual, auditory, and tangible epiphany, God's voice summons a messenger. Isaiah responds: send me!

Psalm 138. The psalmist sings thanks and praise to God, bowing to God's holy temple. God answered the call of the psalmist, and the singer extols God's salvation and faithful love.

1 Corinthians 15:1-11. The good news of Christ's death and resurrection is proclaimed. Paul, the self-proclaimed least of the apostles, witnesses to the grace of God. With proclamation comes belief.

Luke 5:1-11. Jesus goes out in a boat and from there teaches the word of God to the crowd gathered on the shore. He then instructs empty-netted fishermen to cast their nets one more time. The nets almost break for the catch of fish. Simon Peter, falling to his knees, begs for mercy. The fishermen are summoned by Jesus to fish for people and leave everything to follow him.

THEME SENTENCE
God sends us to the world. This news of God is not just for one nation or one group of people. It is for the world. And in order to be shared, this news needs messengers. Messengers include visionaries, ordinary workers, and even the least of the apostles.

A KEY THEOLOGICAL QUESTION
God Sends Us to the World

When theologians consider the calling of Christian believers to go out into the world and share God's word, they often reflect on the disparity between the content of the message we are called to bring and the capacities of the messengers charged to speak. How might a human being who is finite deign to speak about the infinite God? How is it that even the most spiritually attuned among us presumes to know even a whit about who God actually is and what God is up to in this world? Sin complicates matters even further. If "finitude" names our limits in relation to God's greatness; "sinfulness" names our inadequacy in the face of God's goodness. How can we possibly go out into the world and speak God's word to others?

Scripture is clear that, regardless of our finitude and sin, we are called to go and to speak. With visionaries like Isaiah, ordinary workers like the disciples, artists like the psalmist, and even reformed sinners like Paul, we are called to bring words that are hard and words that are beautiful, words that undo and words that bring peace. We go out into the world, even with our inadequacies, because the message we bring is not our own. Rather, it is the message of the God who is holy and glorious; the God who comes into our world in Jesus Christ; the God who dies, and rises, and teaches us to fish.

Those called in today's texts are aware of their limits. The psalmist credits God with strengthening his soul that he might "sing about the LORD's ways" (Ps 138:5) Isaiah, Paul, and the disciples confess their sinfulness. "I'm ruined! . . . I'm a man with unclean lips," says Isaiah (6:5), in response to his vision of the Lord. "I don't deserve to be called an apostle," says Paul, "because I harassed God's church" (1 Cor 15:9). "Leave me, Lord, for I'm a sinner!" says Simon Peter, overcome by the power of that overflowing net (Luke 5:8).

The reality of our limitations should affect how we think about ourselves and what we're doing when we go out. Because we are limited, the words we use for God are also limited. Twelfth-century theologian Thomas Aquinas explains that our language for God is not "univocal" (that is, there is not an *exact* relationship between the words we use and what these words reference). But it is also not "equivocal" (that is, it is *not* the case that there is *no* relationship between the words and their referent). Rather, God-language is "analogical." It tells us something *true* about God without ever exhausting the mystery of God.

Being "fishers of people," then, does not mean we go out into the world as univocal "answer givers" who have nothing to gain from others. We speak what we know to be true, bearing witness to the love of Christ, recognizing that there is always more to learn. Our charge is not to invite others to join us as "insiders" who know better, but to share the news that they have already inherited, with us, God's steadfast love and faithfulness (Ps 138). We approach them with honest testimony to our joy-full surprise that God has called *us*, given the reality of our inadequacy and unworthiness. The point of this is not to put ourselves down, but to highlight the fact that God's claim on each person and all people in this world is immediate, inclusive, and without qualification.

Along these lines, Martin Luther exhorts Christians called to go out into the world to think of themselves "as beggars telling other beggars where to find bread." Contemporary theologians following in this spirit in an increasingly pluralistic and global world would commonly add: "and to learn from others where to find bread (or rice!)." One of the most challenging issues facing us in the decades to come is constructing theologies of evangelism that take into account multiple truth claims without compromising on the good news of the gospel.

Historically speaking, we do great damage whenever we forget our limits—and the limits of what we can know about God. But it is also a problem when we invoke our limits as excuses for not going out into the world. Perhaps the most well-known biblical example of this is the story of Moses in Exodus 3-4. Moses is concerned that he won't be able to explain to the Pharaoh who sent him, that he won't be believed, and that he won't communicate well because he stutters.

Today's texts insist that when we are called to go out into the world, there are more important things to focus on than our own inadequacies. Jesus tells Simon Peter not to be afraid because there is important work ahead. "Don't be afraid. From now on, you will be fishing for people" (Luke 5:10). Following Jesus and doing this work will mean a complete life change, but remembering what it is we're doing can help us overcome our fear. Paul understands that the message he brings is "most important" (1 Cor 15:3); he will not hold back from telling the story of Jesus' death, resurrection, and appearances simply because he has a questionable resumé. And Isaiah can see there is an urgent need to bring to the world this glorious, if difficult, message from God. "I'm here, send me!" he says (Isa 6:8). Sometimes being in the right place at the right time is the most important qualification for going out into the world as God's spokesperson. The question is: are we willing to go despite our inadequacies, and are we committed to speaking not on the basis of our credentials, but out of "the grace of God that is with [us]" (1 Cor 15:10)?

A PASTORAL NEED

It is still difficult for many people to think of themselves as ones who are sent to share God's good news with others. They feel they do not have what they need to speak of their faith. Many folks are happy to leave this to the clergy or to the evangelism and outreach committee. Yet the texts witness to God's call to all sorts of people to be messengers, including "the least of these." The problem may be that many of us do not know what this looks like for our contexts. We may have images in our minds of door-to-door visitations, but we can't imagine what we would say. The nuances of the texts and theological insights help us. We do not go forth to share God's good news thinking that we will have, by our own words, the perfect message to deliver; it is a given that we will fall short. We will not have all the answers to people's questions. But the texts give us wonderful accounts of inadequate persons whom God called and used. Through the story of the visionary, the former persecutor, and the fisherman, we see different types of people altering their lives to become messengers. God calls and equips us imperfect, finite human beings to step out and announce God's abundance to the world. We can trust God's use of our particular situations as we bear the good news to others.

ETHICAL IMPLICATION

Not everyone knows what to say about the good news of God, nor is everyone comfortable bringing words to a situation. Some people are more comfortable listening. Some people are more comfortable swinging a hammer for a reroofing project. Some people are more comfortable providing monetary resources to fund a mission and evangelism program. But the texts suggest lives of witness in which followers of Christ are intentional about articulating the good news with others. While it is wise to help people of all ages find their particular gifts, it is also wise to help Christians articulate their faith. A fine way to begin this work is to provide well-guided venues for people to think about their life stories: Who influenced their faith? What moments of doubt and faith stand out in their memories? What helped them through difficult times? Why are they Christian? These are serious questions that serve as examples of questions people live with. Yet such questions are not part of most people's daily dialogue. In order to have more ease with these sorts of topics, we can begin to recount our stories that are a part of the church's faith. As we recount our stories and listen to one another (perhaps with a good study guide or thoughtful leader) we can be strengthened as we hear ways that God's mercy accompanies our human frailty. This can only help us be patient and caring as we listen and converse as messengers of the good news.

GOSPEL IMPLICATIONS

The thematic statement has an imperial ring to it. It can sound like we are the message bearers, according to the older communication style: message, sender, and receiver. We can easily fall into thinking that we always have the right message to deliver, or, simply, a message to deliver without any need to consider how the receiver's response could have bearing on the content or shape of the message. There are proud and self-important messengers who have gladly carried out their duties in this vein. But that is not the same as gospel action. Instead, the thematic statement loses its sense of imperiousness if we hear the emphasis falling on God's action of sending rather than on our perfection as messengers. God chooses to involve us and does involve us: humans are part of God's mission to the world. Gifted with the Spirit, we are summoned, sent, and resourced, all in spite of our being ones who miss the mark and are incapable of knowing the full grandeur and ways of God. We are not to be overly proud, but neither must we cower at the immensity of the call and commission. We are human, but we are called out disciples. And God equips us for the particularity of each possibility to share the good news.

JENNIFER L. LORD

CYNTHIA L. RIGBY

LAST SUNDAY AFTER THE EPIPHANY [TRANSFIGURATION SUNDAY]

THE LESSONS IN PRÉCIS

Exodus 34:29-35. Moses returns from the mountaintop carrying the two tablets of the law, his face shining from his encounter with God. The Israelites and their leaders feared this. From then on Moses veiled his shining face after he finished speaking with the Israelites and unveiled it to return to the presence of God.

Psalm 99. The psalmist sings of the people trembling before God. God, enthroned on the holy mountain, is to be praised and exalted.

2 Corinthians 3:12-4:2. Through Christ we are able to see the glory of God with unveiled faces. This glory is the glory that is our very transformation by the work of the Spirit of God.

Luke 9:28-36 (37-43). The account of the Transfiguration of Jesus is a theophany in which the disciples are enabled to see the divine glory. In this eighth day mystical mountaintop experience, the disciples have a divine vision of God as light, see the quintessential figures in the lawgiver and the prophet, and hear God's voice issuing divine pronouncement.

THEME SENTENCE

God in Christ glorifies us. The Transfiguration moment reveals Jesus in glory. This same glory had marked Moses' face and now by the power of the Holy Spirit shapes our lives in Christ. We are like mirrors, imperfectly reflecting the glory of God but simultaneously by the Spirit being made to show forth the glory of God in our lives.

A KEY THEOLOGICAL QUESTION
God in Christ Glorifies Us.

Traditionally, Christians tend to equate "sin" with "pride." We often explain the "fall" of Adam and Eve, for example, in terms of them being too prideful—so prideful, in fact, that they want to be like God. While we may disagree about how prideful we are, or resist repenting of our pride, most of us concede that pride is a problem. Not so with the sin that is the "inverse" of pride; sin that theologians have at times identified as "self-deprecation." Because thinking about oneself as *lowly* can look an awfully lot like humility, self-deprecation is often misidentified as a spiritual strength. The texts for today challenge this problematic view, suggesting that self-deprecation is a sin because it resists the reality that God in Christ glorifies us.

The Israelites are *afraid* of Moses because, after his encounter with God, his face shines. Sensitive to the reaction of his people, Moses wears a veil over his face whenever he leaves God's presence and relays God's message. When understood as deference to God's holiness, Israel's fear is, in one sense, commendable. In other words, it might at least initially be understood as that strain of fear that is akin to reverence or awe—fear that is appropriate in the face of a God who is utterly holy and is to be extolled (Ps 99).

The problem is that the Israelites' fear is treated as an interminable, acceptable state. In the midst of a biblical canon in which God and God's emissaries consistently instruct recipients of divine messages *not* to be afraid (e.g., Deut 1:21; Luke 1:30), the fact that Moses' veiling, unveiling, re-veiling routine is established as a habitual cycle should be viewed with suspicion.

In 2 Corinthians, Paul forcefully goes after this problem. The minds of the Israelites were "closed," he says, reminding us "the veil is removed" when "someone turns back to the Lord" (3:14, 16). Paul is not, here, criticizing the Israelites for being overly prideful. He is critiquing them, rather, for resisting their own transformation. Moses' face shines (Ex 34:30), and the Spirit transforms us into the image of Christ (2 Cor 3:18). But the Israelites, hiding behind their fear, insist on establishing a physical barrier to the presence of God.

They, of course, are not alone in resisting God's glory, and in this way their own glorification. Peter, John, and James, for example, privy to the transfiguration of Moses, Elijah, and Jesus, first distance themselves by way of sleep (Luke 9:32) and then by making agitated, knee-jerk, plans to build "shrines" (Luke 9:33). The cloud that immediately then overshadows them and the voice that directs their attention back to the glorified Christ seems a clear correction to the disciples' (especially Peter's) self-diminishing behaviors.

Theologians credit Jewish feminist scholar Valerie Saiving (1960) with the first considered reflection on self-deprecation, which she identifies as "feminine sin." She describes self-deprecation as "feminine" not because it is only women who are guilty of it, but because women seem, sociologically speaking, more prone to think *less* highly about themselves than they should than they are to think *too* highly of themselves. Since 1960, when Saiving published "The Human Situation: A Feminine View," feminist theologians have been careful to recognize this "other side of sin" in their reflection on how difficult it is for all of us to participate in the healing work of grace. While it is, of course, problematic to turn away from the transforming work of the Spirit because one believes one has no need of it, it is just as problematic to turn away because one believes one is unworthy. As was true for the Israelites, and again for the disciples, feelings of unworthiness often manifest as fear, and are often maintained by seemingly humble plans to support from a distance—rather than to truly participate in—the most glorious and glorifying moments.

Today, the idea that self-deprecation is a sin has become mainstream in theological circles. No longer is it an issue addressed predominantly by feminist theologians, or a problem touted as particularly "feminine." Jürgen Moltmann (1993), for example, holds that there is widespread resistance to being glorified in Christ due to our own sense of unworthiness. "God has exalted humanity and given us the prospect of lives that are wide and free," he asserts, "but we hang back and let ourselves down . . . God honours us with God's promises, but we do not believe ourselves capable of what is required of us" (pp. 22-23).

Our spiritual work, this Lent, is not only to repent of the sin of pride. It is also to turn away from the sin of self-deprecation. It is, in part, to cast aside our fear of being transformed by the faces of those who themselves are being changed by the divine presence. It is to wake up and bear witness to whatever transfigurations are going on around us, resisting our impulse to feed our unworthiness, under guise of humility, as a way to escape our own glorification. It is to listen to Christ and to enter into life with him instead of thinking up new ways to serve that ensure our safer, peripheral role. It is to submit to being lifted up and glorified by the one into whom we are baptized—the one in whom we die to old selves and rise as selves made, by the Spirit, altogether new.

A PASTORAL NEED

Many of us need to know that change is not only possible but is also happening right now. The Old Testament account presents the glorified prophet Moses, whose face shines from having been in God's presence. And Christ himself shines on the mountaintop; it is God's presence in the midst of Peter and James. According to these accounts we might then think of glory as God's sole purview, or at least shared only with a most holy human like Moses. But the epistle reading lets us know not only that we can see God's glory with unveiled faces but also that we are being transformed by the Holy Spirit into that glory. This can be corrective news for persons who do not think they are worthy of God's glory. So many people need to encounter this corrective news. A surprising number of persons in any gathering have experienced verbal (or physical) abuse. Perhaps they were abused as children—repeatedly dismissed, put down, called names, and overlooked. People are abused as adults as well—by work environment supervisors, by co-workers, even by friends and family. Cultural messages about individual worth come through television programming and advertising. We receive many messages about what we need to buy in order to look better and live better than we do. Many TV programs are merely a constant stream of gossip, critique, and superficial judgment about people. These days we know that even grade schools struggle to educate children and parents against bullying and all forms of disrespect that take a toll on children's sense of self-worth. What marvelous news, then, that we are being changed from glory into glory. We can open that up for the church, for the world: we are worth more than gold in the eyes of God.

ETHICAL IMPLICATIONS

How can we learn about our worth in the eyes of God? How can our worth in the eyes of God build us up where we need affirmation and caution us when we are too full of ourselves? It seems easy to organize conversations and activities around the first question. Sunday school teachers and youth group leaders can focus on including such affirmations as an ongoing part of their curriculum. Preachers can be sure to speak to this aspect of sin when texts like today's texts open up that focus. Bible study groups and book study groups could choose this topical focus. According to the texts we could say that God needs us to shine to the world. We are to shine with God's Word. We are to shine with God's life for all people. We are to shine because the Holy Spirit is at work in us, constantly taking what we are and working the life of Christ in us. We can affirm each other's unique qualities and gifts in these different teaching, learning, and worship contexts. We can pay attention to people's gifts and look for ways that they can take roles in the work of the church, roles that can be affirmed. In all this, through a focus on God's action being the reason for our glory, we can implicitly and explicitly correct any over-assertion of self-generated worth. Implicitly this can be conveyed through a focus on our creation and redemption in God and the Spirit's work through our gifts. Explicitly this can be conveyed when we challenge each other not to be defined by ways of earning money or by keeping track of status in life but by remembering that we are under construction in Christ.

GOSPEL IMPLICATIONS

According to the Gospel reading, shining with the glory of God is linked to the death and resurrection of Christ. Christ, who shines like the sun on the mountain, comes down from the mountain and turns toward Jerusalem. That is an important framework for us to keep in mind as we prepare sermons on this day. Any talk of glory is to be placed in the larger context of God's glorifying work that involves the life, death, and resurrection of Christ for the sake of the world. Our glorification by God is not something we earn by our own merit; it is how God created us. And it is not for our own sake but it is in us so that we can live as Christ lived for the world. God glorifies us for life in Christ in the world.

Notes

Jürgen Moltmann, *Theology of Hope*, 1993.

Valerie Saiving, "The Human Situation: A Feminine View," *The Journal of Religion* (April, 1960_.

JENNIFER L. LORD

CYNTHIA L. RIGBY

Ash Wednesday

The Lessons in Précis

Lent is the beginning of the forty-day count toward Easter. This is a time of change for those preparing to be baptized and for all the baptized, as we live more fully into the baptismal truth that claims us.

> *Matthew 6:1-6, 16-21.* In the middle of the Sermon on the Mount, Jesus speaks to common pious practices: fasting, prayer, and almsgiving. He declares these things should be done to serve God rather than impress others.

> *Joel 2: 1-2, 12-17.* The horn announces the day of the Lord, and the people are called to repent through mourning, weeping, and fasting. The fast is a holy thing; it is an outward action of inward repentance. The people are summoned to stand before God and beg God's mercy.

> *Psalm 51:1-17.* This prayer for forgiveness is truthful about our wrongdoings and calls upon the mercy and abundant love of God.

> *2 Corinthians 5:20b-6:10.* Paul preaches reconciliation, which is a way that the righteousness of God is signified in our lives. We are reconciled to God and to each other because we have been made righteous in Christ.

Theme Sentence

God makes us righteous in Jesus Christ. These texts are the traditional readings that ground the invitation to Lent and its disciplines. The readings nuance each other as they describe our relationship to God and the ways that inward and outward acts of piety can be a part of our return to God. Thanks be to God that we can return! For we need to be made whole, and God in Christ makes us so.

A KEY THEOLOGICAL QUESTION
God makes us righteous in Jesus Christ.

Christian theology teaches that neither our works nor our practices make us righteous, but rather the grace of God as we experience it in and through the event of Jesus Christ. At the same time, we are instructed by God to engage in spiritual practices including almsgiving, prayer, fasting, and penitential mourning. What is the purpose of these practices, if our righteousness is indeed found in Christ, and not in ourselves by way of the faithful things we do?

In Joel 2:12, the implication is that those being exhorted to return to the Lord with all their hearts have been unfaithful to the Lord. They are experiencing a drought, and a related lack of food and water. These conditions are associated, according to the writer, with the coming day of the Lord—the day, in fact, of the Lord's judgment (2:1). The good news offered is that it is not too late; there is still time to repent and be reconciled to the God who is "merciful and compassionate" (2:13).

Returning to the Lord, according to Joel, takes the shape of fasting, weeping, and mourning. The purpose for engaging in these acts of piety appears to be to facilitate reconciliation with God, which in turn ensures the healing of the land and the preservation of the people. At face value, the text seems to say God punishes the people with drought because they have turned away from God, and that God will likely change their circumstances when—through their fasting, weeping, and mourning—they repent and return to God.

Christian theologians tend to resist such mechanistic, cause-and-effect readings of God's relationship to the trials and struggles of our lives not only because they seem to contradict our confession that God loves us unconditionally but also because such interpretations are elsewhere complicated in scripture. The psalmist makes it clear, for example, that God does not desire acts of piety per se, but rather inward regret and sincere sorrow for sin. "The sacrifice acceptable to God is a broken spirit," he comments (Ps 51:17, NRSV). Ritual acts, including the literal offering of sacrifices, mean nothing to God, the psalmist explains, apart from the presence of a heart that is "broken and crushed" (v. 17). When such a heart is in evidence, however, the offering of sacrifice is a celebration of the fact that we can, indeed, return to the God who is merciful (v. 19).

If Psalm 51 argues our pious acts are worthless apart from the inward state of our hearts, Matthew 6 insists inauthentic acts of piety can actually interfere with our returning to God. If we get caught up impressing others with the eloquence of our prayers or with the severity of our fasting, we risk forgetting that these acts are centered in *God* and not centered in *us*. We are not to engage them for the purpose of retrieving a sense of how righteous and wonderful *we* are. Rather, they are meant to be an expression of our sincere desire to return to the God who knows what we need before we even ask (Matt 6:8). While the instructions offered in Joel include emphasis on public praying and fasting, and while the instructions in Matthew suggest these activities should be done in private, the two texts are utterly consistent with one another in emphasizing that our pious acts are to be centered in God and God's merciful character, rather than in us and our impressive spiritual efforts.

Paul explicitly reminds us in 2 Corinthians that in Christ we are made righteous, by the grace of God. Paul and Timothy have seen it all, suffered all, accomplished all. They, like Joel, are announcing "the day of salvation" (6:2). They, like Joel, are exhorting their readers to be reconciled to God. And while they do not, like Joel, give heavy-duty instructions about how prayer, fasting, and weeping should be engaged, they do plead with the people of God not to accept the grace of God "in vain" (6:1). Living as those who have been reconciled to God in Christ Jesus means becoming part of the "new creation" (5:17) they have earlier insisted. It means being and living altogether different than before.

Ash Wednesday marks the start of Lent, the beginning of a time when we return, again, to the God who is merciful. It is not our acts of piety which accomplish this return, though these acts can certainly be embraced both as a manifestation of our "broken and crushed" (Ps 51:17) hearts and as a God-given vehicle through which we can sincerely express our penitence. Whether trumpets blast or we go into our closets to pray, the focus of our attention is on God and not ourselves. We rejoice that we are free to return to our merciful God again and again, for the righteousness we have in Christ is, by grace, a reality that endures despite our sinfulness, despite our turning away. And yet it matters supremely that we recognize it; it matters that we turn back to remembering whenever we have forgotten. It matters that we know our righteousness in

Christ because it is only when we know it that it can change us into who we really are.

And so we pray, and fast, and weep, and mourn, returning again to the promise of our baptism that God makes us righteous in Christ. We seek again to be reconciled, that we may join in the ministry of reconciliation. We submit again to the work of God, the process of transformation through which we, and all things, will surely become new.

A Pastoral Need

These are the texts appointed each year for Ash Wednesday, the beginning of the Lenten forty-day journey in the Western rites of the church. The traditional disciplines of Lent (prayer, fasting, almsgiving) are not new practices but are the pious practices of the faithful in the Old Testament and in Jesus' time. While some Christian traditions have more familiarity with these disciplines, they can be less known by others or even viewed with suspicion. Yet the practices are based in scripture and are not intended to be a mechanistic form of relating to God. They are a formative, outward way that we express our need to be made right in God. The annual invitation to these classic disciplines underscores the truth that we are in continual need of repentance. We all need to turn to God again and again. And the disciplines have an outward direction: prayers for others, almsgiving for others, fasting that lightens us to be of service beyond ourselves. The texts all point to what we know is true: there are all sorts of ways that we do not live as ones made new. We continue with self-destructive habits (food addictions, time-management issues, "retail therapy"). We persist in ways that we do not live in right relationship with others and creation (e.g., easy categorization of those different from ourselves, continuing patterns of consumption that destroy air and land quality). There is much for which we need to repent, and God is at work even in that repentance.

Ethical Implications

Some communities that have more familiarity with the Lenten disciplines often summarize them with the phrase "giving up something for Lent." Some people select something to give up for the weeks of Lent. It is common for persons to abstain from certain foods, and now some abstain from watching movies, reading mail order catalogues, and being on computer and pdf devices after a certain point in the day. Some persons have turned the phrase around and have begun to promote the days of Lent as a time to "take something on," like an additional prayer discipline, collecting money for a specific charity, or committing to volunteer hours for a local social service agency. The nuances of the texts interacting with the traditional Lenten disciplines should help us see that whatever practices we take on are not solely for our personal growth in God. These disciplines come from scripture and from the historic development of Lent as time of preparation for baptism. Any encounter with these texts and any invitation to the disciplines should send us forth continually to be shaped in God's righteousness that makes us servants in the world. It is hoped that the repeated actions do awaken us to the lifelong form we take as God's people in the world: praying for others, giving benevolently to the world's needs, and practicing a fast that makes us increasingly aware of consumption patterns and lightens us for focus on charity toward others.

GOSPEL IMPLICATIONS

The theme words for the day are somber. Penitence, repentance, and sacrifice all imply aspects of ourselves that need to be put to death. And we are starting again the journey toward our annual remembrance of Jesus' passion, death, and resurrection. Since at least medieval times, these Lenten days have had a somber tone as the faithful contemplate Christ's death. But it is not enough to say that we should consider what in us needs to die because of Christ's death. Instead, following the baptismal pattern of Lent, we know that we are made righteous by a death that is inseparable from resurrection. In other words we do not pretend like we do not know the outcome of the Great Three Days because we do know that after Maundy Thursday and Good Friday we will come again to Pascha, Easter Sunday. God makes us righteous in Christ. It is because God yearns for our full reconciliation, for our abundant life, for our life in God and in community that we turn ourselves over again to the turning we need to do in these days.

JENNIFER L. LORD

CYNTHIA L. RIGBY

First Sunday in Lent

The Lessons in Précis

Deuteronomy 26:1-11. This text gives instructions for the offering of the first fruits. "Once you have entered the land the Lord your God is giving you as an inheritance" (vs. 1) is a reminder at the outset of the abundance of God that engulfs us. Having been given such a gift (land, salvation) we first offer back to God.

Psalm 91:1-2, 9-16. The psalmist sings to God the protector. Dwelling in God's land means refuge from evil, and safety in the midst of danger.

Romans 10:8b-13. Calling on the name of the Lord means salvation. There is power to confessing with our lips, to calling on God. Speaking this truth somehow manifests its reality.

Luke 4:1-13. Even Jesus was tempted. Immediately following his baptism, and "full of the Holy Spirit" (vs. 1), he enters the wilderness. For forty days he abstains from food and is famished. The devil offers bread, glory, and power. Jesus, hungering, cites scripture and resists these temptations.

Theme Sentence

God gives us salvation. The texts give a pattern for Christian life: we have been given the fruitful land of salvation. And we are to return our first fruits from this land. Temptations exist in this land; other allegiances beckon. But God saves in the midst of temptations; we can call upon the name of God.

A KEY THEOLOGICAL QUESTION

God gives us salvation

These texts bear witness to the truth that God gives us salvation, and in multiple ways. God saves us by providing abundantly for our lives (Deut 26). God saves us by protecting us, rescuing us, and granting us long life (Ps 91). God saves us by not shaming us and by treating us generously, whether we are "Jew" or "Greek" (Rom 10), whether we are inhabitants of "a land full of milk and honey" or aliens residing on it (Deut 26:9).

There are myriad theological questions raised whenever the doctrine of salvation is considered. Many reflect our puzzlings about salvation's relationship to the limits of space and time. We know that salvation is, ultimately, an eschatological reality (that is, it names what God wills not only in time, but also for eternity). But will salvation be accomplished, fully, in time? Will it include the literal coming of the Kingdom of God "on earth as it is in heaven" (Matt 6:10, NRSV), or are these words of the Lord's Prayer to be interpreted only metaphorically? Will our bodies be saved, or only our souls? And will *everybody* and *everything* be saved, or only a select few, or a select species?

Another set of questions related to salvation, centers in matters of human need and Jesus Christ's atoning work. Theologians commonly ask, "How is the death of Jesus Christ saving?" Lately, a great deal of energy has been devoted to retrieving the idea that Jesus Christ saves us not only through his death, but also through his life, his teachings, his rising, and his coming again. A good deal of emphasis is also being given to considering not only what Jesus Christ saves us *from,* but also what he saves us *for.* One of the most divisive issues in many Christian churches is the matter of whether all will ultimately be saved in Christ, or whether only those who "confess" and "have faith" will be saved (see Rom 10:9ff.).

The theological question perhaps most commonly asked by Christian believers is, "Why is the salvation God gives not more strongly evident?" We do not always live in abundance (Deut 26). We do not seem especially protected from danger, and our lives are not always long (Ps 91:14-16). Like Jesus, we are tempted to give up on God's promise to save, especially when more immediate paths to sustenance and power present themselves (Luke 4). With Jesus, we are called to stay faithful in the midst of the ambiguity that surrounds us, seeking salvation by calling on God and looking for God's response (Ps 91:15, Rom 10:13).

Theologians are concerned about several contemporary misappropriations of the doctrine of salvation that seem to have developed as people of faith have struggled to understand why what God has promised rarely looks as good as its description. First, they point out that it is a problem when the people of God divorce what they think "salvation" is all about from the present-day difficulties of this world. This often takes the form of "spiritualizing" salvation in such a way that we can say it is present even where people are hungry, and unsafe, and short-lived. Salvation is not really about this life/this world/these bodies, we might convince ourselves. Rather, it is about the life to come, and getting our souls ready to participate in what's ahead.

Another disturbing way of managing the disparity between the character of God's promised salvation and our actual life circumstances is to narrow the recipients of salvation to only those who live long, or stand protected, or share in abundance. In this reasoning, those who are not protected are not actually "saved" and therefore not entitled to any of God's promises. Interestingly, the texts for today challenge faulty, exclusive thinking. Aliens and Gentiles are included along with residents and Jews. "All who call on the Lord's name will be saved" (Rom 10:13).

It is also problematic when people of faith interpret those things that are antithetical to salvation as hidden instances of it. Determined to see God at work, they jump too quickly to identifying God as somehow present in the lack of food, lack of protection, or lack of abundant life. While theologians, including John Calvin and others, have consistently assured us that God, in God's "secret working," is doing more than we can ask or imagine, to hope that God is doing more than we can ascertain is a far cry from asserting that the suffering we see is, in actuality, somehow a good.

Theologians generally insist, in contrast to this, that suffering never takes the form of salvation, even when we can recognize God working *through* suffering. Rehearsing Augustine's insight that the good God creates only that which is good, they return to texts that promise us concrete blessings in this life: abundance of food, protection from danger, longevity, and answers to prayers.

These scholars also suggest that calling out to God for these concrete blessings need not give way to us explaining away, in the name of faith, our sufferings and the sufferings of the world. In fact, the very opposite is the case. In light of God's clear promise to heal all and God's clear desire to include all, our anguish over the suffering of the world is deepened, not alleviated. We look in the face of hunger, and at the abuse of those who are not protected, and we cry out: "how long, O Lord!" Bearing the suffering of the world, especially in this Lenten season, is often exactly what it looks like to claim God's salvation.

A PASTORAL NEED

Because of our constant access to information about our world, other people, and the details of life on this planet, we are confronted more and more by the reality of danger and lack of abundance. Our news feeds come quickly and constantly these days. We have instant access to world information every second of each day: a few quick taps on a screen and we can peruse the day's headline news. But our news feeds these days are both less and more. There is less news: much news reporting is less in-depth, and we have to dig a little deeper to find out more about the stories we read. But news feeds have also increased: we have more snippets of news providing us with more awareness of the multitude of situations calling for our attention. Add to this news mix the dynamics of social networking and the prevalent trend of increased personal disclosure: people are willing to post numerous details about themselves and their activities. These observations, tallied up, give a quick overview of our information overload. Here is the connection to the day's theme: we know now more than ever that we do not always live in abundance. The world seems fragile, and we need to be saved. Life may be good for us some morning, but then we hear of a new assassination in Asia and about more casualties in the war in the Middle East. Health insurance complexities bear down on our sense of control over our self-care. All manner of ecological concerns worry us for the future and the present. Yet we are promised salvation in the midst of danger and ambiguity. Our honest laments only underscore this good news, and we join and wait together on God's promises.

ETHICAL IMPLICATIONS

The Old Testament, Epistle, and Gospel readings depict interactions between persons (and entities). The Old Testament reading instructs the people to make vows honoring God's hand in their lives. Paul speaks to the Romans about calling on the name of the Lord. Jesus interacts with the devil. These texts speak to the importance of speech. This is different than keeping silence in the face of trials, change, and danger. There is an ethic at work as we speak vows to remember whose hand gives all things. There is an ethic of calling on God's name in a way that reminds us to whom we belong. And there is an ethic of spoken resistance. We can practice all of these types of speech. All three of these forms of speech happen in worship: we speak or sing the Psalms and prayers, we recite statements of faith, and we voice our laments in our supplications and intercessions. We can take these patterns of speech with us to our jobs, schools, and general public domains. We may not speak aloud; we may only think of the words. Or we may know them and risk speaking them aloud as we audibly thank God or call on God's mercy in a given moment. By the power of such words we are reminded and remind others that God's salvation is the greater power in our midst. We are reminded that in the end the dangers will pass. God wills the world's salvation.

GOSPEL IMPLICATIONS

Ambiguity is an important word when reading these texts. Though they witness to God's salvation, abundance, protection, rescue, and generosity in our lives, it is true that we do not constantly sense these things. Nor does the world in which we live fully reflect these aspects of God's work in our midst. In fact sometimes the world seems not to reflect these things at all. And it could seem that staying faithful throughout these situations is work we have to do on our own. The Israelites enter God's blessings together and make vows together. Paul speaks to a community that calls on the name of the Lord. We hold each other up as we wait for the fullness of salvation. Jesus is confronted in the wilderness and then heads back to civilization for ministry among the people. By such actions we trust that God is at work in the world and through our lives. We can be signs of salvation for one another, bearing each other up in times of doubt. We are all under the one sign of the crucified-risen One, Jesus Christ, who resisted temptation in order to bring salvation to the world. Even through the good works of each other we can see: God continues to bring abundance.

JENNIFER L. LORD

CYNTHIA L. RIGBY

SECOND SUNDAY IN LENT

THE LESSONS IN PRÉCIS

Genesis 15:1-12, 17-18. God makes a covenant with Abram, granting the promise of descendants, land, and protection. God will be Abram's shield, and God's righteousness will endure for Abram's descendants.

Psalm 27. The psalmist celebrates God's protection in the presence of enemies and beseeches God's presence and protection in the midst of ongoing danger.

Philippians 3:17-4:1. The author of this letter sets out a choice for followers of Christ: live as citizens of Christ or continue to worship earthly things. Citizenship in Christ transforms how we seek and find fulfillment in life. Citizens are assured that all things will be subject to Christ.

Luke 13:31-35. Jesus responds to the Pharisees' report that Herod will kill him. He announces his continued mission to cast out demons and perform cures. He foreshadows his death in Jerusalem and laments the city's violence toward prophets. But he also foreshadows his coming in the name of God as Savior.

THEME SENTENCE

Christ encompasses us. As God promised to be a shield to Abram, so also do we know the all-encompassing promise of God's claim on us through Christ's life, death, and resurrection. God's claim on us does not make us inure from competing loyalties or present dangers, but even in the presence of these things we can know that all things will be subject to Christ.

A KEY THEOLOGICAL QUESTION
Christ Encompasses Us

Biblical portrayals of our relationship to God are tuned to the Trinitarian conception of *perichoresis,* or "mutual indwelling." God does not stand at a distance from us and then bring us into the divine life. God surrounds us from the outset, both without and within. "If I went up to heaven you would be there," exclaims the psalmist. "If I went down to the grave, you would be there too! . . . You knit me together while I was still in my mother's womb" (Ps 139:8, 13). Similarly, Christian theologies do not, at best, recognize Jesus Christ as a "bridge" between human beings and God (however often this metaphor is used in common parlance). Rather, the imagery is participatory: "Remain in me, and I will remain in you" (John 15:4); "In God we live, move, and exist" (Acts 17:28). In short, *Christ encompasses us.* And because Christ encompasses us, this world is not our home (John 15:19) and we are called to live in this world differently, as Christian believers.

Today's texts reflect the idea that our lives participate in the life and work of God (see Col 3:3), exhorting us to carry ourselves accordingly and lamenting when they do not. Paul reminds us that "our citizenship is in heaven" (Phil 3:20), and Abram is told his descendents will be as many as the stars in the heavens (Gen 15:5). Jesus wants to gather Jerusalem's children "as a hen gathers her chicks under her wings" (Luke 13:34). He grieves the fact that they have resisted his close identification with him, noting that the next time they see him will be when he returns there to meet his death.

When one is surrounded by earthly things, it is hard to live as those whose citizenship is in heaven (Phil 3:20). When one has had difficulty conceiving children, it is hard to live as those who trust the promise that there will be many ancestors (Gen 15). It is difficult to be strong and have courage when we are "waiting" on the Lord who has not yet arrived (Ps 27). It is challenging, too, to "stand firm in the Lord" as those who are living in "our humble bodies" and not yet transformed "so that they are like his glorious body" (Phil 3:21; 4:1).

Theologians have often noted that the challenge of Christian believers is to live as those who are "in the world, but not of it." The quandary is this: How can we live with the knowledge that our citizenship is in heaven while still being present to the daily work God has given us here on this earth? How does our belief in God's all-encompassing promise that we are blessed and protected propel us to be with and for the world, rather than licensing us to live at a distance from it?

One theologian who has done significant work on this question is the nineteenth-century Danish thinker, Søren Kierkegaard. Kierkegaard has in mind both Abraham and Jesus when he develops his understanding of the "Knight of Faith." The Knight of Faith, according to Kierkegaard, walks around in this world knowing that this world is not his home, and in this way is able to be more present to it. The Knight of Faith is happy if there is dinner on the table, waiting for him when he gets home, and just as happy if there is not. This is because his hope lies not in whether or what kind of dinner he has but in the promise that God has not forgotten him, that Christ encompasses him. And so he is free to enjoy his dinner even more, because how superb it is or isn't in no way threatens his identity or infringes on his destiny.

Further, Kierkegaard (1983) explains that the Knight of Faith is one "whose hope takes the form of madness" (36-37). The Knight believes not only what is *possible* but also the *impossible* things God has promised. Abraham believes he will be the father of a great nation, despite the fact that he is elderly and has no immediate heir. Paul believes that when Jesus Christ comes again, "He will transform our humble bodies so that they are like his glorious body" and will "subject all things to himself" (Phil 3:21). These beliefs are swimming in hope that is not only unrealistic but also, to all appearances, delusional.

Jesus, a Knight of Faith, knows the fate that awaits him. He will be killed as a prophet in the city he so loves, in the city that will first identify him as the blessed one "who comes in the Lord's name" (Luke 13:35). He knows something of how he will come to participate in the work of the God who encompasses him, but this does not distract him from living in the present. "I'm throwing out demons and healing people today and tomorrow," he says, when he hears Herod wants to kill him, suggesting that Herod will have to bide his time until after the third day, when this work is "complete" (Luke 13:32) God's overarching claim on him frees him to be present to those who need his healing touch in this world and in these moments.

Knowing that this very same Christ encompasses us, our challenge as Christian believers is to live—with and through him—as those who are in the world but not of it. In this Lenten season, we are called to be Knights of Faith: to be freed by our belief in God's impossible promises to live fully in the here and now, in the service of those in need. To live as those whose hope takes the form of madness, looking forward to the day when God's goodness comes to the land of the living (Ps 27:13); when all things are made glorious by the power of Christ (Phil 3:21).

A Pastoral Need

One pastoral need for this day may be to value this life here and now. The texts for this day have enough language between them to support interpretations that our true and best life in God will be in the future. And many people believe this. They have been taught this in their churches. Or they have studied the scriptures and ascertained that the life we live now is less important, something simply to endure. Some people have already suffered such hardships in life that a focus on what is to come is the greatest way of making sense of current realities. Yet the language of the texts speaks to a dual reality, and our proclamation can help reframe views about the afterlife. God's words to Abram are a blessing to Abram's life even as they speak to a future time. The psalmist lauds the truth of God's eternal and lasting presence in the midst of transitory dangers. Paul instructs his hearers to live a good life now, according to the citizenship they have in Christ in heaven. And Jesus, though prophesying about his future coming, speaks of his ongoing work of healing and curing. God's work is intended for us now, even as there are future promises. Citizenship in heaven means something for how we are in the *civitas* of God now. God's power is present now, encompassing us to live according to God's promises now.

Ethical Implications

According to these texts the promises for the future speak to protection, wholeness, belonging, and safety. And we can live in the present according to the promises for the future. We can live not as people who merely endure this life but as people who speak out where the world is not living according to citizenship in Christ. The concept of citizenship in Christ is an all-encompassing concept. It implies his rule over the cosmos, a rule characterized (according to the Gospel reading) by healing and curing. This concept becomes a framework for our lives because it invokes our participation now in all aspects of our lives. In particular this framework can help us pay attention to how we are being good citizens to one another in our congregations and in the neighborhoods surrounding our congregations. But this framework also moves us beyond the work we do in congregations and compels us to see our workplaces, schools, volunteer agencies, and social contexts as places that are also under such citizenship rules. And this citizenship framework can also help us move beyond these local interactions to global connections because we know the promises about the future include past and future generations and a cosmic breadth. We are helped to see that even though we live at great distances from so many others, we are connected as citizens. According to Christ's rule, all humanity is worthy of protection, wholeness, belonging, and safety. Christ encompasses us, and this means we make choices and live lives according to his surrounding embrace.

Gospel Implications

These texts present the tension of eschatology. They point to God's cosmic plan through the words to Abram, the psalmist's song, Paul's description of our civic allegiance in heaven, and Jesus' foreshadowing of the future. Through the language of the texts we learn of God's far-reaching plan for humanity. But eschatology is not only about the future promises. It is also the understanding that the future promises break in on us now in ways that claim us to be in the world but not of the world. By our life in God, in the mutual indwelling of the Holy Trinity, we are brought into this life. We are surrounded inside and out by God and so can live in the world, bearing up one another, with hope. We are gathered under God's wings, under the sign of the empty cross and empty tomb, reaching out to the whole world to gather all in God's love.

Notes

Søren Kierkegaard, *Fear and Trembling*, eds. H. Hong & E. Hong, 1983.

Jennifer L. Lord

Cynthia L. Rigby

THIRD SUNDAY IN LENT

THE LESSONS IN PRÉCIS

Lent calls us to turn from all that distracts us and focus our attention on Jesus and his journey to the cross.

> *Isaiah 55:1-9.* God offers all that we need and more, yet we are inclined to run after things that do not satisfy our deepest needs, and so God calls us to turn back.

> *Psalm 63:1-8.* The psalmist believes that God satisfies our deepest needs and that it is impossible for the believer to flourish when away from God. For this reason, the psalmist sings, "My whole being thirsts for you" (vs. 1).

> *1 Corinthians 10:1-13.* What we do matters. The choices we make matter. Paul therefore both urges us to resist temptation and promises that God will support us as we strive to be faithful.

> *Luke 13:1-9.* We should not look for God's judgment in calamity. God regards all of us equally and requires the same from all of us: repentance.

THEME SENTENCE

God commands and invites repentance. God's call to repentance—turning back to God—isn't for God's sake, but rather for ours. All four readings proclaim that our life, our good, and our hope reside in relationship with God, whose love is made manifest in Jesus' cross and resurrection.

A KEY THEOLOGICAL QUESTION
Sin brings death; repentance ushers in the gift of new life.
Are Christians fixated on sin? In worship, many of our hymns, prayers, and scripture readings are heavily laden with sin-talk. If we're concerned that there's too much talk of sin in Christianity, then the scripture passages today—from Isaiah's talk of wicked ones to Luke's parable of the barren fig tree that gets one more year to show fruit before it's destroyed—could breed more discontent.

It is important to acknowledge that sin-talk can be dangerous talk. It certainly is the case that Christian communities and their leaders have abused sin-talk. Forming rigid delineations between "the sinners" and "the righteous" has been a popular Christian pastime. But into the midst of such finger-pointing comes the opening scene of Luke 13, where Jesus rebukes precisely such judgments. The crowd around him reports on the transgressions committed by certain Galileans. In response, Jesus quickly challenges their haughty assessments, asking them if those Galileans are worse sinners than all other Galileans. Jesus answers his own question with one simple word: no. Rather than serving as an easy way to delineate one from one another, Jesus' reference to human sinfulness suggests a kind of equality. We're all sinful, and Jesus reminds us that we needn't spend our time trying to box up our sins in categories and rank them.

If the value of sin-talk is not found in forming categories of whose sin is worse, then why continue to focus on it? Because, as Paul writes, we all are held captive by its grip (Rom 3:23); we all suffer the consequences of our own and others' sin; and we all stand in need of repentance. This is why Jesus has more to say than simply to point out our sin. He doesn't mince words: "unless you change your hearts and lives, you will die just as they did" (Luke 13:3, 5).

The season of Lent invites us to take stock of our sin and its consequences. Isaiah calls on the wicked to forsake their ways; Luke's Gospel commands us to repent and move into the abundant, fruit-bearing growth God has made possible through Jesus Christ.

Augustine famously wrote, "Our hearts are restless until they rest in you, O God." He understood our restlessness to be a result of our sin; we are restless because of our repeated attempts to take refuge in something other than God. When we mistake any other good thing—whether it be love of another person, food, money, material possessions, sex, you name it—for the Ultimate Good, Augustine argued, our hearts remain restless, unsettled. Augustine knew well the condition reflected in the psalmist's vivid description of life that revolves around lesser goods: orienting our life around that which is not God is like traveling through a dry and weary land without water (63:1).

The consequences of such misdirection can be fatal; wandering too long in a land without water leads to death. In 1 Corinthians, Paul urges new Christians not to forget their history; the people of God have failed God before, and they are in danger of failing again. The temptation to seek other gods, to try to rest in something other than God, is a perennial one. We continue to be caught in the grip of sin's damaging results.

Lent is the time to make a case for the value of sin-talk. We need to talk about sin so we can recognize its destructive effects in our lives.

But that's not the only value of sin-talk. We also need to name our sins and repent of them so that we might have life. Isaiah says, "Listen, and you will live" (55:3). Pay attention to the way sin has us in its grip. To truly repent, we need an awareness of what we've done—and not done—that's led us into this waterless land. Repentance reorients us toward God's love and mercy, where we find sustenance and rest.

Isaiah tells us that God's thoughts are not our thoughts and God's ways are not our ways (55:8). As we look and listen for God's ways of thinking and acting, we turn back to Jesus' parable of the barren fig tree in Luke 13. Jesus offers a life-giving message, if we will only listen. Just like the man who tells the gardener to give the barren fig tree one more year (vs. 8), so God offers us yet another chance to repent, to change our ways. To the gardener, the barren fig tree is a lost cause; but to the man who planted that tree in the vineyard, all hope is not lost.

Lent is the season of "one more year." Rather than consigning us to the wasteland of sin and death, God gives us one more year to repent and embrace the new life possible in Jesus Christ. It is time to return to the Lord so that we might have mercy, returning to God who will abundantly pardon (55:7). Sin-talk, when it points us to repentance, is life-giving, life-sustaining, fruit-bearing talk.

A Pastoral Need

There are few things more alarming for parents than to come upon a beloved child who's gotten into something dangerous, whether pulling bottles from the medicine cabinet or playing with scissors from a nearby desk. With so many perfectly good toys lying around, the child would rather play with these!

That illustration, while perhaps simple, gets right at the heart of these Lenten readings. God has provided a world of good things for us. More than that, God has invited us into relationship with God and with each other. Yet so often we run after other things that are not healthful for us. Tempted by their allure, we imagine they will somehow provide the meaning, purpose, and identity we seek. Such is the essence of sin, which means, literally, "to miss the mark."

Repentance, in the common parlance of our day, typically has negative connotations, implying that we must abase or humiliate ourselves for our wrongdoing in order to appease an angry God. But these passages invite us to reconsider the nature of repentance. God is not angry but lovingly concerned for our well-being. Repentance, in this context, is God imploring us to turn away from those things that would injure us, so that we might return to a right and healthful relationship with God and each other. From this point of view, God acts as a devoted mother who implores her precious child to put away dangerous things and run back to mommy's loving embrace.

Ethical Implication

If God desires so greatly that we enjoy life, then we should encourage each other to choose those things that enrich life and, in particular, nurture our relationship with God and each other. There is, of course, more than one way to do this! Some may read this passage and feel justified in scolding or badgering others, or even judging their sin self-righteously. But is this the way of Christ?

Certainly there are occasions that call for warning. Paul discerns such a moment in his letter to the Corinthians, and Jesus' warning is clear. But notice that the primary impulse of these readings is not to scold, badger, or judge. Rather, through the prophet Isaiah, God enthusiastically invites all people to receive the good food God has prepared. And Jesus goes out of his way to say that no one person is better or inherently more worthy than another. As Paul writes in another place, "*All* have sinned and fall short of God's glory" (Rom 3:23).

How, then, do we encourage each other to lives of righteousness? Remembering that Lent leads us to the cross-strewn hill outside Jerusalem, we may recognize the connection between repentance and compassion. It is precisely because Isaiah loves the people that the visions that come to him are at times painful. Similarly, Jesus does not merely stand back and call for repentance. Rather, he takes on our lot and our life, calling for repentance from a place of absolute solidarity with us. So, too, we might enter into the struggles of those we would call for repentance and welcome others into our own struggles that they may guide us toward greater health and life. Words of repentance not accompanied by compassion and solidarity will most likely fall on deaf ears.

Gospel Implications

Jesus is not a dispassionate judge, weighing our sins against our merits, calculating our faith and our disbelief. Rather, the one who issues warning enters into our situation; the one who calls for repentances embraces our humanity through the incarnation; and the one who judges is judged for us.

Taken in isolation, any call for repentance can distort one's impression of scripture and, more importantly, the God to whom the scriptures testify. Judgment and the call to repentance are weighty, important matters that cannot be avoided in the Christian life. For that very reason it is crucial to recognize that judgment and warning stem from God's great and parental love for us.

Talk of sin and repentance is therefore never intended to humiliate or disgrace; rather, such talk is always motivated by love. We call others from sin to life because we know and wish to share the love of God made manifest in Christ. Similarly, we invite others to call us to repentance because we trust that they, too, have been captured by God's amazing grace. Through it all, we sense the unending movement of God to call us through repentance to grace, life, and peace.

David J. Lose
Deanna Thompson

FOURTH SUNDAY IN LENT

THE LESSONS IN PRÉCIS

Lent invites us to contemplate the lengths to which God will go to restore us to right relationship with God and each other.

> *Joshua 5:9-12.* God not only rescued the Israelites from Egypt but also brought them to the promised land, where manna ceased and the people ate the produce of the land. Through all this, Israel learned that God keeps God's promises.

> *Psalm 32.* There is nothing better than forgiveness—being restored to right relationship, having something that was broken made whole again.

> *2 Corinthians 5:16-21.* Forgiveness, or reconciliation, is not just getting a second chance. It is becoming an entirely new thing—a whole new life, person, and creation. Having received this new life, we are commissioned, invited, and entrusted to share it with others.

> *Luke 15:1-3, 11b-32.* This parable of the prodigal and his brother, perhaps the most famous of all Jesus' stories, reminds us that there is absolutely nothing more important to God than restoring the broken relationship we have with God.

THEME SENTENCE

God forgives, restores, reconciles, and in all these ways creates something new. God's commitment and promise to restore all of creation takes shape in many ways, but it can be seen most clearly in God's intention and activity to reconcile us to God's own self in and through Jesus.

A KEY THEOLOGICAL QUESTION
Through forgiveness of sin and reconciliation of relationship, God creates something new.

What do forgiveness and reconciliation look like? To understand forgiveness and reconciliation, we must first attend to the sin. Sin, in biblical terms, is a condition from which none of us is free (Rom 3:23); it is also a self-chosen act, like knowing the good and not doing it (James 4:17).

The Gospel story of the wayward son highlights the destructive power of individual sin. The son disrespects his father, abandons his family, squanders his resources and his own self-respect, and spirals into a state of alienation and despair. His family counts him for dead; his ruptured relationships, he believes, are beyond repair. It's not too much to say, along with the apostle Paul, "The wages that sin pays are death" (Rom 6:23).

Psalm 32 also offers vivid descriptions of sin's ability to infect our inner life. The psalmist doesn't divulge the nature of his sin, but he admits to burying it internally, where it festers and spreads. Keeping silent about the sin, the psalmist confesses, is both physically damaging—"my bones wore out" (vs. 3)—and spiritually damaging—"your hand was heavy upon me" (vs. 4). Once again, the wages of sin are death.

In the midst of the misery brought on by sin, what do forgiveness and reconciliation look like?

Today's passages indicate that repair of the breach created by sin is work that ultimately only God can do. The parable of the wayward son is nothing less than a resurrection story: the father's radical act of forgiveness of his son's despicable behavior restores his son to life (Luke 15:24). The sins and deceit of the past have been replaced by the gift of new life (2 Cor 5:17).

Even as we are drawn in by Jesus' compelling portrait of God as the father whose forgiving love envelops the sinful son, we must resist the temptation to sentimentalize the father's gift of forgiveness and reconciliation. As Paul writes in 2 Corinthians 5, God's work in overcoming the past, where the wages of sin were death, is costly. Christ, the one who knows no sin, takes on sin and all its destructive effects (vs. 21) so that forgiveness and reconciliation are possible for us. Thinking of forgiveness and reconciliation as easy or automatic turns God's gifts into what Dietrich Bonhoeffer has called "cheap grace." God's reconciling work is accomplished through Christ, whose offer of radical love was met with torture and death. The psalmist's restoration to life and the son's reconciliation with his family became possible only through the costly gift of divine love.

Forgiveness and reconciliation, then, are costly divine gifts that make new life in the world possible for us.

Passionate belief in these gracious gifts of God was behind the sixteenth-century Reformers' calls for reform of the medieval church. According to the Reformers, it is "grace alone" or "Christ alone" that offers forgiveness; God alone—not the church—is the one who sets sinners right with God. God alone is the one who can make things new.

And yet it is important to remember that even in the midst of the God-intoxicated theology of the Reformation, Martin Luther and others held fast to corporate and individual practices of confession. Confession, Luther believed, makes clear that we are sinful and unable to justify ourselves. To practice confession acknowledges that we cannot save ourselves, that we stand in need of the divine gifts of forgiveness and reconciliation.

·   While many contemporary congregations have drifted away from corporate confessions of sin, what we see in these passages, particularly in Psalm 32 and in the parable of the wayward son, is how confessing one's sinfulness is integrally related to receiving the gift of forgiveness and reconciliation. To be sure, confession isn't done in order to earn these divine gifts; rather, it compels us to recognize the ways in which we've fallen short, done harm, and ruptured relationships.

In a culture where "non-apology apologies" too often take the place of true confessions, we need to remember confession's role as part of the process of forgiveness and reconciliation. The season of Lent calls us to reflect on our thoughts and actions. As Kathleen Norris (1998) has written, "If you can never admit to being a wretch then you haven't been paying attention" (*Amazing Grace,* 167). The church can help encourage a countercultural movement to name our sin out loud and ask God—and each other—for forgiveness.

In 2 Corinthians, Paul proclaims that God is doing a new thing in Christ; the old is passing away. Confessing our sins acknowledges and participates in the new way of relating that Christ offers. It prepares us to receive the divine gifts of forgiveness and reconciliation and opens us up to the newness that awaits us in Christ.

A Pastoral Need

"Sin" and "forgiveness" are such familiar words in the church that we may forget how foreign and misunderstood they have become in the common language and culture of the day.

Sin, let us be clear, is not about shame. Rather, sin names the ache deep in our hearts that comes from recognizing the hurts inflicted on ourselves or others that litter the landscape of our lives. Sin names a brokenness in our very being and world that intuitively we know we cannot fix. It may be as small and personal as when a parent verbally lashes out in anger at a child. It may be as large and communal as when a nation engages in war to protect its "national interest" at the expense of the lives and well-being of countless thousands.

Similarly, forgiveness isn't simply saying, "It's okay." Rather, forgiveness is a deliberate releasing of the claim we have on another that creates not only a second chance but also a whole new relationship. Forgiveness refuses to allow the present to be dominated by the regrets of the past but looks instead to the possibilities of the future.

Each of the readings this week, but especially the Gospel, invites us to imagine both the cost and the hope of God's forgiveness not just on a cosmic scale but also in the everyday terms of a father who loves his children enough to forgive one son his foolish waywardness and the other his hardness of heart. If we can imagine forgiveness in such everyday terms, we may also be able to practice it and in this way soothe the deep ache sin creates in our hearts.

Ethical Implications

Three challenges confront us when preaching forgiveness. The first is to avoid having the biblical story devolve into a morality tale. "Because God forgave us, we should forgive others . . . " Of course. We often forget that *receiving* and *practicing* forgiveness are intimately related, and simply *hearing about* forgiveness is not the same as *feeling* God's forgiveness. At its best, true preaching of forgiveness tells us the truth twice: the first time piercing the veils of our hearts to reveal the inner regrets and disappointments so that we may neither deny nor cower from them; the second time making manifest God's profound, even relentless love that will stop at nothing until we know that we are, indeed, God's beloved children.

A second challenge is not to equate forgiveness with a lack of accountability. Forgiveness is at heart a relational category, and so while forgiveness restores relationship, it does not necessarily mute consequences. One can forgive a crime perpetrated against oneself; that does not necessarily reduce the sentencing imposed by civil courts. Christians contend for both justice and forgiveness, not one or the other.

A third challenge is to avoid assuming that repentance must precede forgiveness. Curiously, it is difficult to tell whether the prodigal son is indeed contrite or whether he concocts a confession he expects will restore him to his father's household. As it turns out, the forgiving father doesn't wait to hear his son's confession but instead embraces him. Similarly, we should be cautious to put limits on God's love. Sometimes repentance precedes forgiveness; sometimes hearing the word of forgiveness induces repentance. Our job is to say the word, tell the story, announce the good news, and see what happens.

GOSPEL IMPLICATIONS

Emerson once called the parable of the prodigal son the greatest story told in the Bible . . . or anywhere else. Why? Because amid the variety of confessions about God contained in the pages of scripture, this one seems to get at the very heart of God, who is always more eager to forgive than we are to receive forgiveness, always ready to go to any length necessary to embrace us in love.

But if this is the central message of Jesus, why did people want him dead? I think we forget just how out-of-control we feel when we are forgiven by another. To be forgiven is perhaps the most vulnerable position we can be put in, as we have no claim to make, no rights to argue, no story or excuse to fall back on. Therefore, to those who would rather retain some modicum of control or some semblance of strength, forgiveness is threatening. And so rather than admit our dependence on and need for God's love and forgiveness, we refuse the new creation of forgiveness and, in the case of Jesus, do away with the one who threatens the status quo. Yet God resurrects Jesus, reminding us that God's forgiving love is more powerful than even our fear.

Notes

Kathleen Norris, *Amazing Grace: A Vocabulary of Faith*, 1998.

DAVID J. LOSE

DEANNA THOMPSON

Fifth Sunday in Lent

The Lessons in Précis

As we draw near Jerusalem, we are invited to fasten our eyes on Jesus and his cross so that we might see God's greatest act of love for us.

> *Isaiah 43:16-21.* God delivered the Israelites from Egypt long ago, but God is not finished. God continues to create, redeem, and restore.

> *Psalm 126.* The psalmist remembers the mighty acts of God in the past and boldly asks God to restore Israel in the present.

> *Philippians 3:4b-14.* Although Paul did everything right according to the law, he discovered in Christ a whole new way of being in relationship with God and neighbor. This new way made everything else look meager by comparison.

> *John 12:1-8.* Mary's act of devotion in anointing Jesus signaled his coming death. While Judas did not recognize this because of his greed, Jesus did because of his commitment to give his life for the sake of the world.

Theme Sentence

God is not finished! God has acted throughout history to repair and restore God's relationship with all humanity. God's mighty acts in the past only foreshadow God's greatest work of reconciliation in and through Jesus' cross and resurrection.

A KEY THEOLOGICAL QUESTION

Glimpsing God's Future

In both Isaiah 43 and Psalm 126, the Israelites are summoned to look to the future, to a time when God will do "a new thing" (Isa 43:19). While Old Testament writings overflow with calls for Israel to remember God's mighty acts of the past, the accent in our readings from Isaiah and Psalms is on what God will do in the future. In the New Testament epistle reading, Paul's message to the Philippians goes so far as to commend "forgetting what lies behind" (Phil 3:13, NRSV) in order to focus on what lies ahead. The message comes through loud and clear: God is not done, and the struggles, sorrows, and tears of the present will not define God's future.

In the mid 1990s I heard a white South African pastor speak about his congregation's struggle to be the church in the midst of apartheid. His congregation was one of the few Afrikaner churches that consistently opposed apartheid rule. They worked against this evil system, and prayed that God would "make a way in the wilderness" (Isa 43:19, NRSV) through apartheid's oppression and brutality.

Like every South African opposed to apartheid, the pastor and his congregation rejoiced and celebrated its demise in the early 1990s. But the next part of his story was unexpected: after apartheid ended, the pastor admitted, he and his congregation struggled to envision a way forward. Suddenly they were on the cusp of "a new thing," a new way of being in the world, and they were stuck, unsure of what they should do and how they should act. Being against apartheid could no longer be their primary way of being in the world, and what they should work for was not yet clear.

In the biblical texts for today, the people of God are called to look forward to the new thing God is about to do for them. But sometimes our imaginations fail us, and we can't quite see through to this new way of being. In the newly-post-apartheid South Africa of the mid 1990s, for instance, it was hard to imagine what it meant to be the church with no apartheid to oppose. Where do we fit into the new thing God is about to do with and for us?

The post-apartheid story in many ways confirms Jesus' claim to Judas, "You will always have the poor among you" (John 12:8). Apartheid is officially over, but staggeringly high levels of poverty, violence, HIV infection, and inadequate housing and education persist. The high hopes ushered in under South Africa's first black President Nelson Mandela and other new leaders seem tragically distant now.

During a trip to South Africa in 2008, I witnessed the gnawing disillusionment of many South Africans who had been so full of hope a few years before. At the same time, lodged within the regions of despair were glimpses of how God is about to do a new thing. One such glimpse came from Bishop Paul Verryn, pastor of Central Methodist Church in downtown Johannesburg, a church renown for taking in recent refugees from Zimbabwe. The bishop reported that his church currently housed over three thousand refugees within its four walls. At one point in his talk, the bishop let out an exasperated claim, "I spend more time talking about sewage than I do about the gospel."

I tried to make my way to the bishop after his talk, but the line was too long and the evening too late. I had hoped to ask the bishop if he could see—amid the staggering challenge of housing thousands of homeless—the work of Central Methodist Church as anticipating God's future, of God doing a new thing. Could it be that sewage talk *is* gospel talk of the highest order? Could it be that God's "new thing" might be about waste as well as generativity?

Within the unrelenting challenges of refugees and poverty and sewage problems, perhaps it's possible to glimpse something new. But such glimpsing requires careful attention, attention similar to the kind Mary gives Jesus in John 12.

In the Johannine text, while Judas suffers from a failure of imagination in his inability to see God ushering in a new way of being in the world through Jesus, Mary is able to glimpse something new. At some level, Mary understands that Jesus is about to upset the structures in which Judas and so many others are caught. Mary's act anticipates that God in Christ is doing something new.

In this season of Lent, we pray along with ancient Israel as well as those who take refuge in Central Methodist Church in Johannesburg that those who sow in tears will reap with shouts of joy, that even in the midst of great suffering we can glimpse the new thing God is doing in our midst. In Lent we "press on toward the goal" (Phil 3:14, NRSV) of living in the newness of life given us in Christ. In Christ, God created and continues to create new possibilities for life, even in the face of death.

A PASTORAL NEED

Why would anyone stay in an abusive marriage? Or in a job that brings little satisfaction? Or in a pattern of living that is destructive? Why, in short, is it so difficult to trade a difficult present for a possibly richer future? Because, of course, the future is unknown and therefore somewhat frightening. The present, even if it's troublesome, is at least a known quantity. Though we may not be flourishing, we are at least surviving. This typical way of thinking shortchanges the future God offers.

The texts for this Sunday invite us to imagine a future crafted and given to us as a gift by God. In the first reading and psalm, we overhear promises made to Israel about restoration. In the second reading, Paul extols how much richer and more satisfying his new life in Christ is compared to his previous life. In the Gospel, Jesus embraces the difficult, immediate future of the cross because of his trust in God and love for God's people.

Promises about the future create hope and faith by helping us envision something we had not expected or imagined. Speaking of the future actually helps create that future by granting us the vision to see it and the courage to move toward it. Yet promises can seem fragile, even frightening—what if they're not kept? We gather on Sunday because we need to hear these promises over and over again. By looking to the promises God kept in the past, we gain confidence that God will keep promises about the future . . . even and especially for us.

ETHICAL IMPLICATIONS

Talk about the future is always a little slippery. Not only can promises seem fragile, as mentioned above, but they can also seem vague, general, or even insubstantial. Such promises carry little power to shape imagination or create trust. For this reason, the Bible is remarkably confident about the future it envisions. While not attempting to pin down the details, it nevertheless speaks in vivid terms about God's future action to restore, redeem, and save.

Two particular patterns in biblical promises are worth remembering. First, promises about God's future action are rooted in God's past action. Isaiah locates the trustworthiness of the promise about the future restoration of the currently exiled Israelites in God's past action to redeem Israel from slavery in Egypt. Today, those same promises God made through Isaiah and later kept serve a similar purpose for us—by remembering God's faithfulness in the past, we are more likely to believe God's promise about the future. During Lent in particular, we look to God's past action in Jesus to take on our lot and our life and identify with us fully as a token of God's trustworthiness.

The second element of biblical promises is that while they may speak about the future, they are actually addressed to the present. Promises about the future create faith, hope, and courage in the present. Paul's letter brims over with a present-tense confidence rooted in God's promises. Similarly, we are encouraged to care for our neighbor, the environment, and all the world now because in spite of whether our present actions succeed or fail we have God's promises 1) to be with us (a promise made concrete in the cross of Jesus), and 2) to redeem all things (as signaled in the resurrection). Because God has promised to take care of the future, we are free and empowered in the here and now to love, sacrifice, risk, and die, trusting in the God who raised Jesus from the grave.

Gospel Implications

If there is a single theme in the readings on this day, it is that God is not yet finished. The God who acted in the past to save Israel, to usher Paul into a previously unimagined relationship with God, and to send Jesus to demonstrate God's love for us has more in store for us and all the world. In short, the future is God's.

But that doesn't make it easy to embrace that future, as the Christian life is rarely easy. Whether it is being faithful in our relationships and responsibilities, or caring for the poor in South Africa or our own community, the challenges of living into the future to which God has called us can be daunting. For this reason, we must temper all talk about the future to which God invites us with the reminder of just how much God loves us in the present. And these passages, particularly the Gospel reading, help us to do so, as they bring us to the very brink of the passion of our Lord. Earlier in John's Gospel, Jesus says that he is the good shepherd, that he gives his life of his own accord for the sake of the sheep (10:17-18); in today's Gospel reading we see him ready to do this. Why? For one reason only: to show us God's tremendous love for us (3:16).

Armed with the promise that the future is God's and assured that God loves us and is with us here and now, we can keep faith in the present and march confidently into God's future.

David J. Lose
Deanna Thompson

GOOD FRIDAY

THE LESSONS IN PRÉCIS

We dare call this darkest of days "good" because of what God accomplishes through it.

> *Isaiah 52:13-53:12.* God is at work through the suffering servant to redeem Israel. No one would have imagined that this servant—beaten, rejected, cursed—is God's chosen instrument, but he is.

> *Psalm 22.* It is agonizing to feel cut off from the Lord. The psalmist therefore cries out for comfort, eager to tell of God's steadfast mercy and sure help.

> *Hebrews 10:16-25.* In Jesus, God has kept God's promise to make a new covenant that grants us access to God's grace, apart from sacrifice.

> *John 18:1-19:42.* Jesus is betrayed by Judas, arrested, denied by Peter, sentenced to death, and crucified. John portrays a Savior who embraces his destiny and accomplishes all that is set for him, fulfilling what Jesus had said earlier: "I give up my life so that I can take it up again. No one takes it from me, but I give it up because I want to" (10:17b-18).

THEME SENTENCE

God comes not as expected, but as necessary. The whole Bible witnesses to God's steadfast commitment to redeem God's creation. The readings appointed for Good Friday testify that this redemption is unexpected and costly. We are bid to watch, marvel, and be transformed by God's love poured out in Jesus.

A KEY THEOLOGICAL QUESTION
Dare we call this day "good"?

"Good Friday was not a good day for Jesus" our pastor said as he began his Good Friday sermon. In the pregnant pause that followed, our daughter's young voice broke the sanctuary's silence:

"Why wasn't it a good day for Jesus?" she asked.

Polite chuckles and discreet head-turning ensued. Unhappy with what seemed like a dismissal of her question, my daughter looked up at me with earnest eyes. She had asked a serious question; she wanted a serious answer.

Why wasn't Good Friday a good day for Jesus?

This question ushers us into conversations about atonement, about how it is that God saves us through Jesus Christ. On Good Friday, we're faced with Jesus' agonizing death, and questions about the relationship between his death and God's gift of salvation are front and center. Did Jesus have to die in order to save our sins? Was Jesus' death actually a "good" thing? What does it mean to say that Jesus saves?

One pop culture response to these questions came in Mel Gibson's 2004 film, *The Passion of the Christ*. The film begins with a passage from Isaiah 53:5 that ends with the words, "by his wounds we are healed." While these words appear on the screen in English, the rest of the movie follows in Aramaic, Hebrew, and Latin. Gibson originally intended to present the whole drama without subtitles, wagering that the visual images—that is, the prolonged torture and suffering of Jesus, played by Jim Caviezel—would speak more loudly than any dialogue. According to the film's theory of atonement, the focus is Jesus' death. On the screen, his living and his rising remain in the shadows behind the bleeding, the suffering, and the dying.

The view of atonement the film sets forth is most closely aligned with the satisfaction theory of atonement, where Jesus' death is the most crucial element of the story. In his treatise, *Cur Deus Homo?* (Why Did God Become Human?), medieval theologian Anselm insisted that the death of Christ satisfies God's righteous anger at human sin and that the cross alone restores humanity's relationship with God. Many of the verses from Isaiah 53 lend support to Anselm's view: Jesus, in the role of the suffering servant, bears our infirmities, is wounded for our transgressions, and is punished so we can be made whole (53:4-5).

Before we grow too comfortable with this formulation of atonement, however, a few verses from the passages for today encourage us to think again. At the beginning of Psalm 22, for instance, the psalmist challenges God. Not only does he express feeling forsaken by God, but he also laments, "I cry out during the day, but you don't answer; even at nighttime I don't stop" (Ps 22:2). That Jesus echoes the psalmist's call of alienation (Matt 27:46) raises the question of whether substitutionary atonement theory is able to encompass the breadth and depth of biblical interpretations of Jesus' death.

The history of theological interpretation acknowledges a wider biblical framework in its reluctance to officially endorse a single view of atonement. From the theory of Christ the Victor (e.g., Col 2:15) that sees God and the forces of evil locked in cosmic battle that is ultimately overcome by the resurrection (Gustaf Aulén), to medieval theologian Abelard's moral influence theory that emphasizes Jesus' life of love that leads to his death (e.g. John 15), we see in both the biblical text and the church's doctrinal traditions that just how it is that Jesus saves is not easily reducible to one theoretical response. We can see in John's Gospel that Jesus' life of extraordinary love leads him to the cross of death and ultimately to the resurrection. It's the entirety of who Jesus is and what he has done that brings salvation.

But for now, we're stuck within the parameters of Good Friday, a day that certainly wasn't good for Jesus. The scripture readings talk of Jesus' betrayal in deed by one he calls friend (John 18:1-5), his denial by one who had promised to be faithful to him (18:15-18, 25-27), his beatings and humiliation by the Roman soldiers (19:1-3), and his continued mistreatment until his last breath (19:28-29). The words of the prophet Isaiah speak of the servant who is crushed with pain (Isa 53:10). The psalmist's words tell of despair over God's apparent silence in the midst of cries for help. All of this builds a strong case to suggest that Good Friday was not a good day for Jesus.

If Good Friday was so horrible for Jesus, dare we call it "good"? In the midst of the scripture's detailed descriptions of suffering, betrayal, desertion, and alienation, we also glimpse something more. The author of Hebrews talks of "the certainty that our faith gives" and holding fast "to the confession of our hope" that Good Friday is not the end of the story (Heb 10:22-23). The psalmist moves from lament to joy, rejoicing in the deliverance of "to those not yet born" (Ps 22:31). The reason we can call Good Friday good comes from the promise that there's more, that Jesus' claim, "It is completed" (John 19:30), is about the end of death rather than the end of hope.

Good Friday is good only because Easter has the final word.

A Pastoral Need

There is a lot of confusion about Jesus' death that rarely gets articulated for fear, I suspect, of seeming impious or ignorant. In particular, many Christians wonder *why* Jesus had to die, or if he even *had to* die. We know the story, but we don't know the meaning. While the service of Good Friday is not the day to launch into a lengthy theological discourse on theories of atonement, be assured that those theories are lurking behind what we say about the cross, and it is well worth our thinking deeply and clearly about atonement theology so that the few words we do offer have the desired impact.

One way to think about the three major theories of atonement mentioned above is to ask what each discloses about God's primary character. With Anselm—and even more for those who later developed Anselm's theory—the primary attribute of God's character is justice: Jesus dies to appease God's righteous anger caused by our offending God's justice. With Aulén, it is victory—Jesus dies and is raised again in order to trick the devil and thereby achieve God's victory over death. With Abelard, it is morality—Jesus lives and dies to offer us an example of right living.

While each of these readings aptly describes elements of God's essence, none gets at the core character of God as expressed in John's Gospel: love. "God so loved the world . . . " (3:16), Jesus says earlier. Later, at the beginning of his extended passion narrative, John writes in reference to Jesus, "Having loved his own who were in the world, he loved them fully" (13:1). That is why we dare to call this day "good," because in it and through it God makes manifest God's love for us and all the world, a love so strong that even death cannot keep it down. The need for such a love is one of the clearest pastoral needs on this day.

Ethical Implications

"God so loved the world . . ." (John 3:16). "I give up my life so that I can take it up again. No one takes it from me, but I give it up because I want to" (10:17-18). "Having loved his own . . . he loved them fully" (13:1). "Am I not to drink the cup the Father has given me?" (18:11). "Woman, here is your son . . . Here is your mother" (19:26-27). "It is completed" (19:30).

John's Gospel is full of statements by Jesus that witness to two interrelated affirmations. 1) What happens in this story is no accident—Jesus embraces, rather than falls into, his destiny. 2) Jesus chooses to give himself for us out of love, as he cares both for our lives here and now as well as in the age to come.

But these aren't simply affirmations about Jesus, they are also characterizations of the Christian life. While we are not in control of everything, there is much over which we have discretion, including our time, our wealth, our talents, our interest, and our compassion. To follow Jesus is to choose, as he did, to offer our lives for others out of love. How? By recognizing, accepting, even basking in God's great love for us. The cross invites us to recognize that loss, failure, and death are not the greatest obstacles in this life; rather, to live without love, to take no risks for fear of failure, to hoard what we have—these are what rob us of life. Jesus invites us to identify with others as he has identified with us, and in this way to find our lives by losing them in love.

GOSPEL IMPLICATIONS
Good Friday and Easter are in every way two sides of the same narrative coin. While we observe them on two distinct days, only together do they tell God's story. Apart from Good Friday, Easter makes no sense. And apart from Easter, Good Friday can only be considered the story of one more noble and innocent victim to the world's penchant for violence. Taken together, they tell the story of God's tremendous love for the world, a love that was willing to endure the humiliation, shame, and pain of the cross, a love that was too strong to be kept captive to death.

We should therefore, remember that just as Good Friday is not the final or pinnacle day of the Christian calendar, so also death does not have the last word. We can bear to look at the cross only, perhaps, because we know the story is not finished. Similarly, we can bear to look at the difficult places of our lives, trusting that God has not abandoned us. And we can bear each others' burdens because we know that as we do so, we see God crucified and risen for us and all the world.

DAVID J. LOSE

DEANNA THOMPSON

Resurrection of the Lord (Easter Day)

The Lessons in Précis

Easter celebrates God's victory over death, a victory we share.

Acts 10: 34-43. Peter summarizes for Gentiles the story of Jesus: God chose Jesus, but he was rejected and put to death by the religious authorities. So God raised Jesus from death, and all who believe in him are drawn into new relationship with God.

Psalm 118:1-2, 14-21. The psalmist praises God's marvelous work to redeem and save.

1 Corinthians 15:19-26. The resurrection, according to Paul, is the first scene in the final and climactic act of God's drama to redeem the world. The resurrection creates hope in believers in this life and for the life to come.

John 20:1-18. Mary goes to the empty tomb. Resurrection is unsettling, even confusing, but ultimately it is consoling and comforting, as Jesus calls Mary by name and commissions her to share the good news that he has been raised and will ascend in triumph to God.

Theme Sentence

Life wins! When God raises Jesus from death, God affirms that life is stronger than death, that love is stronger than fear, and that forgiveness is stronger than judgment. In all these things, we see that God keeps God's promises.

A KEY THEOLOGICAL QUESTION
Recognizing the New Resurrection Reality

After the dark days of Lent and the grief of Good Friday, Easter brings palpable relief. Just as spring is emerging around us, we hear good news of great joy: that death does not have the last word. In the resurrection of Christ, God overcomes the destructive forces of sin, suffering, and death and gives us life. On Easter, we can sing with the psalmist that "you answered me, because you were my saving help" (Ps 118:21).

Today's scripture passages suggest that we, like the apostles, are called to be witnesses to the difference Christ's life, death, and resurrection makes for life in the present and in the future (Acts 10:39). We are called to witness to the resurrection reality that God ushers into the world through Christ. Christ has died, Christ has risen, and life and death are no longer the same.

But just how resurrection changes things is not immediately clear. The resurrection story in John 20 begins with confusion. The disciples visit Jesus' tomb only to discover the corpse has gone missing. When Mary arrives, she meets a stranger and asks him where they've taken the body. Mary does not yet understand this new resurrection reality; she, too, is confused and disoriented. It isn't until the risen Christ utters her name that she recognizes him and calls him *Rabbouni*. Christ, her teacher and Lord, is alive. What does it mean for Mary to live within this new resurrection reality after she thought her teacher and Lord was dead?

In answering that question, we need to linger for a moment over the remarkable Johannine claim of the unrecognizability of the risen Christ. Mary, who accompanied Jesus to his death, cannot recognize the risen Lord even as he stands next to her and talks to her. Mary was one of Jesus' most loyal followers—some even call her the first apostle—thus it's jarring and unnerving that even she cannot recognize Jesus and his resurrection reality right away. We learn from Mary's encounter that the risen Christ is strangely different from the not-yet-crucified Christ. As Archbishop of Canterbury Rowan Williams (2008) writes, "It's the risen Christ and not the suffering Christ who is the savior" (76). The risen Christ is about the future rather than the past, and it takes Mary a while to catch up.

When Christ uses her name, he calls Mary into a new resurrection reality; and in her recognition of Christ as the resurrected one, Mary's disorientation, grief, and despair over the loss of her Lord begin to fade. But the story doesn't end there; instead, the risen Christ tells Mary that the resurrection reality in which she now lives is not about clinging to him or to the past. Rather, it's about being commissioned to go and tell others of the resurrection and the new reality it brings.

In Acts 10, Peter and the other disciples are helping the Gentiles recognize the new resurrection reality as well. Peter and the others are witnessing to the life, death, and resurrection of Jesus. Their stories lift up Jesus' gift of healing all who were oppressed whom he encountered during his ministry. But the Gentiles to whom the apostles are preaching do not immediately recognize that the resurrection reality created through the rising of Jesus, the Jew, includes them. Therefore, Peter informs them that the God who raised Jesus "doesn't show partiality" (vs. 34); the Gentiles, too, are part of the new resurrection reality where Christ offers forgiveness of sins.

Resurrection reality changes not only life in this world but also what we can hope for beyond the grave. In 1 Corinthians, Paul describes the resurrection reality as one in which we are all made alive in Christ. But Paul also adds to the strangeness when he says that living fully in the resurrection reality—when the last enemy, death, has been overcome—means living in a largely unrecognizable reality. Indeed, Paul's point is that this new reality where death is no more will be disorientingly different from the life we live now. No more predictable patterns, no more presidents or kings or legislative bodies; all of these will be gone (15:24). All created things will pass away.

While most of us take comfort in God's promises of life beyond the grave, it's likely we're also unnerved by talk of how different life will be in the full resurrection reality. Twentieth century Christian writer and theologian C.S. Lewis (1960) addresses this unsettling reality in the wake of his beloved wife's death. And while Lewis acknowledges the disturbing lack of recognition that he believes, with Paul, is intrinsic to the full resurrection reality, he also points to the deeper recognition of God's love that grounds and sustains us through the unrecognition. Lewis writes:

> When we see the face of God we shall know that we have always known it. . . . In heaven there will be no anguish and no duty of turning away from our earthly Beloveds. First, because we shall have turned already . . . from the creatures He made lovable to Love Himself. But secondly, because we shall find them all in Him. By loving Him more than them we shall love them more than we do now (139).

Eschatology—theologians' fancy word for talk of God's promised future—is first and foremost about the resurrection reality offered the world through Christ's rising from the dead. But this reality is disorienting and often unrecognizable. In the resurrection, though, we are promised eternal life with the one who loved us into being and the one who will love us through our taking leave of all that is familiar. Christ is risen. Hallelujah!

A PASTORAL NEED

There is a significant feature of each of the Gospel stories about that first Easter morning that we often leave out. When the heavenly messengers first announce the news of Jesus' resurrection, no one says, "Praise God," let alone, "I knew it!" No one, that is, at first believes the news. In one story the women flee the tomb in terror and silence (Mark 16:8), and in another their testimony is dismissed as "nonsense" (Luke 24:11). In John's portrayal, Mary Magdalene draws what seems the obvious conclusion when Jesus' body cannot be found: someone has taken it.

Amid all the special music, flowers, and celebrations that attend our Easter services, it's easy to forget that news of Jesus' resurrection is as incredible and hard-to-believe as ever. Jesus wasn't just in a coma for a few days. Nor was his body merely resuscitated. No. The scriptures testify that Jesus died. And that God resurrected him—that is, created in him a whole new life that lasts beyond this mortal life.

No wonder it's hard to believe. We have no experience with resurrection. But if the scriptural witness is true, then it changes everything. If God can raise Jesus, death no longer has the last word. If God can raise Jesus, then we need not fear the grave . . . or anything else for that matter. If God can raise Jesus, then all things are possible. If God can raise Jesus, then we, like the apostles in Acts, have no choice to tell this incredible, life-changing story.

ETHICAL IMPLICATIONS

New life brings new possibilities. When we confess that God has raised Jesus from the dead, we confess that salvation—for us and for all the world—is ultimately and completely God's responsibility. Resurrection is beyond us—we cannot create such a miraculous act. But we can celebrate it, tell about it, and live out of the confidence and courage resurrection brings. Because God has raised Jesus from the dead, that is, we can trust God's promise to renew all of creation and throw ourselves into that work, feeding the hungry, housing the homeless, helping those in need, caring for the environment, and visiting those who are isolated.

And this is true even if we don't see the outcome of our efforts. Because God's raising of Jesus is what Paul calls the "first crop of the harvest" (1 Cor 15:20), we can lend our strength and support to all that is life-affirming and life-giving, trusting that whether we succeed or fail, God will redeem all things in time. This grants tremendous freedom to Christians both to dare great things and to keep faith in smaller ones, as we hear in the cry "Christ is Risen" the promise that no effort for good— whether great or small—is done in vain but is caught up in God's great act of redemption signaled by Christ's resurrection.

So look around—what is ailing that needs support, who is afraid that needs courage, what is dying that needs new life? Throw yourself into these worthy pursuits without fear, for Christ is risen and will come again to redeem each and all of us and, indeed, all the world.

Gospel Implications

The Easter story is the climax and pinnacle of the biblical drama, but it is not the end. One of the amazing things about the Bible is that it begins in the very beginning with Genesis and closes only at the very end in Revelation, which means that we all live somewhere between the Acts of the Apostles and Revelation. Therefore, we are invited to take our place with all those who from Peter onward confess faith in the resurrected Christ.

This may be daunting to some of our hearers, as we don't typically think of ourselves as connected with the biblical "heroes" we've heard about at church. Further, many may think they lack the faith to play any meaningful role in God's ongoing story. But I suspect we draw a much sharper line between doubt and faith than the Bible does. Consider the main characters in today's readings: Peter who denied his Lord; Mary who did not recognize Jesus and assumed his body was stolen; Paul who at first persecuted the early Christians. Yet God used all of these people to spread the good news of God's purpose to save, bless, and redeem the world. If God can work through these imperfect persons, then surely God will also use all that we have and are, as well.

Notes

C.S. Lewis, *The Four Loves,* 1960.

Rowan Williams, *Resurrection,* 2008.

DAVID J. LOSE

DEANNA THOMPSON

Second Sunday of Easter

The Lessons in Précis

Throughout Easter we witness the growth of the disciples' faith and the spread of the gospel.

> *Acts 5:27-32.* The resurrection creates in the disciples the faith and courage to witness to those who oppose them.

> *Psalm 118:14-29.* Upon realizing all that God has done to renew, redeem, and save, the Psalmist can only profess faith and give thanks: "This is the day the Lord acted; we will rejoice and celebrate in it!" (vs. 24).

> *Revelation 1:4-8.* Everything John wants to say to these seven churches stems from his vision of God's grace, mercy, and majesty made manifest in and through Jesus the Christ, the Alpha and Omega, the beginning and end.

> *John 20:19-31.* In the presence of the risen Christ, Thomas is called to believe. Jesus' final words to Thomas are less rebuke of him than blessing of us and all those who "don't see and yet believe" (vs. 29).

Theme Sentence

Resurrection creates faith. The Easter proclamation that "Christ is risen!" does not describe a neutral or passive event. News of the resurrection affected the earliest witnesses, and it still affects us, giving us faith to witness, persevere, serve, and give thanks for God's abundant blessing.

A KEY THEOLOGICAL QUESTION
The Difference between Faith and Certainty

On a recent summer road trip, we visited the town of Independence, Missouri, home of former President Harry S. Truman. Alongside the Truman history filling the town, we discovered a Mormon Temple site that Joseph Smith and other church leaders believed to be the exact location of Christ's second coming. The plaque on the site memorializes their certainty: Independence, Missouri, will be where Christ will come again.

Medieval theologian Anselm's dictum that theology is "faith seeking understanding" offers a different version of faith than that of Joseph Smith, a version that offers illumination of the readings for today. Rather than coming to certitude about the great questions of faith and then resting on those answers, Anselm described the process of living with faith as a continuous quest of seeking to understand. Our understanding is always partial; and as we come to understand faith and the questions of faith more deeply, we seek an even deeper wisdom regarding the answers.

If we are on a continuous journey with faith, we need to acknowledge that there will be moments of impatience, moments where we want the "hows" and the "whys" to become clearer and more understandable. Much like the disciple Thomas in John 20, we want to be certain of what it is we believe. In John's story, Thomas demands evidence. He needs to see the wounds on Christ's hands; he needs to feel the holes caused by the nails. He wants to be certain. Christ gives Thomas what he wants, even as he commends those who have faith in the absence of such convincing evidence.

Indeed, many Christians in the twenty-first century crave the kind of certainty Thomas demanded. In the midst of challenges from the "new atheists" like Sam Harris, author of *The End of Faith* (2005), we may wonder what proof we can offer to answer the critics' assaults. Harris contends that we religious types unwisely abandon our reason in order to believe. How might we respond to such demands for certainty, for reason in place of faith, in our day?

The book of Revelation, which many of us level-headed Christians in the contemporary world often prefer to avoid, seems only to make things worse. In the first chapter, the author writes about Christ's second coming, saying, "He is coming with the clouds"; a few lines later we're told that God is "the Alpha and the Omega," "the one who is and was and is coming" (1:7-8). Such scriptural imagery of the return of the risen Christ and the power of God takes language and stretches it to its limits. In Revelation, we're given an apocalyptic vision, one that sounds more at home in the fantastical world of Harry Potter than as part of sensible talk about faith in a society that purportedly values rationality and evidence for one's beliefs.

Joseph Smith is just one among many persons of faith who take such apocalyptic visions and reduce them to affirmations of certitude. Scripture says Jesus "is coming with the clouds," so we take such imagery and proclaim that Jesus is coming with the clouds all the way down to Independence, Missouri. While many of us in mainline Christianity today might be highly critical of such a move, at the same time we can appreciate the desire Smith and others have had for certainty about matters of faith.

If we approach faith more as Anselm did, however, we can return to Acts 5, to the part of the story where we hear that the God of Jesus Christ is the same God as the God of ancient Israel. The apostles tell the high priests of the temple that "the God of our ancestors raised Jesus from the dead" (Acts 5:30). What they offer is a different vision than the priests expect or accept, a claim about God's redeeming action in Jesus Christ based more on faith than on certainty. The priests don't like it.

What does the apostles' testimony mean for us today? Indeed, the apostles risk their lives to share the message of God's redeeming work in the world. Jesus was killed; but God did not allow death to have the final word. As we, the people of faith, seek to understand what this means, we acknowledge that we sometimes crave the certainty Thomas demanded in John 20. But we hear in Acts the command to trust in the testimonies of those ancestors in the faith; to embrace the resurrection reality as God's gift to us. As the author of Revelation proclaims, we are God's, from beginning to end. Let us continue to seek a deeper understanding of what such proclamations mean for a life of faith.

A PASTORAL NEED

As far as I'm concerned, Thomas has gotten a bad rap. He asks for nothing more than what the other disciples got: a chance to see Jesus in person, to know that word of his Lord's resurrection is no cruel hoax. Thomas isn't so much a doubter as he is a realist. After all, when the disciples recognize that if Jesus returns to Judea he will likely be stoned, it is Thomas who urges the others to follow Jesus to that death (John 11:16).

Pictured as a realist, it is easier to hear Thomas' skepticism as akin to that of a terminally-ill person who, resigned to their fate, is told of a new miracle cure. Three days earlier Thomas had watched as his teacher and friend was nailed to the cross, and so he wants proof when he hears Jesus is alive. Few things cut more deeply than the shards of a broken dream, and Thomas has bled enough.

It may be that we have many Thomases in our congregation— hard-boiled realists who cast a weary and skeptical eye to news that life can be any different than what they have experienced thus far. To these persons, this reading may sound at first like a rebuke, yet I suspect that Jesus' words are not so much a rebuke of Thomas but an encouragement to all of us who "don't see and yet believe" (John 20:29). John shares this story both to acknowledge how hard it is to believe at times and to encourage all of us in faith—even and especially the Thomases.

ETHICAL IMPLICATIONS

The readings appointed for this day say a lot about faith: where it comes from and what it makes possible. First, the readings testify to the power of telling and hearing Jesus' story to create faith. The passage from Revelation captures the dynamic nature of promises about the future—"Look, he is coming with the clouds!" (1:7)—to create faith in the present. John's statement in verses 30-31 reveals the purpose of his gospel and, indeed, all proclamation: to create faith in Jesus and thereby enjoy abundant life.

At the same time, faith is more than knowledge. Hearing the story of Jesus grants us courage to follow him, daring to give testimony like Peter and the other disciples, even in the most difficult of circumstances. Other passages in Acts highlight the acts of mercy and kindness undertaken by the earliest disciples. Caught up in faith in Jesus, they conformed their life to his example.

But I think these passages also hint at how to regard those of differing faiths. There is, after all, no way to prove our faith. Thus, as we saw in the story of Thomas, faith can be hard. It is, at heart, a gamble, a risk, a wager that against all odds God's love prevails over hate and that the life God offers is stronger than death. When we meet those who do not believe as we do, we might therefore recognize that whatever faith they have is similarly a brave gamble. For this reason, we can interact with believers of other traditions with a measure of respect, joining them whenever possible in caring for God's world and people.

GOSPEL IMPLICATIONS

Talk about faith can quickly get derailed in two ways. First, faith can seem largely like a "head thing," a cognitive assent to doctrinal formulas. Scripture, however, imagines faith as a way of being, not just a way of thinking. Those who are called to faith are called, like Thomas, Mary, and the original disciples all the way through Dietrich Bonhoeffer, Martin Luther King, Jr., Dorothy Day, and even us to live out their faith in ways that are tangible.

Faith can also seem like one more thing we should do, a feat of the will that marks true Christians from a lesser breed. But notice that in each of the readings faith is more of a response by those who have been gripped by God than a choice or decision. The disciples testify because they must obey the Spirit, even when it puts their lives in jeopardy. Thomas' skepticism is swept away, and all he can do is confess Jesus not only as his Lord but also as his God. John the Seer writes to the seven churches because he can do no other.

Faith is a gift—not something we can muster or dredge up, but rather something that takes hold of us, leading us in directions we may never previously have imagined treading. Where, we might ask our people, will this dynamic and unpredictable faith lead you?

Notes

Sam Harris, *The End of Faith: Religion, Terror and the Future of Reason*, 2005.

_____

DAVID J. LOSE

DEANNA THOMPSON

THIRD SUNDAY
OF EASTER

THE LESSONS IN PRÉCIS

The 50-day period of expectancy between Easter and Pentecost allows God's people to continue experiencing the dawning awareness of disciples who, in the power of the Spirit, discover the meaning of Jesus' resurrection.

> *Acts 9:1-6 (7-20).* Saul of Tarsus, a dedicated defender of Judaism, experiences a world-altering vision of the resurrected Jesus as leader and Lord of the community he once hated. Saul's life and the cause of Christianity are forever changed because he surrenders his limited understanding to become the "agent" of God (vs. 15).
>
> *Psalm 30.* Although we may weep at the dark night of life's setbacks, "joy comes with the morning" when our confidence in God remains unmoved (vs. 5, nrsv).
>
> *Revelation 5:11-14.* Were the living and powerful risen Christ to be fully revealed to us, our call to ascribe glory to him would be all-encompassing.
>
> *John 21:1-19.* When the risen Lord beckons, Peter casts aside the limits of his own understanding to respond to the call of Christ to serve people in need, whatever the cost.

THEME SENTENCE

Christ's world-altering purposes often transcend our limited understanding. Like Peter and Paul, how often our carefully constructed assumptions about living faithfully may be challenged when we confess to a limited understanding of God's purposes, whether in our vocation or in our work with a community of faith.

A Key Theological Question

As universally definitive as it is, and as the historical event of which nothing greater can be conceived, Easter in and of itself is insufficient for full faith in God. A faith inspired by Easter yearns for the breath of Pentecost. While before Easter fear for one's faith as a possession may have funded hatred of the "other," the first flush of Easter can raise a fear that one's new faith is insufficient. Fear foments violence and weakens zeal for the good. Christian joy is born from Easter yet needs strength to follow eagerly the crucified and risen Christ. We cannot imagine how stymied we would be suddenly to have to begin a new life of faith and discipleship based upon the premises against which our "old" lives had been dedicated. We need help. We need instruction. We need the deep and abiding vision that comes only from Christ's Spirit presiding in the members of the new Christian community. During and after "conversion," we cannot make our own way and we cannot make ourselves up, no matter what the self-authoring premises of postmodernity may claim. God's wisdom and action in and with others will mean that it takes the others in Christian community rightly to make us up and to aid faith's erasure of fear.

And so it is also with Paul, Peter, and all other Christian faithful. Saul's Damascus Road trip was his own cipher for a journey that began with an Easter shock and was strengthened by catechetical placement in the Spirit-community he had meant to destroy. The well-schooled Saul would be re-forged by both mystical means and daily communal habits over a long while. His actual discipleship/leadership journey would not end until Rome. Not-so-schooled Peter would become a leader after abandoning the biggest haul of fish he ever got and being told to love and feed Christ's flock. Like Paul, Peter would need much longer, cruciform instruction to become a servant leader and apostle who rightly loves. Common to both would be God's conversion of them from their dogmatic dispositions to loving like Jesus, from mere "orthodoxy" to "orthophilly." God would form them with surprising means. God shapes each of us toward and beyond Easter, according to our given circumstances. But common throughout God's formational pedagogy is the employ of the Spirit and the New Community to bring the would-be faithful into deeper faith and understanding.

The difficulty of discipleship is compounded when the instructions challenge our core convictions, lifestyle, and worldview. One cannot imagine how impossible it must have seemed to Saul of Tarsus to "move on," then, after having been thrown off his high horse and turned inside out by the person and community he so zealously persecuted. Jesus Christ and the new community of his church represented everything Saul opposed. They threatened cultural stability, tradition, the moral code, and the whole social order, even if that order had accommodated to empire. Now Saul/Paul not only had to accommodate those who threatened all he was about, but he also was fully dependent upon and led into a whole new life by these same threatening revolutionaries. As Luke Timothy Johnson observes, Saul's conversion—no immediate thing!—was a terrifying story of being "struck blind by a great light, overwhelmed by a commanding voice, led helplessly by the hand to the city, sitting in darkness, fasting, praying, waiting . . . for what?, and finally being brought by means of greeting as a brother, and the laying on of hands, and the pouring of water, into the community of those he had hated" (Johnson, 1992, 169).

These texts are addressed to both the unbelieving seeker and the already converted. And they are addressed to everyone in between. That would be us. We are shown here God's means for anyone to grow in faith. We are also given the insight that the people to whom we are given and who are given to us in the new community are like those in the old. How often we moan that people inside the church are as "bad," if not worse, as those outside. We rue that congregational life is dysfunctional, pathogenic, and just plain hateful of those "others" outside who challenge our stabile church and culture, and how even more hateful the church can be to those inside who have crossed our own personal norms and expectations. Maybe a lack of external enemies for sinners means we naturally turn toward attacking our own. But God's healing pedagogy gives us differences that we fear and might even hate. Thereby our own lives may be shaped into forms we could never have recognized before. This is grace for the individual and the church. And it gives but a hint of the wily and witty means by which God will love and heal the world.

God's power of Easter is surely the most dramatic act of all. Still, the journey from Saul to Paul, self-absorbed Simon to Peter, old Adam to new, unbeliever to disciple, takes time and involves many. It takes the new community to "raise the dead" and to forge a sword of fear into a plowshare of grace. In God's so doing, the community itself is shaped into deeper discipleship along with the new disciple. Though we will be changed in a moment, our Easter on this side of mortality is not completed in a day. The journey from Easter to Pentecost is one from pretended self-confident independence to a humble, communally empowering faith sufficient for daily discipleship. Taking us beyond fear, God makes us God's instruments in, with, and through fearless community. Yet, no matter how far we think we may have progressed onward from Easter, we will find that Christ's cross figures high between both Easter and Pentecost.

A Pastoral Need

For many of us, our lives are works of art crafted by our own hands sometimes quite intentionally and sometimes seemingly by happenstance, but always by the tracks we lay down each day, providing forward movement. We try with God's help to secure a future for ourselves and for those we love, so much so that we are often shocked when the well laid tracks are rocked and our lives become derailed. A family member is diagnosed with a terminal illness; our child whom we worked so hard to protect has been seduced into a world of aimless rebellion and drugs; the vocation we worked so hard to perfect has been bypassed by the jobs of a digital culture; the congregation in which we have worshipped for decades no longer appeals to the families of our community. We cry, "God, I don't understand."

We thought God was on our side. We confused our limited understanding of God's purposes with our own carefully constructed assumptions about what living faithfully should look like. To live as a Christian has never meant that life will be heartbreak free. But the good news, whether in Saul's story of redemption or Peter's story of surrender is that no one becomes an instrument of God's purpose unless in the midst of struggle he or she learns to trust God. And no one learns how to trust God like this apart from a community that helps us overcome our fear of whether God is in this with us.

ETHICAL IMPLICATIONS

It has always been too easy for religious worship to slip into and almost be eclipsed by our own nationalism or sense of ethnic privilege. The irony of being struck blind in order to see how his defense of the faith had turned into hatred provides an important text for exploring how Saul of Tarsus' dogmatic dispositions had turned his fervid orthodoxy into violent orthopraxy toward others.

In the summer of 2010, the question of erecting a mosque at the site of a building where the roof was destroyed by falling debris from the World Trade Center towers was debated throughout the United States. Some argued that locating this worship center would be a counter monument not unlike the mosque built over the destroyed temple in conquered Jerusalem. For others, this was a question of a Christian commitment to religious liberty and love of neighbor in which the Park 51 Center for Islamic worship became a ground zero example of similar efforts to stop people from building mosques in Murfreesboro, Tennessee, in Temecula, California, in rural Wisconsin, etc. As reported in *The New York Times* such efforts represent a growing "gloves off" approach to the spread of Islam in America, conceding that the problem is "Islam itself." Fear of Islam is frequently stirred up by speakers, often hosted by Christian congregations, who "quote passages from the Koran and argue that even the most Americanized Muslim secretly wants to replace the Constitution with Islamic Shariah law" (Goodstein, 2010).

Gospel often confronts our core convictions and worldviews. It challenges us to examine whether our response to others is fear or a willingness to lay down our own agendas to be an instrument God can use.

GOSPEL IMPLICATIONS

In the time between Easter and Pentecost, a transformation occurs for disciples who first gathered in fear behind locked doors but eventually burst forth with a message of transcendent assurance that "God has made this Jesus, whom you crucified, both Lord and Christ" (Acts 2:36). Fear often circumscribes our ability to see God's purposes. It may be the fear of Peter, who returns to his former vocation and needs Christ to help him see his true calling. It may be Saul of Tarsus, who needs to surrender his agenda to serve God in order to see that God plans to bring him before Gentiles, kings, and the very people he sought to protect. It may be Ananias, who trembles with amazement that God wants him to reach across the barricade of hate to invite Saul into a community of disciples where he learns, with love and patient care in community, how to become Paul—the person who shares the grace of God in cross-cultural outreach to the world. "Weeping may stay all night, but by morning, joy!"—we trust in God's provision (Ps 30:5). Perhaps we, too, will understand and glorify God from the vantage of eternity. Gospel invites us to see it now.

Notes

Laurie Goodstein, "Around Country, Mosque Projects Meet Opposition," *The New York Times*, August 8, 2010, Section A, 1.

Luke Timothy Johnson, *The Acts of the Apostles*, 1992.

ROBERT STEPHEN REID

DUANE LARSON

FOURTH SUNDAY
OF EASTER

THE LESSONS IN PRÉCIS

The 50-day period of expectancy between Easter and Pentecost allows God's people to continue experiencing the dawning awareness of disciples who, in the power of the Spirit, discover that Christ overcomes even the purported finality of death.

> ***Acts 9:36-43.*** Peter, like Jesus before him, reclaims life from death. The resuscitation of Dorcas is a prophetic seal of God's blessings and the peace richly experienced by the emerging church of Christ followers.

> ***Psalm 23.*** Depicting YHWH as Shepherd and Host, this psalm has always been read as symbolizing the pilgrim journey of life triumphing over the shadow of death and death itself.

> ***Revelation 7:9-17.*** A great multitude of white-robed people from every race and nation gather in eternity to praise Christ as the great Lamb of God whose worthy life vindicated their lives as eternally worthy.

> ***John 10:22-30.*** Jesus' response challenges a limited conception of Jewish Messiahship that would promise a better but perishable life for people with a declaration that he gives his followers eternal life that will never perish.

THEME SENTENCE

Christ leaves death behind. Living leads to dying, but the resurrection of Jesus means that the Great Shepherd will continue to lead disciples to the water of life and that God will wipe away every tear from our eyes as we participate in Jesus' unfinished story.

A KEY THEOLOGICAL QUESTION

Peter raises Dorcas from the dead. Those who sing with the psalmist lack for nothing in God. The sealed and saved servants washed by the last Passover also lack for nothing. And the Great Shepherd simply will not let his followers go. The new life in the risen Lord is not yet complete, to be sure. But the texts together for this day of proclamation emphasize that our new roles in God's great drama will mean the end of tears.

Is this too optimistic a word for a world like ours? How could it ever be that there shall be no more pain and sorrow? How many times has this been promised by religion and myth through the millennia? How can we hear and do this word without cynicism from our weakness within and disparagement from the powers without?

On the large scale of human history, the human wreckage is bloody indeed. Our hands are red both by human intent and by nature's "tooth and claw" (Tennyson). William James once observed, with some humor, that even if finally only one cockroach was clicking his grief of being lonely, still all would not be right with the world. Judging by its history, evolution's future bears no healing promise. And human being purportedly apart from nature (were such a thing even possible) is more horrid in its voluntary violence. Though John's Revelation, too, is bloody; it is the end of death that he sees on the grandest scale. And that is the point—that new life puts death behind. Still, how can we be sure?

We cannot. No one can. No scientist or theologian, other than the most fundamentalist and non-empirical of either sort, can guarantee the certainty of human knowledge. The question instead is how one can trust in a promise. Even so, there are no human promises that can be eternally trusted, for humans die. But here God promises. God's promise is of a wholly distinct category, as the director's promise to the new actors is of a different category than those the actors make among each other; better, as an aged and wise mentor who has seen and been through it all can make a promise that is categorically different than the kind made by the apprentices whom she or he would guide. In this case, our trust in God's promise will deepen as we see not only how far God has journeyed to accompany us on "our" side, but also that God will cross many more dangerous borders yet.

Even when God promises, however, humans can put reason unreasonably in the way. For example, the John text, full of suggestive themes, is often read even "unconsciously" in the traditioned language of "election." "I know my own sheep and they know me" (10:14). Supposing that the "problem" is one of why some people follow Jesus and others do not, it seems reasonable to conclude that some people are simply disposed to hearing the Shepherd speak. They have the ears to hear. So, we conclude, some people are predestined or elected, and some evidently are not. This is one way of reading and hearing the text, and it has a history that deserves respect.

Another perspective is to suppose the text is primarily about Jesus' unity with the Father. We hear or read Jesus' "I and the Father are one" (10:30) substantively or ontologically, as a claim of mutual identification. Thus one may infer and proclaim this word as a foundation for the doctrine of the Trinity and could; so it becomes a Trinitarian text. This, too, is a traditioned interpretation to be respected.

Suppose, however, that the reader/hearer/proclaimer emphasizes the intentionality behind certain verbs. The sheep who know Christ *will not* be let go. Jesus' father and he *are* one. Hear both words not only ontologically, but also as resolve, intention, gracious willfulness, and absolute promise. Jesus and his father are one in their resolve to save their sheep, heal the world, raise the dead, and wash tears away forever. Heard this way, the promise is so great that what counts is not even election, with all its premises still of tribalism and distinctions between those who are in and those who are out. The promise is so intention-full that Easter *will* mean that death is put behind; such is the grandest strategic plan spun from God's love. It is a "problem" only for those who would trump love with election, for those who value their own paternity and posterity over compassion for those of "the other side." God's love in Christ, however, is so large that he suffered death on the cross—truly a journey of compassion to the "other side"—and then raised Jesus Christ from *that* death, not just any death, so that death is put behind life forever.

That is a story larger than any other that has ever been told. It includes us yet in its unfolding drama. Those who would turn an ear to the "sheep whisperer's" voice will discover they can trust him.

Phyllis Tickle has written that the contemporary paradigm for the life of Christian faith is not Christendom's "believe, behave, belong," but just the reverse: "belong, behave, believe" (159). This puts the priority right; relationship with God in Jesus Christ, who first gives himself to us, is more important but not separate from knowledge about God. One never relates without knowing, but knowing without relationship is hardly to know at all. At the outset of a faith journey like ours, we do not need to "know" the answers first. It is enough to trust that God is intent that we belong. And we do, by Christ's promise. The rest of behaving and believing will happen in their due time in the new life of Easter faith.

A Pastoral Need

Six weeks after Pastor John Claypool's daughter Laura Lue died on schedule from childhood leukemia, a Jewish rabbi who was also a good friend met him during local hospital visitation. He caught Claypool off guard by asking, "Honest, man to man. Did God do anything for any of [your family] in the midst of all that circumstance?" Claypool knew it was a genuine question from a man who had also struggled with grief: Is God truly present in meaningful ways in our darkest hours?

Claypool told his friend that God came to them in an unexpected way—through the gift of endurance to face the unendurable. Living through a tragedy of such immensity had taught him that, "Having sensed how powerless I was to hold on to her life, having sensed that I could do so little for someone I loved so much, has made me much more anxious to take every day as the gift that it is, and not to take for granted the people that I love, but to look on them as a kind of windfall, a kind of grace, and a kind of gift" (Claypool, 2006, 49).

Even as he walked in this valley of the shadow of death, Claypool learned that God was with him. How do we face death? Could you say Christian hope might come as a gift of endurance? As a belief that our life itself is truly a gift from God?

Ethical Implications

We who regularly recite the Apostles' Creed in community proclaim, "I believe in the resurrection of the body." Whether we view death as the great enemy to be finally vanquished as does John the Revelator or welcome it as release from whatever infirmity keeps us from living robustly, the Easter story stands central to the Christian faith; death has been swallowed up in the victory of Christ's resurrection. A belief in the ability to transcend death is intimately related to what it means for Christians to "believe, behave, belong" in community where the meaning of one's life is measured by something greater than its longevity or achievement.

Living in the middle of God's story with humankind, we may forget how stunning the news of Easter faith was for people who had staked everything in the ministry of Jesus. Whether it is the story of Jesus taking the little girl by the hand and saying "Get up" (Luke 8:54) or Peter prayerfully telling Dorcas to arise, biblical stories of raising the dead or restoring life are core to our hope in God. We know that such hope can too easily be traduced by irresponsible palliatives, such as seeking to comfort mourners with claims that God needs a person more than we do, or in quelling the fears of children by assuring them that grandma now watches over them from heaven's clouds. N. T. Wright maintains, "What we say about death and resurrection gives shape and color to everything else. If we are not careful, we will offer merely a 'hope' that is no longer a surprise, no longer able to transform lives and communities in the present, no longer generated by the resurrection of Jesus himself and looking forward to the promised new heaven and new earth" (25).

GOSPEL IMPLICATIONS

In one of the shortest confessions of faith in scripture, Paul reminds Christians in Rome: "Because if you confess with your mouth 'Jesus is Lord' and in your heart you have faith that God raised him from the dead, you will be saved. Trusting with the heart leads to righteousness, and confessing with the mouth leads to salvation" (Rom 10:9-10). This notion of being healed, or made whole—saved—is at the heart of this confession and at the heart of Jesus' promise to followers held in the hand of his and the father's purposes that they will never perish.

Many of our favorite Christian hymns actually have odd theologies about what the *English Book of Common Prayer* describes as the "sure and certain hope of the resurrection." In his song, *The Riddle*, Christian musician Ken Medema manages to capture something fundamental about the nature of God's promise of new life:

Finding leads to losing, losing lets you find,
   Living leads to dying, but life leaves death behind,
Losing leads to finding, that's all that I can say;
   No one will find life another way.

Jesus and the father are fully resolved to save their sheep, to heal the world, to raise the dead, and to wash tears away for those whose life leaves death behind.

Notes

John Claypool, "What Can We Expect From God?" *This Incomplete One: Words Occasioned by the Death of a Young Person*, ed. Michael D. Bush, 2006.

Kenneth Medema, "The Riddle," Retrieved at http://www.baptistprinciples.org/Biennial09/MEDEMATranscript062709.pdf

Phyllis Tickle, *The Great Emergence: How Christianity is Changing and Why*, 2008.

N. T. Wright, *Surprised by Hope: Rethinking Heaven, the Resurrection, and the Mission of the Church*, 2008.

ROBERT STEPHEN REID

DUANE LARSON

FIFTH SUNDAY
OF EASTER

THE LESSONS IN PRÉCIS

The 50-day period of expectancy between Easter and Pentecost allows God's people to continue experiencing the dawning awareness of disciples who, in the power of the Spirit, discover that Christian identity must transcend nationality.

Acts 11:1-18. Through a vision and experience Peter grasps: "If then God gave them the same gift that he gave us who believed in the Lord Jesus Christ, then who am I? Could I stand in God's way?" (vs. 17, author's trans).

Psalm 148. The Psalmist invites the assembled faithful to affirm manifestations of God's glory in both the heavens and the earth.

Revelation 21:1-6. The central claim is the affirmation: "Look! God's dwelling is here with humankind. He will dwell with them, and they will be his peoples. God himself will be with them as their God."

John 13:31-35. Christian identity is to be rooted in the new commandment of love for one another rather than in racial or ethnic identity.

THEME SENTENCE

The Holy Spirit surprises us with God's inclusiveness. We humans inevitably seem to make a religion out of our ethnic or other identities, but God puts challenge to such gospel divisions, often using the Holy Spirit as teacher of the Way.

A Key Theological Question

There is certainly no lack of identity obsession today. The more the globe becomes a village, the louder and more violent grow the gasps of those who intend only their own and absolute truths and absolute privileges. It also can seem that the closer humankind comes together, the more disposed are the once-privileged toward defining the other, rather than allowing others to define themselves. Midway in our liturgical journey from Easter to Pentecost, perhaps the proclaimer of God's word can help hearers experience the first disciples' discovery that Christian faith both transcends all other identity obsession and practices hospitality toward all "others."

And as happens with middle journey consciousness—that time when we begin to appreciate the real cost of an arduous trip—the hearer will recognize how daunting, even still crucifying, the challenges along the way are and will be. With popular culture already having begun to forget the awe and power of Easter just a month before (It takes more prompting now to get a congregational response to "The Lord is risen."), a spiritual ennui can afflict both the proclaimer and the hearer. The band Stealers Wheel once complained in song about "clowns to the left of me, jokers to the right." Is the Christian stuck in the middle, xenophobes to the left and acedia to the right? The likely answer is worse, that we have something of each deeply within ourselves. But the journey from Easter to Pentecost blesses us both by naming and healing our malady, orienting us to Christ as our Presider, and by gathering us to each other, convened by the Holy Spirit as a holy community of mutual instruction.

Neither Peter nor his apostolic colleagues originally expected their community to extend beyond the comfortable bounds of their Judaism. Peter's radical boundary crossing toward the other, the uncircumcised, was roundly condemned at first by his "first" community. His defense— that God had spoken in dreams to him and to Gentiles (this in itself an interesting source of authority) and then that the Holy Spirit had fallen on those gathered in Caesarea without their yet being baptized (this in itself is an interesting underscore of the Spirit's intended inclusivity)— persuaded his peers into praise. God has given the Gentiles, as well as the Jews, thus all humankind, "the repentance that leads to life" (Acts 11:18, NRSV).

Both the Psalmist and the seer St. John add their amen, that God's glory is manifest everywhere and God will dwell with mortals as God's own. There is no suggestion necessarily of "universalism" here. But the promise of God's grace unto inclusivity is as clear as an Easter day. Not only did God cross a religious boundary by humbly assuming mortality, suffering sin unto crucifixion, and transcending death by embracing it and rising over it (*transcending* does not mean erasing but rather assuming, keeping, and overcoming). God in front of Pentecost promises to cross to the "other" side—humanity and all the creation—once again and finally, to live among and with us as our God. The theology of the cross, that which describes how God acts on the basis of exactly what God did in suffering the death of the Son, is fulfilled in this promise that God will for the final time come over to the other side.

Just as the theology of the cross means that God chooses to side with those who do not get to choose sides, so also God's going to the other side erases all sides. Christian community means divine inclusivity. The Holy Spirit will surprise us. But the Spirit is doing what the Spirit does. It is because there are jokers and clowns in our hearts that the Spirit's work surprises us. The faithful Christian will praise God when we realize that this is what should have been expected all along.

The new community naturally practices hospitality. The practice also comes by Jesus' own command. "Just as I have loved you, so you also must love each other" (John 13:34). This is a more radical command to a new practice than we may at first realize. Across most human cultures and religions, we are indeed and positively disposed to the Golden Rule. Christians default to Jesus' commands to love God and one another "as your selves." Fine as this is, Jesus commands something more difficult: that we love like he did.

It is one good thing to follow the Christian version of the Golden Rule. But perhaps Jesus the mentor saw something in his brief three years with his protégés that changed his mind about his earlier command. Maybe Jesus realized that loving one's neighbor as one's self may not always be good news for the neighbor. Just how well and healthily do we love ourselves? So Jesus clarifies. Love like he did. Do so, and we will see the world changed, and our own lives with it.

We have much to learn from the Holy Spirit. The Spirit's convening of us into God's holy, inclusive community calls us to exercise our best thought and care for each other. God's Spirit is using us even to make each other more personal: inclusivity with hospitality equals authentic community. We are quite making each other up. But this new community is not a utopia, something humanly imagined and constructed. This new community is, thankfully, God's strategic plan made real with the likes of us. God crossed major borders to make it so, and we will see more such border crossing yet. There will be fear of others here and spiritual sloth there. But the cross of Christ is at the border gates, and God is working to erase the borders altogether. How exciting this journey with God's Holy Spirit is becoming!

A Pastoral Need

In defending his actions at having baptized Gentile converts, Peter concludes his argument by saying, "Who am I? Could I stand in God's way?" (Acts 11:18). Standing in God's way has a specific focus in this story. It speaks to those moments when we tend to reify our own homogenous ways rather than act intentionally to be inclusive of others.

A homeless person has worshipped with a congregation for several months. During Advent a member gives this person a wrapped Christmas gift. Try as she may and with tears in her eyes she cannot resist opening it. The gift is a can of spray deodorant. She no longer worships there.

A group of parents decide summer would be a great time to provide an intergenerational educational event. When several of the congregation's non-middle-class children show up for Sunday school without parents, they are excluded from participating. The design requires parents to be with their children. These kids are told there is no Sunday school for them this summer.

Several key leaders in an intentionally multiracial congregation become disturbed when they discover that the worship leader actively maintains diversity records of lay members assisting in serving the Eucharist/communion. The worship leader wanted to insure that the congregation was being intentional in its effort to reflect its multiracial commitment. Other leaders see an imposition of a quota system: "Stop trying to force it," they demand. "Just let it happen."

We hinder God whenever we refuse to be intentional in welcoming the other and make choices that assume our group's interests best serve God's interests.

ETHICAL IMPLICATIONS

A challenge for the church is that too often we love our neighbor best as we love our selves; i.e., when our neighbor looks like us, is in the same social class as we are, and has needs to which we can respond without overly complicating our busy lives. Nancy T. Ammerman, the Organizing Religious Work project director for the Hartford Institute of Religious Research reports that, "Mainline folks, for all their talk about diversity, lag significantly behind" conservative and Catholic congregations in the efforts to be intentional about realizing diversity as a missional focus for congregational identity (Dart, 2001).

For much of the preceding century, we have tended to read these Acts conversion stories as narratives of the young church accepting Gentiles into Christian community or as stories concerning the difficulty the early Jewish-Christian community had in overcoming its holiness regulations. What can too easily be missed is how a story like this provides a missional challenge for Christian congregations to become equally intentional in their cross-cultural refusal to permit distinctions between "them" and "us."

As it was for the Jerusalem Christian community (see Gal 2), this ministry challenge of implementing intentional racial and social diversity can be just as difficult to face today. In *United by Faith*, Paul Curtis DeYoung and his coauthors note,

> When religious people make choices based on their individual rights, they largely end up in homogeneous congregations. Answering the question about whether we ought to end up in uniracial congregations requires that we draw on a more powerful tradition. Given that overwhelmingly the largest percentage of religious people in the United States is Christian—nearly 90 percent at the time of this writing—it makes the most sense to draw on that tradition (2004, 4).

Stories like these, where Peter claims he would not choose to "hinder God" (Acts 11:17, NRSV), lift up this "more powerful tradition."

GOSPEL IMPLICATIONS

Benjamin Barber has masterfully argued that the twenty-first century will be characterized by *Jihad vs. McWorld*, two opposed forces that in their worst evocations would make of us all either troubled tribalists or complacent consumers. At its worst McWorld flattens in the name of interconnectedness, fosters artificial social cooperation, requires integration and uniformity, makes consumers of everyone, and needs all borders to go away. At its worst Jihad pits cultures against cultures, people against people, and tribe against tribe; fights against interdependence; lauds self-determination; and recreates borders.

Gospel, the force in the redemptive death of Jesus that rends the curtain between the temple courts (Luke 23:45), challenges us to surrender all tendencies to make tribe our faith and self our center. If the theology of the cross means that God chooses to side with those who do not get to choose sides, Christians must be intentional in exploring their tendency to surrender to either of these competing worldviews, neither of which is worthy of living faithfully. Stated again, perhaps the proclaimer of God's word can help hearers experience the first disciples' discovery that Christian faith both transcends all other identity obsession and practices hospitality toward all "others." After all, everyone who is a disciple of Christ was once on the outside and has been welcomed in, through no merit of our own.

Notes

Benjamin R. Barber, *Jihad vs. McWorld: Terrorism's Challenge to Democracy*, 2003.

Curtiss Paul DeYoung, Michael O. Emerson, George Yancy, and Karen Kim, *United by Faith: The Multiracial Congregation As an Answer to the Problem of Race*, 2004.

John Dart, "Hues in the Pews: Racially Mixed Churches an Elusive Goal," *Christian Century* (February 28, 2001), Retrieved at http://hirr.hartsem.edu/cong/articles_huesinthepews.html

ROBERT STEPHEN REID

DUANE LARSON

SIXTH SUNDAY
OF EASTER

THE LESSONS IN PRÉCIS

The 50-day period of expectancy between Easter and Pentecost allows God's people to continue experiencing the dawning awareness of disciples who, in the power of the Spirit, discover that Christian identity must transcend nationality.

> *Acts 16:9-15.* Paul grasps that the gospel is meant not just for Semitic peoples but for other Mediterranean peoples as well.

> *Psalm 67.* The intention is for all people to revere God: "Let the people celebrate and shout with joy because you judge the nations fairly and guide all nations on the earth" (vs. 4).

> *Revelation 21:10, 22–22:5.* The tree of life in the New Jerusalem will be replenished by the water of life flowing from God's throne; God's purpose is realized in the healing of all the nations.

> *John 14:23-29.* A disciple asks Jesus, "Why are you about to reveal yourself to us and not to the world?" (14:22). Jesus confounds Jewish Messianic expectation by promising the Spirit of God will reveal God's purposes to all who believe.

THEME SENTENCE

The Holy Spirit opens Paul's vision to a multiethnic view of God's church. Whenever we would reduce worship of God to worship with only our own kind, the Holy Spirit will challenge us with God's gospel vision of a cross-cultural gospel with multiethnic congregations that transcend ethnic exclusivity.

A KEY THEOLOGICAL QUESTION

While our socially-networked and technologically-tied world gets smaller and even "flatter," new life in Christ's Spirit opens to a huge new world. The scriptures for this Sunday are uniquely unified in their testimony and coherent with the trajectory we have been on. The gospel of God's grace is meant for everyone; all nations will be glad; God's tree of life will heal the nations; the Spirit of God will accompany and equip all who believe. The new life of faith takes us into a world far bigger than the one we think we know, and the Holy Spirit will in-spire us to engage the new world with love and peace. So Jesus directly told his disciples. So Paul also discovered when he was led by the Spirit to cross borders he had never before encountered.

The journey from Easter to Pentecost opens new dimensions of understanding. What we had thought were limits are now opportunities. What we feared as unfamiliar may now be the signs of homecoming. Those whom we disliked, we may find now as God's doorways to the beloved community that both excites and heals us. What might have seemed a familiar journey is now charged by awareness that something is radically different about the world around us and the world within. We may indeed want to run or hide or look fearfully over our shoulders, so different the air seems. But journey on from Easter into Pentecost we must, even as we wonder if this electricity and call are truly God's work. A journey with the Spirit, especially one wherein we believe the Spirit leads us but is not yet wholly manifest, fills us with questions, even trepidation, about what God is doing. We also know that where challenges mount, they can be signs of the last gasp of our former selves and the old world. Those challenges belong to the birth pangs that precede our full transformation by the Spirit of God.

The Holy Spirit already is showing us and leading us into the fullness of life on this mortal side. God is giving us a preview of how life shall be at its fullest. It will not be "the same ol' same ol'." It will not be monochromatic. It will not be mere refrain of behavior made perfect and individuals only singly made happy. God intends that we will be God's and that we will be, finally, wholly "ourselves." But this will happen only by God's intention of our being members of a new, mutually in-forming, community.

The African concept of *Ubuntu*, that a person cannot even *be* without deep relationship to the neighbor, exemplifies what God is up to in this new Spirited creation project. More fundamentally, this is how God the Trinity works. God—the loving, triune community of diversity, Father, Son, Spirit—intends human persons to enjoy such communion and mutual transformation in, with, and through each other. This was the work Jesus began in his three years of earthly ministry. It is the work he promised would continue and compound under the Spirit's advocacy. Be clear that a commitment to diversity is no mere politically correct principle separable from Jesus that he merely exemplified. Those who encounter and relate to Jesus Christ discover that self-giving and other-receiving is precisely the dynamic life of God the Trinity. This is the distinctly Christian life then that will evangelize the "other" with gracious hospitality. No wonder life will be abundant and full of grace, for there is so much yet to receive! Such a broad, deep, and truly communal life, wherein individuals are not erased but even further built, cannot truly be full without God's transcending also of the human and tribal boundaries that inhibit hospitality and mutual construction. As the contemporary hymn invites, "All are welcome in this place" (Haugen, 1994).

So we are invited to reflect on what God is doing in knitting together a diverse community centered in Christ. Precisely at a time when the old world is daunted by its compaction and nations are afraid of cultural and religious pluralization, God calls the church to exhibit the divine difference that is hopeful, hospitable, and evangelical. Yes, the counter examples to God's intentions are worrisomely plentiful. Who could have imagined that the nation that gave the world the democratic liberalism of liberty, equality, and fraternity would prohibit a woman's right of religious expression? And while countries are beset by problems of insecure borders and religious intolerance, who would have predicted that honorable leaders would descend to demagogy so to feed fear rather than hasten hope?

Of course, this happens all the time. So again God is calling the church to change the conversation by employing a more humane and Spirited language. It was not so long ago that church growth experts argued strongly that a growing church must be based on a principle of sociological homogeneity. Today, however, the churches of the "Great Emergence" are growing because they embrace diversity (Tickle, 2008). They speak a larger language of hospitality to those who had been excluded from God's house. Perhaps Paul's dream of a Macedonian beckoning him to visit was not only for Paul. Now, all who are represented by "Macedonia"—those who are not welcome to the homogenous table, those outside formal borders, those who look or act differently outside our more personal borders—look to the church to live Christ's life.

The old world's backdrop still of xenophobia may indicate that God is allowing the challenges to deepen so that the church may more strongly respond and lead in hope. Ultimately, the necessary human efforts toward justice cannot achieve our best and most noble aspirations because of our finitude. But that we drive toward them displays God's goals. Thus Christ's disciples will lovingly strive together in this life to be a prequel of God's abundant life intended for all. And God is still calling us toward the true Pentecost, even very particularly through the "other."

A Pastoral Need

In *For the Healing of the Nations*, Justo L. González (1999) reminds us of people who speak longingly of finally getting to live their dream in retirement, like owning a wilderness cabin and spending all day fishing by a stream in the woods. Retirement will be living the dream. But ask such a person, "What are you doing now in your free time?" and that person says something like, "I just love going to the stock car races" and then says he has even started building a car of his own (105).

The disconnect between that man's espoused values and his real practice is obvious to everyone but him. In the same way, González writes, "If we really want the world to believe the proclamation of the Reign of God, then, both as individuals and as a church we had better begin living as a people that is practicing for the reign of God . . . [For] worship is a rehearsal and an act of proclamation" (105; 110).

The challenge is that many of us already live in a multicultural world, not unlike that found in Paul and John's day, yet still worship in Christian communities primarily with people who share our distinctive customs and similar social worldviews. Like the Macedonian man who once pleaded with Paul to reach beyond his boundaries, González calls for Christians to become intentional in creating multicultural congregational worship "not simply because our society is multicultural, but because the future from which God is calling us is multicultural" (112).

ETHICAL IMPLICATIONS

Too often we have read the book of Acts as a blueprint for engaging in cross-cultural *missions*—a challenge that began in Jerusalem, then in Judea, Samaria, and, with Paul's missionary journeys, taking it to the ends of the earth. His response to the vision of the Macedonian man pleading for him to come and proclaim the good news has become the emblematic text for Christian missionary effort. In our enthusiasm what we too often have missed is that cross-cultural mission historically has had trouble distinguishing its dominant culture understanding of the gospel from its unseen colonial and now post-colonial ideologies. Mission matters. But it must be re-imagined.

What we have missed is how the first churches embodied a multicultural reality, whether beginning with a God-fearing Gentile woman praying by the river in Philippi or the people depicted as praising God from every tribe, language, people, and nation joined in worship in the New Jerusalem of John's Apocalypse (Rev 7:9, 15-17). Our challenge in the twenty-first century is to discover ways to transcend the univocal homogeneity of building congregations based on ethnic identity or common, class-based cultural values.

The question is not whether the homogeneity principle works. The question is whether such efforts create Christian communities that embody the purposes of God. Brian Blount (2001) argues that,

> Jesus called for the apocalypse of worship, the realization of its end-time multicultural reality. In the first century it meant a temple where Jews and Gentiles could worship as one; in the twenty-first century it surely must mean churches desegregated along lines of race, ethnicity, and culture, and integrated toward the vision of inclusive communities of faith. . . . The hope lies in what the destruction of the fruitless institutions of homogeneity will bring—not death, but new life, a transformed life whose future is so unlike the present that the present must die before it will yield (27).

GOSPEL IMPLICATIONS

N. T. Wright (2008) draws our attention to the fact that Rev 21-22 says the river of life that nourishes trees, the leaves of which are "for the healing of the nations" (22:2), flows *out* of the New Jerusalem. Yes, there is a final judgment against evil, and there is worship of the eternal one in the City. The mystery of hope is that diverse peoples yet to be healed are still out there. Clearly, answering theological questions about heaven and hell is not God's end game; nor is answering questions about personal destiny in the afterlife. Rather, the central, framing question here as in all of scripture is one of "God's purpose of rescue and re-creation for the whole world, the entire cosmos" (184). The question is not just, as Paul so eloquently makes apparent in Romans, "How is God going to rescue Israel?" but how is God going to rescue all humanity through this one man, Jesus Christ (Rom 5). As Paul stood on the Macedonian shores of one world and saw the invitation of the next, the church stands on similar shores that invite us to envision the "healing of the nations" as Christ's *next* world—and to make every effort to embody this other-centered reality *now.*

Notes

Brian K. Blount, "The Apocalypse of Worship: A House of Prayer for All Nations," *Making Room at the Table: An Invitation to Multicultural Worship,* eds., Brian K. Blount and Lenora Tubbs Tisdale, 2001.

Justo L. González, *For the Healing of the Nations: The Book of Revelation in an Age of Conflict,* 1999.

Marty Haugen, "All Are Welcome in This Place" (GIA Publications, 1994), Retrieved at http://www.giamusic.com/sacred_music/index.cfm

Phyllis Tickle, *The Great Emergence: How Christianity Is Changing and Why,* 2008.

N. T. Wright, *Surprised by Hope: Rethinking Heaven, the Resurrection and the Mission of the Church,* 2008.

ROBERT STEPHEN REID

DUANE LARSON

Seventh Sunday
of Easter

The Lessons in Précis

The 50-day period of expectancy between Easter and Pentecost allows God's people to continue experiencing the dawning awareness of disciples who, in the power of the Spirit, challenge the ways of the world so the world will know God's ways.

> *Acts 16:16-34.* Human avarice and ethnic divisiveness become the occasion for a Philippian jailer, saved from death-deserving disgrace, to be saved by actual grace, believing in the Lord Jesus.

> *Psalm 97.* Words spoken about YHWH addressed to all nations are balanced by words spoken about YHWH addressed to people who love YHWH.

> *Revelation 22:12-14, 16-17, 20-21.* The Spirit and the bride invite everyone who hears, everyone who is thirsty, and anyone who wishes to take the water of life as a gift to come to God.

> *John 17:20-26.* The task of followers is to overcome all divisive difference so that the world may see that God's purposes challenge the ways of the world, so that "the world will believe that you sent me" (vs. 21).

Theme Sentence

The Holy Spirit and the heavenly Lord empower followers to overcome division. In so doing the world is to know who sent Christ. The church exists as the presence of Christ in the world so that people everywhere will have the right to "enter the city by the gates" of saving faith (Rev 22:14).

A Key Theological Question

We have interpreted this journey to Pentecost as a time of preparation for the manifestation of the Spirit, even while the Spirit already works in us. This work means to open us more to the gospel's significance for a new and larger, though compact, multiethnic and multi-religious world. This is the same situation into which the first disciples were sent.

One could argue that our situation is more complex. In this day's postmodernity, when the pluralistic character of the world is deepened by the reduction of language among the philosophically elite into mere power exercises that do not and cannot refer to facts, when it is most commonly agreed at least in practice that there are no grand narratives, the would-be Christian is perplexed not only by diversity's challenges, but also by how even to speak to them. The scripture texts for this week speak further to this challenge against speech. They also invite more complex theological reflection.

To understand Jesus' prayer as the "high priestly prayer" casts the interpretation in an overly ecclesial frame. This default proof text for the ecumenical movement's goal of visible unity has made such structural unity a rationale for evangelical outreach. Failure in the latter can then be explained rightly or wrongly by the failure to achieve the former. The church's disunity in form and in moral activity has indeed provided justifiable cause for disbelief. It has even become a bullet point for aggressive atheism.

Jesus' prayer asks a certain unity in form and witness. But the prayer concerns much more than mere structure. It bears on the theological— even the ontological ("real")—reality of Jesus' relationship to the Father. If the world in its given diversity is to know its own divinely-intended wholeness and oneness, then the followers of Jesus must show forth their own unity as example, witness, and inspiration to a fractured world. The unity of the followers of Jesus, in turn, can be based only on the creative gift of God the Trinity, the author of creation who sublimely lives and loves in a unity of three-personed diversity.

So why should the disciples be one? There are at least two related answers. First, God who sends them forth as God's own icons to the world is One, even as a diverse and other Trinitarian One God. Thus God would shape redeemed humanity in God's own Trinitarian image. Jesus' prayer is for a new creation. We can see it after Easter as a *creatio novum ex nihilo*. Second, because God who so loves the world yearns that the world in its freedom would know fully the love that is celebrated in reconciled diversity and by which the world so abundantly can live. Many Johannine themes themselves come into a bright unity of focus in Jesus' "high priestly prayer."

Yet this doctrinal core to Christian faith is not easily explained. It does not work to preach doctrinally *about* the faith to people (ourselves!) who so need a re-creative word for health and wholeness. Tolstoy, for example, famously complained that a church focused on the Nicene Creed was turned in on itself and ethereal salvation, while a church focused on Jesus' beatitudes was truly devoted to justice in the world. Tolstoy therefore dismissed the church as irrelevant to contemporary human life and chose Jesus as the way toward an authentic world peace. Faced with unity or virtue, Tolstoy chose the latter, and built a movement on that de-religionized platform.

Many Christian theologians themselves argue similarly that creedal foundations for faith must be dispensed for their now-irrelevant dependence on "essentialist" philosophy. It is not necessary to go that far. The unity of which Jesus speaks is a unity of love between Father and Son. And love has its own "will power." The prayer for unity *will* be answered by the gift of the Spirit, who *will* bring together followers of Jesus in deep love, mutual respect, and individually gifted diversity. Their unity *will* be one of divine love's resolve. Those in the Spirit's breath *will* resolutely be one, and not for structure's sake but for love's sake, itself unending and irrepressible. So it *will* out-reach. It *will* be evangelical. God intends that the world be a diversified one. God also intends that it be "won" by his love in Christ. The resolve of God's love is divine promise to us. There is no other reason for God's so wooing. Thus Jesus' prayer bears an evangelical dimension: that the world would see and know intimately the unity of those claimed by Christ.

We know from the record of God's mighty acts that such seeing and knowing happens in deep, personal encounters in the Spirit. How interesting it is that a fortune-telling slave girl and a Philippian jailer, the former who was as good as dead in her bondage and the latter who was as good as dead for not adequately performing his security detail, both find new life in the direct and authoritative words of Paul. True, these stories do not cohere with the Western modern worldview. Contemporary Western Christians may be inclined to read these events as symbolic. A postmodern form of charismatic Christianity, however, may argue with sophistication that one should take the Bible literally not because that is the only way to have genuine referentiality, but because only by living seriously in such a narrative can one experience the power of the Spirit. In either case, to speak authoritatively with God's creative care for the health of the neighbor and the community's wholeness is to be life-transforming and life-giving. When God's words are stewarded gently yet faithfully as transformational gifts, the proclaimer conducts the power of creative love between God and new persons rising out of human clay. So diverse people like jailors, enslaved women, and we ourselves discover grace in surprising trips from death to life. Thereby God makes us one and whole.

A Pastoral Need

It is the rare individual who is reasoned into faith in God. Behind the metaphor of *thirst* in the words of the Risen Lord and the Spirit (Rev 22:17) and behind Luke's stories of two people who turn to Paul for help, both *as good as dead*, lies the acknowledgement that people come to faith in God out of need. The Philippian jailer asks, " 'Honorable masters, what must I do to be rescued?' [The disciples] answer, 'Believe in the Lord Jesus, and you will be saved—you and your entire household' " (Acts 16:30-31).

We initially come to faith in God because we need a new life. Scripture is filled with stories in which God meets people at their point of need and turns that need into a story of new creation. "Consider Abraham," Paul urges in Galatians 3:6. All Abraham actually wanted was a son. If not for his own life to be renewed, at least for this new life to carry his name and memory forward into succeeding generations. It wasn't much to ask. But God wanted more. From this need for new life, the most basic of personal needs, comes what the Bible repeatedly refers to as the story of new creation. It stands at the beginning of God's covenant call to a people who would be his own. Between Easter and Pentecost we learn that saving faith can become new creation, that conversion is but the beginning of a journey that was intended to embody divine love's *resolve*.

ETHICAL IMPLICATIONS

The texts we explore between Easter and Pentecost reveal the dawning awareness of disciples who, in the power of the Spirit, challenge the ways of the world so the world will know God's ways. But if this is to continue today, people need to be able to move beyond conversion faith (need-meeting faith) to discipleship (missional) faith. People still reduce mission to a noun rather than understand it as the central defining verb of a purposeful faith. In *Treasures in Clay Jars,* Darrell Guder (2004) notes, "Dallas Willard has said that our churches are full of converts who do not intend to become disciples. Another way to put it would be this: Our churches are full of people who are there to receive the benefits of grace without knowing that they are receiving such blessings 'in order to be a blessing'" (60).

The church is intended to be the presence of Christ in the world so that people everywhere will have the right to "enter the city by the gates" of saving faith (Rev 22:14), but with this right comes responsibility. Too often church leaders have focused on unity of belief as unity in doctrinal or denominational affirmations when true unity that makes Christ known occurs when Christians move beyond need-based faith to be formed by Christian practices that witness to the reign of God. For Guder, a missional orientation asks,

How does God's Word call, shape, transform, and send me . . . and us? Coupled with this openness is the awareness that biblical formation must mean change, and often conversion. Christian communities may discover that their discipling will require repentance and that their way of being church will have to change (70).

The problem of the convert who never becomes a disciple is that she believes faith is supposed to improve rather than change her.

GOSPEL IMPLICATIONS

Depending on context, the word translated "saved," in the Philippian jailer's question can as readily be rendered by "healed" or "made whole" as by "rescued." Every generation of Christians inherit culturally shaped conventions clarifying how they construe the question, "What must I do to be saved?" One need not look back too far generationally to see how these responses have differed. They have been shaped just as much by class, culture, ethnicity, education, ideologies, and social differences as they have by the biblical witness. As a result, the generational responses have bequeathed us denominational distinctions and a wide variety of public-private expressions of faith. Some have argued that such tensional differences have kept Christianity divided, while others have argued that these differences have fostered a vibrancy of faith. But the danger of difference is that it can too easily collapse *coming to faith* into one of these meta-frames, a collapse that eventually dissipates the power of the gospel, dissipates the power of the *divine resolve* expressed by the Father, Son, and Spirit as grace and love. Yet, it is this Spirit that continues to challenge even these ways of the world to become, yet again, saving expressions of creative care for the health of the neighbor and the wholeness of communities. Thus finally the question becomes, "What has God done to save you?"

Notes

Darrell Guder, "Pattern Two: Biblical Formation and Discipleship," *Treasure in Clay Jars: Patterns in Missional Faithfulness*, Jointly authored by Lois Barrett, Darrell Guder, Walter Hobbs, George Hunsberger, Linford Stutzman, Jeff Van Kooten and Dale Siemer, 2004, 59-73.

———

ROBERT STEPHEN REID

DUANE LARSON

DAY OF PENTECOST

THE LESSONS IN PRÉCIS

The 50-day period of expectancy between Easter and Pentecost culminates in God's people, who are released in the power of the Spirit, proclaiming the gospel in every language and dramatizing that the gospel should never be reduced to privileging one people and one language.

> ***Acts 2:1-21.*** The resurrection and ascension of Christ make possible the gift of the Holy Spirit at Pentecost to empower congregations of believing people to reach all nations and overcome all ethnic and religious division in the world.

> ***Psalm 104:24-34, 35b.*** The true extent of God's mastery of all aspects of creation is extolled.

> ***Romans 8:14-17.*** We receive a spirit of adoption, as we cry out to God, and the Spirit is given to us as a witness that we are children of God.

> ***John 14:8-17 (25-27).*** Questions of faith prompt Jesus to say that people who believe in him will do not only "the works that I do . . . [but] even greater works than these, because I am going to the Father" (v. 12).

THEME SENTENCE

Pentecost is not about the "pyrotechnics of theophany"; it is about becoming a Spirit-empowered *theodromoi.* God's Spirit-empowered *couriers* are people who find the language and the means to communicate God's redemptive purposes in Christ in order to see identities that divide people overcome through Christ.

A Key Theological Question

There is no dearth of drama at Pentecost. No human-made machines are required for wind, fire, and compelling speech. The compelling speech, especially, is not in the campaign style of "what we will do for you." It is not a forecast. It is about God's promises fulfilled. God's promises of "drama," prophesied by Joel, are indeed fulfilled on Pentecost. The "last days" had come with the Wind. The old days are done. A new time is begun with the full manifestation of God's Spirit. If Epiphany is the showing forth of God's powerful humility in a babe, Pentecost is the showing forth of Christ's gracious power in humble people of every age, gender, and class. Pentecost is not for the elite, not for self-appointed tribes or clerocracies, but for "other" people of every kind and land.

Pentecost's effects today, whenever and wherever Pentecosts happen, have no lack of drama either. The Spirit's power reaches forth from humble pockets all around, in the amazing miracles of compassion, reconciliation, and forgiveness; in relationships newly prospering and human rights newly recovered. While powerfully local, the Holy Spirit has truly gone global again, too. Since the Azusa Street revival in Los Angeles at the beginning of the twentieth century, Pentecostalism has grown dramatically in size, respect, and contribution to robust theological reflection. Since the latter two decades of that same century, a Pentecostal character has defined the massive surge of Christianity in the southern hemisphere, now where most Christians live. The affective and attractive power of Christian religious experience that is confident in its open subjectivity of faith and growing sophistication of "objective" theological reflection is an old and new thing which we "westerners" need to appreciate positively, as Philip Jenkins (2002, 2006) has so well informed us. But for all this evocative drama, it is not the most important activity of the Holy Spirit.

It looks like the Holy Spirit is calling, gathering, enlightening, and sanctifying (Luther's words) in a manner foreign to us. We've preferred hegemony and homogeneity. We've even come from acknowledging that Sunday is the most segregated time in America to arguing affirmatively for homogenity's role in growing congregations. But Pentecost shows definitively that the Spirit objects. The Holy Spirit today is up to something far different. Tribal identities are being transcended, but not by a new hegemonic language that flattens out all particularities (even if empire still looms large backstage). Cultures are being "crossed," but not so that the end result is their erasure or exclusion. Even other religious tones are being translated into a larger score and new key without violence to their particularity and in affirmation of their positive contribution to human being.

Sure, religious extremism throughout the world within any religion would seem to put the lie to these claims. But the very term *extremism* underscores that an emerging and larger hospitality is taking hold and assuming normativity. Without losing its own conviction and finally normative witness to God's graciousness, Christianity is at the center of this global dynamic, and it is part of the Spirit's movement. Now, Pentecost is any day when Christian preachers point to what God's Holy Spirit is doing and always has been doing, as signaled in the great manifestation (theophany) of our liturgical Pentecost. The Spirit is reconciling the world while simultaneously deepening identities of difference that are constructive for selves and communities.

How do we know these activities as of the Spirit? Michael Welker (1994), as the first among many contemporary theologians, has shown that the work of the Spirit is to reconcile opposite trends without loss to the positive value of each. In these days of social media, for example, it is fairly easy to communicate across the globe and "make friends." But how authentic is that? It rightly gives many pause when we hear of televangelists who would transmit their congregational preaching as live video and even have plans to make it holographic. The ability to communicate with depth requires time, care, and embodied presence. Even if emerging technologies address some of these depth issues and will get better yet in so doing, discipleship formation is an embodied and embodying process.

Humans, it seems, can achieve massive and broad mediated communication, but broadcasting necessarily lacks depth, nuance, contextual appropriateness and particularity. On the other hand, the best of human communication occurs in more localized situations and with a particular people. Even at our best, we can go wide but not deep, or deep but not wide. The Holy Spirit does both. The Spirit's communication comes with intimate engagement and evokes narrative. This process intends that our biographies each and intact will enrich the story of God with God's people. The Holy Spirit communicates and mediates communication in both ways; no other can. This is why such communion is holy. The Holy Spirit does likewise in building a community of believers of the most diverse sorts. Thus the church, the body of Christ, is remarkable by its unity even while simultaneously building particular identities. In the intersubjective power of Pentecost, Christians more than virtually "make each other up." Also, we actually come to understand each other! How is it that we each hear God's word from another in our own way, in our own language? It happens, according to the Pentecost witness, because God's Holy Spirit has come upon the most unexpected beneficiaries in fulsome grace and is doing among humans the humanly impossible.

The journey on which we have been to Pentecost, liturgically and symbolically, of course, will have no end. Even heaven itself could not be "static" in its perfection, but will offer ever deeper relationship and communication. So Pentecost points to ever deeper joy. In such joy, barely tapped in Peter's impulsive jump into the sea so to hasten toward the Risen Lord, Pentecost impels believers to reach out to everyone. The world is our sea, and all its creatures are to be heirs of God's grace in love. Only in the power of the Spirit will we with Peter be able to love Christ and feed his sheep. Only by the empowering love of Christ poured prodigally and dramatically on his own friends, will we go where we would otherwise not choose. The journey of discipleship will be difficult. But we are empowered now to walk, love, feed, and serve.

A Pastoral Need

Anyone reading the story of Pentecost quickly stumbles on the fact that the recipients of this first "baptism in the Spirit" manifest their experience by speaking in what is perceived to be the diverse languages of the Mediterranean world. Peter's subsequent sermon also draws attention to the manner in which this Spirit, now gifted to God's people, will tear down former divisions of age, class, and gender in witnessing to God's purposes. So, why it is so hard for congregations to embody this same diversity as witness to the work of God today?

James Forbes (2003) describes how the congregation of the Riverside Church in New York eventually had to adopt what he calls a "75 percent" philosophy:

> A truly diverse congregation where anybody enjoys more than 75 percent of what's going on is not thoroughly integrated . . . Be prepared to think, "Hey this is great. I enjoyed at least 75 percent of it," because 25 percent of you should grant . . . somebody's precious liturgical expression that is probably odious to you; otherwise it's not integrated. (p. 82)

A congregation that decides to claim its Pentecost birthright will need to become intentional in discovering how to become inclusive of different worship styles as well as being inclusive of who participates in worship. Worshipping in the power of the Spirit may put challenge to the assumptions that the goal of worship is to meet individual needs; it may even give rise to manifesting a Pentecostal witness in diversity as the expression of God's very gospel purposes.

ETHICAL IMPLICATIONS

Luke Timothy Johnson (1992) notes that in relating the Pentecost story Luke's point is not to focus on "the pyrotechnics of theophany, but spiritual transformation. The real 'event of Pentecost' is the empowerment of the disciples by the Holy Spirit" (p. 45). The question is, "To what purpose?" The answer might seem self-evident in Peter's interpretation of this witness; he says the Spirit was "poured out" so that those hearing his message might "know beyond question that God has made this Jesus, whom you crucified, both Lord and Christ" (Acts 2:36).

Perhaps one of the more overlooked aspects of the story is this way in which this ideal depiction of international linguistic diversity experienced by these listeners embodies the heart of the matter. Note how the text begins and concludes with references to portents (1-2; 19-21), describes the Spirit as poured out (3-4; 16-18), notes the confusion of observers (5-6; 14-15) and also their amazement (7; 12-13), and then builds to the central and climactic enumeration of the variety of languages experienced by the witnesses of this event (8-11). We typically speed past the reading of lists, yet here is the central point. Pentecost then and now invites the church to imagine tearing down all walls of division between people. Worship in and through the Spirit of Pentecost should never be age-, class-, gender-, or color-blind. Such inclusive worship requires effort.

The story of the earliest Christian communities as depicted in the New Testament demonstrates that this was never easy. Overcoming difference is hard. Congregations must become intentional if they are to realize this vision. But, ideally, nothing should detract them from trying to overcome all such distinctions in Christ. The degree to which Christian communities can live into this vision is a great part of living into the church's missional challenge in the twenty-first century.

GOSPEL IMPLICATIONS

While being transported to Rome where he was to be martyred for his faith, Ignatius, the third bishop of the congregation at Antioch, wrote letters to congregations that had hosted him on his journey. In his letter to the famed Polycarp, bishop of Smyrna, he asked this deeply respected Christian leader to appoint a courier, a *theodromos* (God's courier) to hasten spreading a witness to faith among the Syrians. This courier should "glorify your zealous love to the glory of God" (*Ignatius to Polycarp* 7.2). In the Mediterranean world of this era, such runners were the source for all news, good or bad. One way we can choose to understand Luke's story of Pentecost is to think of the Spirit, manifested by this linguistic witness to "mighty works of God" (Acts 2:11), as a kind of cross-cultural testimony of God's grace. In other words, *Pentecost is not about the "pyrotechnics of theophany"; it is about people becoming Spirit-empowered theodromoi.* God's Spirit empowered *couriers* are people who find the language and the means to communicate widely and deeply God's redemptive purposes in Christ in order to see identities that divide people overcome through Christ. Pentecost grace continues whenever Christians trust in God's Spirit to help tear down walls of division the world builds up.

Notes

James Forbes, as quoted in Curtis Paul DeYoung, Michael O. Emerson, George Yancey, and Karen Chai Kim, *United By Faith: The Multiracial Congregation as an Answer to the problem of Race*, 2003.

Luke Timothy Johnson, *The Acts of the Apostles*, 1992.

Philip Jenkins, *The Next Christendom: The Coming of Global Christianity*, 2002.

Philip Jenkins, *The New Faces of Christianity: Believing the Bible in the Global South*, 2006.

Michael Welker, *God the Spirit*, 1994.

ROBERT STEPHEN REID

DUANE LARSON

Trinity Sunday

The Lessons in Précis

Proverbs 8:1-4, 22-31. Wisdom is personified and portrayed as a living creation of YHWH We are first called to listen to Wisdom, and are then given the reasons why. Verses twenty-two through thirty-one delightfully lay out Wisdom's close connection to the created order.

Psalm 8. Like Proverbs 8, Psalm 8 directs us to the work of creation, to its grandeur and beauty, and to the comparative smallness of humanity. Yet God has given humanity something special that even so sets us apart.

Romans 5:1-5. A classic Trinitarian text, Romans 5 shows us the three divine Persons working in concert to make us new creations, justified by grace and engulfed by the anointing of God's love.

John 16:12-15. God's revelation to us is not static, as Jesus' words here make clear. The Holy Spirit will never cease in leading us to fresh and new insights and understandings of our salvation and of the creation in which we live.

Theme Sentence

Father, Son, and Holy Spirit give us all we need to flourish in creation and in the redemption that brings us to New Creation. These passages remind us of God's great enthusiasm for creation and of God's desire that we thrive in it now and forevermore!

A KEY THEOLOGICAL QUESTION

Anyone who has had the opportunity to stand outside in a remote area and observe the night sky cannot help but wonder with the psalmist, "What are human beings that you are mindful of them, mortals that you care for them?" (Ps 8:4, NRSV). And if simple observation were not enough, the reality about the place of humans in the universe is certain to leave people with the feeling that human existence does not count for much in the broad scheme of things. Humans are, after all, positioned on a planet in a universe so vast that when we look out with sophisticated equipment to what are thought to be the edges of this universe, we are looking back in time billions of years. As Paul Jewett writes, "Were one to compress the history of the universe into a year, planet Earth would appear during the last month of the year, and the first humans would strut onto the stage of life on the last day of the last month of the year at about 10:30 in the evening" (Jewett, 1996, p. 4). What would make us think that we matter at all?

The texts for Trinity Sunday are but a small selection of scripture texts that demonstrate God's great love and concern not only for human beings but also for the planet they inhabit. The universe did not come into being by blind chance, as some would have us believe. Nor is the God who creates the god of the pagans who makes war with rivals or copulates and gives birth to this world. It is the work of the Triune God, Father, Son, and Holy Spirit. God is the one who "established the heavens," "marked out the horizon on the deep sea," and "marked out the earth's foundations" (Prov 8:27, 29). God "established the earth on its foundations" and "covered it with the watery deep" (Ps 104:5, 6). God is present in the beginning with the Word (John 1:1-2) and the Spirit (Gen 1:2), giving form to what was formless, creating the universe by his command (Heb 11:3).

The world was created by Father, Son, and Holy Spirit working in perfect unity, not out of necessity or because God was lonely but because of his great love. From eternity, God has had a communal life within himself. God did not need to create in order have community. Rather, creation flows out of God's communal life. Given that God's interior life consists of mutual love and regard for the other, creation can be understood as an act that is fitting for God. It is what one could expect from a gracious, loving, and hospitable God.

The pinnacle of creation is humanity. God made humans not as slaves of the gods, but "only slightly less than divine" (Ps 8:5) and "let them rule over [God's] handiwork" (Ps 8:6). Humans are "fearfully and wonderfully made" (Ps 139:14, KJV). Similar to the love of a married couple, which flows over into a desire to share that love with a child, so the love within the Triune God overflowed into a desire to share that love with beings who could freely respond in love. The Father, Son, and Holy Spirit created humans, inviting them to share in the life of God.

Unfortunately, humans abused their God-given freedom and rebelled, choosing to listen to the voice of a deceiver rather than the voice of love (Gen 3:1-7). By so doing, they cut themselves off from the source of life and were cast out of the presence of God, rather than sharing in the dynamic communal life of God. If that was not bad enough, the consequences of human sin reached beyond human persons, subjecting the whole created order to corruption and frustration (Rom 8:28-29).

God does not abandon his work, however. The same Triune God, who as an outworking of his great love created all things, loves his creation so much that he becomes part of the creation in order to restore it. Because God chose to send his Son to become a sinless second Adam, humans are once again invited to share in the life of God. "We have peace with God through our Lord Jesus Christ," writes Paul (Rom 5:1). The Holy Spirit now lives in believers and fills them with the love of God (Rom 5:5). This outpouring of God's love through the work of the Spirit into his people enables them to let God's love flow to others, restoring broken relationships, offering mercy and grace to those they come into contact with every day. Paul describes restored humans as "the new creation" (2 Cor 5:17).

The work of restoration is not limited to human persons, however. Although the application of Christ's death and resurrection restores human persons to communion with God, humans are only the first-fruits of the new creation. The scope of restoration is cosmic. Because of Christ's saving work on the cross and through the ongoing work of the Holy Spirit, God is reconciling the cosmos to himself, promising at some future time to make *all* things new (Rev 21:5). This *is* God's world and, enabled by the Holy Spirit, Christians should live in harmony with all things as a demonstration to all of the future harmony of the eschaton anticipated by the prophets. The Bible closes as it opened: with the creation of heaven and earth. The story has moved from creation to New Creation. This is the end, the *telos*, of the hope of God's people.

A Pastoral Need

Everywhere people turn today, they receive the message that science is steamrolling religious faith because science reveals a world that is so ancient, so sprawlingly vast, that it is merely deluded thinking to conclude that human beings matter. Even if there were a god in existence somewhere out there, he'd have to strain and squint to pick out the speck of dust that is the planet Earth, much less be able to take note of any puny person who lives a fleeting four score of years on that speck. Humanity is a cosmic footnote.

In truth, science need not lead to any such dire conclusions. But those intent on downsizing humanity have grabbed a lot of big bullhorns through bestselling books, appearances on "Larry King Live," etc. And it gets a little depressing. People feel shook up. We don't need to return to the day when we thought the Earth was the center of everything, but we'd sure like it if we could feel a *little* better about our place in the grand scheme of things.

The quartet of Lectionary passages for Trinity Sunday in Year C can help. Here we see God's great enthusiasm for his project of creation, the attention God pays to it, and the intense divine desire—shared equally among the three persons—that human beings get along well in this creation. So intense is God's desire for this that God launched a massive salvage operation to set things right again. It is a project fueled by grace, and it is one that, by the Holy Spirit's leading, will go on and on until that day when we arrive at the glory that will be the New Creation.

Ethical Implications

Christians do well to admit that in history, the human claim to being "the crown of creation," and thus bearing a special place in the grand scheme of things, has led to significant mayhem. We have been too self-referential, too selfish, and too consumeristic in gobbling up the resources of this planet, as though it was God's intention all along that we spoil and pillage as we go. It has taken many centuries—and the ecological catastrophes since the Industrial Revolution—to at long last awaken the Christian community to its first, best calling as earthkeepers and shalom tenders.

On Trinity Sunday, we can receive a bracing reminder to treat creation with respect by taking our cues from Father, Son, and Holy Spirit. The delight with which Wisdom is portrayed in Proverbs 8 indicates how much God wants creation to flourish and be maintained as the source of divine delight that it is. What's more, the self-deferential spirit with which the three persons within the divine community treat one another likewise sets the tone for humanity—made in the image of this very God—as it carries out its entire existence. We, too, are here to serve one another and the creatures with which we share this planet. Selfish attitudes and wanton polluting or consuming of the creation is simply not fitting for people because it would so clearly not be fitting for God.

The three persons in God worked in concert to create this cosmos. They worked in concert to redeem this cosmos. It is now our delightful task to see what they do and then do likewise in celebrating and maintaining a grand and glorious creation.

GOSPEL IMPLICATIONS
Evangelical Christians have for too long pinned the entire work of salvation on Christ Jesus alone, even as they have for too long viewed the target of Jesus' death and resurrection as the redemption only of human souls. It's the old "Me and Jesus" scenario, as I sit in a dew-covered garden waiting for Jesus to speak to me alone.

The passages of this Year C Trinity Sunday correct our theology, reminding us that in both creation and redemption the entirety of God— Father, Son, and Holy Spirit—was intimately involved in each step along the way. No one flew solo in creation. Jesus did not fly solo in saving us, either. The Triune God who created all that exists retains a zestful ardor for that creation and uses Word, Wisdom, and Spirit to direct us down paths that will lead to greater understanding, greater appreciation, and greater zeal to celebrate the works of the Triune God.

God was in Christ reconciling the world—the cosmos—to himself. As Paul wrote in Colossians 1, God is invested in "all things" (vs. 16). The gospel of Christ tells us that followers of Jesus have a similarly broad and capacious view on the works of Father, Son, and Holy Spirit.

Notes
Paul K. Jewett, *Who We Are: Our Dignity As Human*, 1996.

_____

SCOTT HOEZEE

MARY VANDEN BERG

Proper 4 [9]

The Lessons in Précis

1 Kings 18:20-21 (22-29) 30-39. Elijah's triumph over the priests of Baal is the ultimate showdown as to who is the real God. But as important as the heavenly focus is, the double-minded Israelites, who worship both YHWH and other gods, are key to understanding this great story.

Psalm 96. The in-your-face nature of praise is well displayed here. God's people do not praise God in private for their own benefit—they worship God in public so as to invite the whole world into the choir!

Galatians 1:1-12. Paul drops the usual pleasantries and goes after the Galatians for having adopted a false view of the gospel and, thus, of the God who brings us that gospel.

Luke 7:1-10. Jesus marvels over the faith of this centurion, a foreign person who is an icon of all that is loathsome to the Jews. But Jesus does not merely compliment this man's faith—he goes on to lament that God's own people could learn a thing or two from this centurion's example.

Theme Sentence

God will not leave himself without a witness. All people—including the people of God—tend to refashion God into someone a little nicer, as if they were doing a divine makeover. But the true God will shine through the fog of idolatry that we pump into our worship sanctuaries.

A KEY THEOLOGICAL QUESTION

In Psalm 96, listeners are called to "declare God's glory among the nations" (vs. 3). *Glory* is an interesting word. If my Bible software is correct, the word occurs throughout the Bible 351 times, not including occurrences in the Apocrypha. But what is glory? And what does it mean to declare it? A quick glance at a thesaurus offers synonyms such as "magnificence," "credit," "splendor," "grandeur," "fame," "praise," and "success," among others. The biblical text is likewise quite diverse in its use of the term.

Even when the term is used in conjunction with God, the meaning varies. For example, sometimes glory is something humans do to or for God, as is the case in Psalm 96 (vs. 3, 7, and 8). Sometimes it is something that humans see, a representation of God (e.g., Exod 24:16-17; 40:34-5). And at other times it seems as though glory is something God possesses, something associated with his name that identifies him and rightly belongs to God alone (Isa 48:11).

The Hebrew word for glory is *kabod,* meaning "heavy" or "weighty." With that in mind, perhaps one way to think about glory as it relates to God is that God is not to be dealt with lightly. There is a certain gravity associated with God. The Israelites found that out as God extravagantly displayed his power and glory through the very weapons the people associated with Baal: lightning and thunder. When the fireworks were over, the Israelites fell on their faces in fear and proclaimed God's glory: "The LORD is the real God! The LORD is the real God!" (1 Kgs 18:39).

The failure of Israel's faith leading up to the confrontation on Mt. Carmel is nothing new. In the six hundred year history since God delivered them from Egypt, Israel repeatedly turned away from worshipping the true God by building golden calves, taking the gods of the surrounding nations as their own, and blending worship of those gods with worship of YHWH. It is as if they are hedging their bets, covering all the god bases. It is not that they deny that YHWH is a god. It is that they deny that YHWH is the only true God. They rob glory from YHWH by giving to other gods the glory God is due. It is as though the weightiness of having only one God who can fulfill all their needs is too much for them to carry.

The Galatian Christians bear an eerie resemblance to Israel. Not content with the gospel message about God's plan of salvation, the Galatians have added adherence to the law as a requirement for a relationship with God through Christ. Paul points out, in a rather cranky tone, that this addition distorts God's message of grace into something completely different, something that is no gospel at all (Gal 1:6-7). By distorting God's message, they distort the God who offers them this message of grace. For some reason, the God of grace is too hard to handle, so they refashion him into someone more to their liking, someone more manageable.

By contrast, the Gentile centurion in Luke's Gospel seems to understand glory. There is no indication that he thinks he needs to add a prayer to Jupiter or give an additional offering to Apollo. He does not even expect Jesus to come all the way to his house. He trusts that Jesus' word alone will heal his servant (Luke 7:7). He gives glory to God by trusting his word. His faith appears to astonish even Jesus (Luke 7:9), perhaps because glory is usually recognized after the miracle is performed, not before (John 2:11; 11:3). The centurion appears to have recognized in Jesus the glory that John associates with the Word who became flesh (John 1:14).

If Christian worship is any indication, it seems that God's glory is only rarely declared in a way that would cause people to fall to their faces as Israel did on Mt. Carmel. Perhaps it is because God's people today have, as Neal Plantinga (2006) suggests, mistaken real glory for the publicity associated with athletes, entertainers, or politicians (p. 150). Christians are more comfortable worshipping and giving glory to a god who resembles their modern perceptions of glory than a dangerous God who ignites soaking wood on a flooded altar or comes to us as one despised and rejected (Isa 53:3).

It is not easy to get comfortable with glory that is displayed most prominently on a cross. But what could be a more weighty display of love than a God who pours out his own life to rescue people who have rejected him? That is true glory, and maybe that is why people are so uncomfortable with it—because we cannot imagine giving our lives for someone who hates us. That, however, is the heart of the glory of God. Authentic Christian worship should focus on the glory of Christ's death and resurrection proclaimed through word and sacrament. Insofar as that happens, we will fall on our faces and respond in union with the centurion, "Lord, I am not worthy to receive you, but only say the word and I shall be healed" (see Luke 7:7).

A PASTORAL NEED

The human heart, John Calvin observed, is a perpetual idol factory. Of course, most people today regard idolatry as passé, as the kind of thing that shows up only in nineteenth-century adventure novels or in the parts of the Bible we seldom read. Idolatry is long ago and far away, most assume; it is not today.

Alas, no. But no one likes having his or her false—or even semi-false—view of God corrected or challenged. I know I don't. But to paraphrase C.S. Lewis, God is the great iconoclast who perpetually shatters our false images of God in ways, frankly, we all need. But for preachers this is not an easy task, in part because there is always the danger that in helping people to recognize their own idolatrous pictures of God, the preacher could inadvertently send the message that the real God is, of course, the one *the preacher* envisions!

That equal but opposite sin must be avoided. But there is no denying the need to help people realize that, despite all the "God Bless America" and "My country right or wrong" rhetoric that is prevalent today, God cannot be neatly identified with one nation, one cause, one political viewpoint, or any given political party or figure. As Anne Lamott once observed, "You can safely assume that you've created God in your own image when it turns out that God hates all the same people you do" (*Traveling Mercies*). Preachers need to let God use them to unmask such idolatry.

ETHICAL IMPLICATIONS
Humility and modesty where one's conception of God is concerned can help head off some of the most terrible things people have done to each other in the name of God across the ages. If I accept that not every jot and tittle of what I believe to be God's point-of-view may not be correct—or at least that it is not necessarily the whole story—then I am open to having my views expanded by even the religious person whose views I do not fully share. At the very least I will be less likely to want to harm or kill that other person on account of the theological or religious differences that divide us.

Of course, having a perpetual desire to gain as accurate a picture of God as possible means recognizing that a New Testament perspective, where the definitive revelation of God came through a humble and suffering servant named Jesus, likewise steers me away from theology-sanctioned violence. Any time my picture of God starts veering toward the Rambo end of the divine spectrum or looking more like some lightning-bolt-wielding Zeus, a glance at the cross should be the equivalent of fire on the Mount Carmel altar or a bright light shining down on the Damascus Road. I am undone by the real God and am called to set aside the more (conveniently) violent pictures of God I am prone to reach for when confronted with enemies in the world.

Gospel Implications

We assume God does not have infinite patience with the false religions that have appeared across history. But based on the Bible we'd have to extrapolate to discern exactly what God thinks of the cult of the ancient Egyptians or religions like Hinduism or Buddhism as they exist today. Granted, we can generate Bible-based critiques of these other faiths, but we cannot quote chapter and verse in parsing other faiths. The Bible does not mention them.

The same cannot be said when God's own people get it wrong. The Old and New Testaments provide ample evidence of what God thinks of the idolatry cooked up by his own people. Whether it is the double-minded Israelites in Elijah's day or the restrictive and punitive faith of the Pharisees in Jesus' day, we know that God gets plenty upset when his own people get things singularly wrong.

Jesus' sacrifice on the cross is radiant for more reasons than we can recount. But among the most luminous truths of the cross is that *this* is the definitive revelation of God. God is love, God is grace. That is the real God against whom we need to measure our every conception of what we think God thinks, how we think God might act in a given situation, and how we think God might treat the person standing in front of us at any given moment of life.

Notes

Anne Lamott, *Traveling Mercies: Some Thoughts on Faith*, 1999.

Neal Plantinga in Timothy George, *God the Holy Trinity: Reflections on Christian Faith and Practice*, 2006.

SCOTT HOEZEE

MARY VANDEN BERG

PROPER 5 [10]

THE LESSONS IN PRÉCIS

1 Kings 17:8-16 (17-24). Elijah comes to a bereft widow and her son and provides life in a time of death. Even when the worst comes to the widow in the sudden death of her boy, God brings life through his servant Elijah.

Psalm 146. God's help is worth more than any help earth could provide. And this God has a soft spot in the divine heart, especially for the most vulnerable in our midst.

Galatians 1:11-24. Seldom does God unmask a false picture of himself more poignantly than with Saul of Tarsus. This passage is Paul's first-person account of his jaw-dropping change from a dealer of death to a bringer of (gospel) life!

Luke 7:11-17. The ultimate social cipher—a childless widow—has life restored to her in a holy flash as Jesus' heart takes pity on her and restores the life of her dead son. When Jesus gives the mother back her son, he restores to her the world in its entirety.

THEME SENTENCE
God is always on the side of life and never more so than with those whose flourishing is precarious in every way. The widow, the orphan, and the stranger always caught God's eye in the Old Testament, even as the lepers and the poor caught Jesus' eye in the Gospels.

A KEY THEOLOGICAL QUESTION
It is not too difficult to get bogged down on any given day by the amount of suffering in the world. Across the same week when this article was

written, the news carried reports of a teenage girl killed in a car accident, a father of four mauled to death by a grizzly bear, a six-year-old boy drowning in a lake, and a devastating mudslide that killed almost one hundred and fifty people. For theists, particularly Christian theists who claim to have a relationship with a loving and gracious God, it is hard to circumvent the skeptics who question what sort of God allows these events. In fact, those questions sometimes rage inside our own heads.

The readings for today show a God who is not only keenly aware of the results of evil in the world but is also the ever present helper of the victims of that evil. As we read the story of the widow of Zarephath and the man of God, we hear echoes of Luke's story of the grieving widow of Nain. Both stories deal with a widow, one of the lowest persons on the societal totem pole. In both cases, the widows' only hope—their sons— has died. And in both stories, God comes and restores life and hope to the widows, and by so doing reveals something of God's character.

In the story about the widow of Zarephath God comes represented by his prophet Elijah, a prophet whose very name bears witness to the God he serves (*Elijah* means "my God is YHWH"). The widow of Nain, however, is visited by God himself, the second person of the Trinity, "true God from true God." The woman from Zarephath proclaims that Elijah is indeed "a man of God" who speaks the truth (1 Kgs 17:24). The people of Nain, after the boy is raised from the dead declare, "God has come to help his people" (Luke 7:16). In both cases, help comes to these women not from mortals "in whom there is no help" (Ps 146:3, NRSV), but from the "God of Jacob . . . the maker of heaven and earth, the sea, and all that is in them" (Ps 146:5-6).

The problem with these stories, is that it is often difficult to understand why God seems to be so willing to help these women yet is strangely absent in our own world. A related problem is the potential to think that God merely pops into the world to help people every now and then but spends most of the time in blissful distance from the day-to-day troubles that plague us, with an often disproportionate amount of those troubles landing on the most vulnerable, like the widows in our stories for today.

While it may be tempting to think of God in these terms, the Bible reveals God as one who is intimately involved in and cares deeply about the world. The psalmists repeatedly refer to God as "my help" (e.g., Ps 22:19; 40:17; 63:7, NRSV), cry out to God for help (e.g., Ps 35:2; 70:1; 109:26; 121:1-2), and even describe God as the only true source of help (e.g., Ps 60:11; 108:12; 146:3). This crying out for help should not, however, be understood as a cry for God to show up, as if God is not already here. Quite the opposite. Psalm 104 depicts God as causing the grass to grow for cattle and human beings, watering the cedars of Lebanon, causing both night and day, and being thoroughly involved in everything that happens in this world. In the New Testament, Paul reflects this general understanding of God's providential care of the world in his sermon to the Athenians, where he affirms that God is not "far away from any of us" (Acts 17:27). According to Paul, God's involvement in the world is so comprehensive that apart from God's sustaining presence in the world, we would cease to exist, for only in God do we "live, move, and exist" (Acts 17:28).

This close relationship between God and the world begs the earlier question, however, about the presence of evil. There are no easy answers to this perpetually vexing problem. Perhaps the best we can do is remind ourselves that God has not abandoned this world, but rather has expended himself as a sacrifice for this world in order to begin the process of setting things right. Evil does not have the last word. God's "yes" is always stronger than the "no" of evil. Further, God promises to use even the evil in the world for the salvific good of his people (Rom 8:28). Nothing can "separate us from God's love in Christ Jesus our Lord" (Rom 8:38-39). God's power as Creator and sustainer authenticates his ability to help. God's love as Redeemer assures us of his desire to help. This knowledge prompts us, as the sixteenth century Heidelberg Catechism states, to "be patient when things go against us, thankful when things go well, and for the future . . . have good confidence in our faithful God and Father that nothing will separate us from God's love."

A PASTORAL NEED

The Bible provides more than sufficient evidence that it has always been a struggle to see and to identify with those who live on the margins of society. But if this has been true throughout history, it is only magnified today as the omnipresent mass media constantly shines the spotlight on only the best, the brightest, and the most beautiful. About the only time we hear about the truly down-and-out is when their fortunes are suddenly reversed by winning the lottery. Then (and only then) will Joan Rivers stick a microphone into the faces of once-hapless folks to ask how it feels now that they are really *somebody*.

But the nobodies of this world are always somebodies to God, and yet it remains a constant struggle for the people of God to adopt a similar ability to see those whom society mostly overlooks. We all hear about the big tragedies, the high profile sudden deaths that come to people with names like Kennedy and Travolta. But God sees the quiet tragedies, the tears that widows cry in the dark watches of the night. God sees the injustice that keeps people trapped in cycles of poverty that ricochet from generation to generation.

Preaching needs to open people's eyes to the invisible members of society. No one sermon can accomplish this. But over time the compassionate sensibilities of God need to get ingrained into Christians so that they can do what Jesus is so often depicted as doing: lifting up his eyes and *seeing* those whom everyone else simply overlooked.

Ethical Implications

If you use the pulpit to talk about just laws concerning the poor, it won't take long before somebody accuses you of grinding a partisan political axe. Not long ago one of the most fiercely conservative TV talking heads in the United States told his viewers to flee their churches in case their pastors started to talk about social justice since that is manifestly code talk for communism and socialism. This person did relent (a bit) when it was pointed out to him that it is actually code talk for the perspective of God and for the gospel of Christ Jesus.

How we treat the most vulnerable members of society is, biblically speaking, a sign of how holy we are. The book of Leviticus seems to be as outdated and odd a part of the Bible as one can find. But as the preacher Rob Bell said to his just-forming congregation years ago, Leviticus asks a basic question: What would life look like if you believed God lived in your very midst? Bell went on to found his new congregation with a sustained sermon series on Leviticus, noting that how we treat the poor, the widow, and other invisible members of society has a lot to do with responding to the presence of God.

Some of the most lyric stories in the Bible involve God restoring life to those facing a world of death. Elijah's raising of the widow's son, Jesus' raising of the dead, Paul's bringing new life to the Gentiles who had so long been shunned by even God's own people: all of these are testament to God's fierce determination that we should *all* have life and have it abundantly.

GOSPEL IMPLICATIONS

The story of God's covenant began when God uprooted a man named Abram and forced him to become a wanderer, a stranger in a strange land. Ever since, God told his people to take their cue from that and to make a concerted effort to identify with the aliens within their gates as well as with the economically disadvantaged (who were never to remain perpetually poor if laws like the Jubilee were followed). From Abram to Ruth to a host of others, the story was always the same: God wanted his people to keep an eye out for the marginalized. And it all comes to a head in Jesus, the ultimate stranger in a strange land, the One who, as the Evangelist John reminded us, came to his own people but even there was rejected.

The incarnate Lord Jesus literally *embodied* the Bible's focus on the poor and the stranger. That's why he told stories about a good Samaritan and a poor man named Lazarus. That's why he constantly reached out to those whom the religious authorities deemed to be the wrong people. Jesus never failed to see those whom others could not or would not see. But then, that was Jesus for you, the Son of God who was his Father all over again.

_____

SCOTT HOEZEE

MARY VANDEN BERG

PROPER 6 [11]

THE LESSONS IN PRÉCIS

1 Kings 21:1-10 (11-14) 15-21a. Ahab sulks, Jezebel acts, and an innocent man is deprived of not only his God-given allotment of the promised land but also his very life. And God took note.

Psalm 5:1-8. God cannot and will not abide the perpetrators of evil. He will, however, see their wicked deeds even as he most surely will hear the cries of those victimized by evil.

Galatians 2:15-21. The death of no less than God's own Son was required to get human beings out of the calamitous series of sin and evil that has marched through history from the Garden of Eden onward.

Luke 7:36-8:3. A sinful woman lavishes Jesus with a love that his more upstanding hosts carefully withhold. Jesus uses the occasion to highlight the true nature of gratitude and who it is that really "gets it" when it comes to loving God for a forgiveness so great.

THEME SENTENCE
A holy God cannot abide sin and evil but has found a way in Christ to *forgive* that sin and evil. The same God who despises sin became incarnate so as to get close enough to actual sinners to save them from the inside out.

A KEY THEOLOGICAL QUESTION
Sin is not something most people like to talk about. In fact, the word "sin" has fallen on hard times. Even in church, the language of "mistakes,"

"errors in judgment," or "missteps" frequently replaces the word "sin." Sin has become the "S" word.

Sin is a difficult topic to overlook in today's texts, however. Ahab wants a piece of property that does not belong to him and that he cannot legally obtain under the inheritance laws of Israel. As king, he ought to know this, but he pursues the land anyway in complete defiance of God's law. Frustrated with Naboth's righteousness, Ahab pouts and tells his evil wife Jezebel about his problems. True to form, Jezebel takes matters into her own hands, trumping up false charges against Naboth that result in his death. She reports the good news to Ahab, and he grabs the land. But God is not pleased. Elijah identifies Ahab's actions as "evil" and announces God's judgment against him (1 Kgs 21:20-22).

The Gospel reading also involves sin, as we meet a woman from the city who is considered a sinner but who discovered Jesus was dining in a nearby house. Luke does not tell us what her sinful life entailed, but whatever it was, her reputation was clearly well-known. The Pharisee who was from that town and had invited Jesus for dinner knows that she is a "sinner" (Luke 7:39).

Like the Pharisee in Luke's story, people are often experts at identifying sin in someone else. No one has a problem looking at the actions of Ahab and Jezebel and calling those actions "sin." The problems arise when we are called to look at our own lives. Suddenly, intentional deceit becomes an error in judgment, yelling at one's spouse or child becomes a mistake, and cheating on one's taxes becomes a misunderstanding.

These language games lead to self-deception, to a fundamental misperception of who we really are. John Calvin identifies the two parts of all true knowledge as knowledge of God and knowledge of self. He asserts that one cannot really know God unless one knows oneself; conversely, one cannot really know oneself unless one sees oneself in the light of the glory of God. In other words, it is vitally important that our self-assessment is accurate.

When we underplay our sinful actions and perceive ourselves as pretty good people, particularly in contrast to "really bad" people like Ahab, we underplay God's majesty as well. If we are not actually all that bad, it is difficult to understand why the Creator of heaven and earth would have chosen to step down, take on human flesh, and die for the forgiveness of our sins. Like the alcoholic, we have to admit that we have a problem in order to grasp the solution. Calvin writes, "We cannot seriously aspire to [God] before we begin to become displeased with ourselves" (*Institutes*, I.1.1). To put it another way, before we can accept the grace offered in Jesus Christ, we have to recognize that we are as displeasing to God as Ahab and are in need of God's forgiving grace.

Furthermore, the story of the sinful woman points out that when our self-knowledge is distorted, gratitude for God's work on our behalf and the love that flows out of that gratitude will shrivel. The Pharisee, who (mistakenly) thought he was a righteous person, stands in judgment over both the woman, whom he identifies as sinful, and Jesus whom he thinks should know better than to cavort with such a person. The Pharisee's problem is not that he does not have much that needs forgiving. His problem is that he does not *think* he has much from which to be forgiven. He is so busy judging others by his own standard that he fails to see that by God's standard he is just as sinful. He lacks the sort of love the woman shows to Jesus because he has failed to recognize himself as a sinner in need of God's grace.

The psalmist writes that God will not dwell with the wicked, the arrogant, those who tell lies, and those who are violent and dishonest (Ps 5:4-6). Paul tells the Corinthians that idolaters, the sexually immoral, the greedy, and even slanderers will not inherit the kingdom of heaven (1 Cor 6:9-10). Jesus identifies the wicked as those who do not offer food, drink, clothes, and comfort to those in need (Matt 25:41-46). The more one listens to God's word, the more difficult it becomes to ignore that "all have sinned and fall short of God's glory" (Rom 3:23). We are sinners in the sight of God. To think more highly of ourselves than that, to think that the sins we commit leave us less stained than the sins of Ahab or the woman in Luke's story or those who commit the various sins in the Pauline lists is to end up like the Pharisee. Better to end up like the sinful woman who leaves the story with a new identity. Although still a sinner, she is a forgiven sinner (Luke 7:48). As such, she has been adopted by God as God's own child (Gal 4:5).

All followers of Christ are forgiven sinners. We were dead in our sins, unable to love God or each other, but we have been made alive in Christ (Eph 2:5). We have been crucified with Christ; we no longer live but Christ lives in us (Gal 2:20). We are God's handiwork "created in Christ Jesus to do good things" (Eph 2:10). By recognizing who we are—sinners who have been forgiven much—we open the door to loving

God with all of our heart, soul, and mind, and loving our neighbor as ourselves (Matt 22:37).

A PASTORAL NEED

Dealing with the reality of sin is always dicey. On the one hand we are committed to sanctified lifestyles, to holiness, to being like Jesus. On the other hand, we cannot escape the sinful behavior of people in society. But so often the reaction of Christians to sin is so harsh that grace gets swamped. Christians often give the impression that they are *shocked* that there are people in the world who disagree with the church on things like sexual morality. As a result of that shock, some end up carrying signs and placards at public rallies—signs that are so hateful, the gospel looks like bad news instead of good news.

For his part, Jesus never seemed shocked at sin. He was sometimes surprised to encounter strong *faith* but he is never shown fainting at having encountered a prostitute or some other sinner. That was the reaction of the Pharisees, who would have nothing to do with people whose holiness did not rise to the level of their own. Yet Jesus was a magnet for those with many sins. Those who had the most sins to forgive actually sought him out. It's a painful question to ask, but we do well to face the question of why we scare sinners off in ways our Lord generally did not.

ETHICAL CONSIDERATIONS

How can one extend the love of Jesus to sinful people without appearing to be "soft on sin"? Anyone who preaches grace as exuberantly as possible knows that sooner or later some in the church will push back so as to reintroduce themes of justice and judgment. Grace is fine, but let's not fail to take sin seriously, too. And anyway, doesn't the church run the risk of getting snookered if it offers up grace a little too quickly? Can't we all tell stories of how welcoming the church once was to a certain person from the community who later stole from the church or did some other sinful act that ended up hurting a lot of people? Grace can be exploited.

Perhaps the example of Jesus is properly instructive. After all, Jesus never failed to detect the presence of sin. I sometimes use a musical analogy: if you do not know music very well, then you can listen to a performance of an orchestra and not catch the mistakes it made. But someone trained in music will catch far more of the orchestra's misplayed notes. The conductor will catch more yet, even as the composer will hear every goof. Jesus was like the composer. He could not fail to hear all the dropped notes that took place around him. Yet when faced with sinners, he did not become shrill with them. Jesus knew that humility and sacrifice would heal this world's sins in a way fire and brimstone never could. He was confident in that. Maybe Christians today need to share such confidence. We do not condone or commend sin but neither is it *our* job to fix it—for that we can but point people to Jesus and pray that the Holy Spirit will do the rest.

Gospel Implications
The joy of the gospel is experienced best by those willing to admit how desperately they need what only Jesus can give. As Paul says in Galatians, there comes a point where we realize that the only life we have is the one Jesus gives to us through his cross and resurrection. The better we appreciate that, the more inclined we are to spread that joy to others.

The perennial problem Christians face is their unwillingness to admit that everyone needs the same amount of grace. I do not need less grace than does the drug dealer who strings out twelve-year-old girls. Notorious criminals do not need a higher octane grace than does my saintly grandmother. Grace is grace is grace. But good deeds are easier to see than invisible grace. And so after a while we in the church start to think that the difference between reckless sinners in society and saintly folks in the church is not grace but works (or maybe I still need a *little* grace but mostly I've got things covered through my upstanding lifestyle).

If the grace of the gospel does not cause our hearts to skip a beat each time we hear it, it may be time to wonder if we really know that the life we live is Christ's alone.

Scott Hoezee
Mary Vanden Berg

PROPER 7 [12]

THE LESSONS IN PRÉCIS

1 Kings 19:1-4 (5-7) 8-15a. Elijah has about had it with the ups and downs of ministry, but God is not yet finished with him. After feeding and reassuring the prophet, God puts Elijah right back to work.

Psalms 42 and 43. The psalms pull no punches when it comes to the fact that we all get discouraged. Sometimes the memory of God's faithfulness in the past is all we have to go on until God brings us to a new and better day.

Galatians 3:23-29. By the grace of faith, believers get to put on Jesus like a garment. So clothed, the differences that divide us disappear in the unity of baptism.

Luke 8:26-39. The power of the kingdom comes to the people of the Gerasenes, and it scares them half to death. Apparently one demon-crazed man was easier to deal with than the idea that God might just upset everything we have foolishly come to accept as "normal."

THEME SENTENCE

God rescues us from the perils of life that enslave us and bring us down. But God's power does not always come in the form we expect and often upends our tidy lives. Still, the power of salvation really does make all things new and equips us for ministry.

A KEY THEOLOGICAL QUESTION

One of the attributes of God that the Christian tradition has always recognized is omnipotence. God is able to do anything that is logically possible to do. While modern people have raised many questions about what might be considered logically possible, the Bible does not worry about such problems. The Bible presents God as all-powerful, the one who is able to do even more than we could ask or imagine (Eph 3:20).

Today's texts all have to do with the power of God in one way or another. Elijah has just had perhaps the most victorious moment of his life. While Elijah is surrounded by Ahab, the prophets of Baal who want to kill him, and the people of Israel who have abandoned God, God makes himself known as the only true God through a spectacular display of power. But once Jezebel gets wind of the demise of her four-hundred prophets, she vows to kill Elijah, and so he must flee for his life. In today's text Elijah is exhausted and asks God to end his life (1 Kgs 19:4).

God does not grant Elijah's request. Rather God comes to him, displaying his power much more quietly than on Mount Carmel. God sends an angel with freshly baked bread and a jar of water (1 Kgs 19:6), offering precisely what Elijah needs at that moment, caring for him by providing for his most basic needs. This is not exactly the fireworks displayed to the wayward people of Israel in the previous narrative, but it is no less miraculous.

The Gospel reading for today focuses on a man in dire circumstances. He lives a tortured life among the dead, tormented day and night by a legion of demons. Like Elijah, he is oppressed by evil. But he does not cry out for help or ask God to end his life as Elijah did. In fact, when God-incarnate shows up, the man yells at him, questioning what Jesus wants with him. The man is too weak even to know what he needs. But Jesus knows, commanding the demons to come out of him as soon as he sees the man (Luke 8:29). Once again, there are no fireworks, just a man, a legion of demons, and a herd of pigs. And as with Elijah, God comes to the man and gives him exactly what he needs. God had not forgotten this man, and the man responds by obeying Jesus and telling the people in his town how much God had done for him (Luke 8:39).

The cry of the psalmist in Psalms 42 and 43 is also the cry of one suffering because of evil. This pair of psalms functions as one extended cry to God. One can even imagine that the thoughts of the psalmist were like the thoughts of Elijah as he lay down under the broom tree. The cry of the psalmist is the cry of one who has been taunted, particularly because of his belief in God. The cry is a cry of one who is downcast, feeling oppressed by her circumstances. But even more important to recognize is that the psalmist's cry is a cry of faith in the all-powerful God, the only one who is truly able to change the psalmist's circumstances. The psalmist reminds readers that the ultimate hope of the persecuted, depressed, and downtrodden is God.

Sometimes God displays his power in a spectacular way, igniting a soaking-wet altar in order to demonstrate that he, not Baal, is God (1 Kgs 18:16-39). Sometimes God's power comes more quietly, providing food to one who is discouraged, or bringing peace to a man tormented by demons. In each case, God displays his power in ways that defy our imagination. The most stunning display of God's power, however, came not in a fiery demonstration on a mountain or even in casting out a legion of demons but on a Roman cross on a hill outside Jerusalem, followed three days later by the empty tomb. Paul says this power is foolishness to the world, but to Christ's followers it is the power of God for our righteousness (1 Cor 1:18, 30). It is the power of the cross that broke human imprisonment to a law we could not keep (Gal 3:23-25).

Through the power of the cross God makes people into new creations (1 Cor 5:17). Having accepted Christ by faith, God clothes his people with Christ (Gal 3:27), giving them the ability to live not as slaves to sin but as God's own children (Gal 3:26). Paul himself is the premier example of the power of God to turn life around (Acts 9:1-19). Paul, as much as anyone else, knows how God's power can remake a wretched sinner into a brand new creation. Perhaps that is why he writes so passionately to the Galatians who have turned back to slavery to the law after receiving the gospel of grace.

Unfortunately, despite the fact that we are new creations, the world as a whole continues to await the "glorious freedom of God's children" (Rom 8:21). Like the psalmist, there are times when, because of our circumstances, tears are our food day and night (Ps 42:3). There are times when we feel oppressed by our enemies and forgotten by God (Ps 42:9). We are downcast. At those times our cries of faith rise to heaven with those of the psalmist of old, and we are reminded that the power of God is with us. The power of God, so different from the power of the world, is actually made perfect in weakness (2 Cor 12:9). When we are weak, God is strong (2 Cor 12:10). With that in mind, we can put our hope in God and praise him, for he alone is our Savior and our God.

A Pastoral Need

Unless we insist on wearing rose-colored glasses, it is not difficult to see boatloads of suffering, depression, disorientation, and hurt everywhere we look. As a friend of mine used to say, go up to almost any person in a pew on a Sunday morning, scratch the surface of his or her life, and you will likely find hurts aplenty. Whatever else being a Christian means, it does not insulate us from grief. In fact, those of us who have a better vision for how life in God's creation should be often find far *more* to lament than those without such a better vision. When a tsunami wipes out a whole population, even atheists ask the hard question of "Why?" But those of us who believe in a good God find that question to be far more acute.

The church is chock-full of hurt every Sunday morning. People come to church desperate for a Word from the Lord, desperate to hear that God really can heal and restore us and make all things new. We want to be lifted out of the depressions that beset us. We want to be healed of the diseases that ail us. We want to be delivered from the things that hold us in thrall. On any given Sunday, we'd all like to be like the man in the Gerasenes: we'd like to go home clothed and in our right minds, restored in Christ to all God desires us to be.

Ethical Implications

It's time that more Christians in the church take a stand against those who insist on putting slogans like "We're Too Blessed to Be Depressed" on their church signs. It's time to let people know that being a Christian does not mean that every day we "Put on a Happy Faith." It's time that we ask that "Praise Teams" not try to send semaphore signals to the congregation that everyone should look and feel and just flat out *be* as beatific and blessed as the members of the Praise Team are so earnestly trying to display. (Maybe, as a friend once suggested, it's time to balance Praise Teams with "Lament Teams" who can get up to give voice to the other emotions that are in the sanctuary every single Sunday.)

Christians have a holy obligation to embrace the tensions of the faith, a key one of which is that Christians struggle with discouragement and depression. And the reason they struggle is not because their faith is weak. The believers in the Old Testament had the courage and the pluck to expect a lot from God (and to let God have it when they didn't get it).

The faith that fueled psalms of lament was not a weak faith but a strong one. As people now clothed with Christ, we too have high expectations for life and a keen hunger for righteousness. When we see how far we and the world (and also the church) fall short, we have reasons to grieve. But we also have reasons to hope that our holy grief will not have the last word. As Jesus once said, blessed are those who know how to mourn because the day will come when they will be comforted!

GOSPEL IMPLICATIONS

Christ Jesus came to make all things new, but the old still has some life left to it. In Luke 8 we are shocked that the people of the Gerasenes failed to celebrate the miracle that had taken place. Did they love pigs so much and this once-crazed man so little that they were blind to the good thing that had taken place? Or were they scared silly by the sheer power of God's kingdom? Can God's power actually frighten people? It appears to have done so in the Gerasenes.

But are we sometimes afraid of the kingdom, too? C.S. Lewis once said that we like to think becoming a Christian is like teaching a horse how to run a little faster when really it's more like outfitting a horse with a pair of wings and teaching it to fly. The passages in this set of lectionary texts are partly about how life sometimes goes and partly about how things can become radically new when the Spirit of God cuts loose with kingdom power. We are often caught between the two, but the good news is that Christ really can step into the hurts of our lives and make us all new. We need not be afraid!

SCOTT HOEZEE

MARY VANDEN BERG

Proper 8 [13]

The Lessons in Précis

2 Kings 2:1-2, 6-14. Elijah departs, but God's spirit comes upon Elisha in great power. The prophets are encouraged— the work of the Lord God of Israel will continue.

Psalm 77:1-2, 11-20. God's power is in the service of God's people in ways that the very creation respects. Deep waters are not an obstacle when God leads the people along. The creation respects its Creator.

Galatians 5:1, 13-25. God has set us free in Christ. However, we are "free" not to do whatever we want but to be what God created us to be in the first place: people bearing bumper crops of spiritual fruit that nourish all around us.

Luke 9:51-62. Jesus turns his face to Jerusalem and all that awaits him there. Having done so, his words on the cost of discipleship sharpen. What lies ahead is not for the half-hearted! To follow Jesus is to arrive finally at a cross.

Theme Sentence

God's salvation marches through the valleys and streets of this real world because it is this world that God aims to redeem. The Creator has not abandoned creation in favor of some misty spiritual realm. Salvation emerges in the world, and its fruits need to be on display in this world, too.

A Key Theological Question

Since Trinity Sunday, the Old Testament readings have been following the story of Elijah. Today's text records the story of the end of Elijah's life. But God does not leave his people without a prophet. The text also tells about the equipping of Elijah's successor, Elisha. Elijah asks Elisha, "What do you want me to do for you before I am taken from you?" (2 Kgs 2:9). Elisha replies, "Let me have twice your spirit." (2 Kgs 2:9) That seems like quite a bold request, but Elijah grants the request if Elisha can see him taken away. After seeing Elijah taken away in a fiery chariot, Elisha walks away from the scene with Elijah's cloak. He splits the Jordan while the company of prophets watches and subsequently affirms that Elisha indeed has inherited Elijah's spirit.

As with the story of Elijah and Elisha, throughout scripture the Spirit is associated in one way or another with power: power to split the Jordan river, power to speak in different languages (Acts 2), and power to proclaim the word of the Lord (Isa 61:1; Acts 4:31), to name just a few examples. Although it is not clear from the immediate text whether the spirit of Elijah and the Spirit of the Lord are exactly the same thing, it is clear that the spirit Elisha has inherited gives him power. Furthermore, the power that he displays over creation indicates that the spirit is none other than the Spirit of God.

Although the power of the Spirit is sometimes displayed in miraculous ways like those just mentioned, the same power that splits rivers and casts out demons is available in the equally miraculous production of fruit from a formerly unfruitful life. In Galatians, after explaining the freedom in Christ that Christians have, Paul enjoins his readers to "be guided by the Spirit" (Gal 5:16). His description of life in the Spirit, however, can sound quite intimidating. The Spirit-filled life disallows not only those behaviors that are relatively easy to avoid, such as witchcraft and orgies. It also prohibits behaviors such as jealousy, envy, and selfish ambition. But Paul does not stop with only those behaviors that should be rejected. He goes on to list "fruits" or positive characteristics of life in the Spirit. This familiar list of fruits includes "love, joy, peace, patience, kindness, goodness, faithfulness, gentleness and self-control" (Gal 5:22-23). One is tempted to respond to all of this as Jesus' followers at one time responded to him, "Then who can be saved?" (Matt 19:25).

This is exactly where the gospel of grace comes in. Paul, the preacher of grace, makes clear that this list of dos and don'ts is not a new law. The fact that Christians are no longer under the law but under grace is precisely his point to the Galatians who seem to have slid back into a law mentality. The list is not about living a life in order to become right with God. Paul's letter to the Galatians is all about the fact that his readers are already right with God because of God's grace in Christ. But being right with God is not the whole picture; this new life should be evident in their behavior.

While the Galatians should relish their freedom in Christ, it is not freedom to indulge in sin (Gal 5:13). The good news is that because they have been incorporated into Christ through baptism (Gal 3:27), God's Spirit lives in them (Gal 4:6). Because God's Spirit lives in those who belong to Christ, they are empowered to live in actuality the Spirit-filled life described by Paul. Good fruit is not optional; it is an indication that a person has truly been made one with Christ. That leads to the further question, however, of why the lives of Christians do not often clearly display these fruits.

That question brings us back to Elisha. He asks Elijah for a double portion of his spirit. Matthew records Jesus telling his disciples that if they ask, God will give them good gifts (Matt 7:11). In a parallel passage Luke quotes Jesus saying that as surely as a father gives good gifts to his children when they ask, so will God give his people the Holy Spirit if they ask God for this gift (Luke 11:13). While different theological traditions understand the giving of the Holy Spirit in varying ways, one thing seems clear: if we ask God to empower us by the gift of his Spirit, God surely will empower us. Perhaps we look at Paul's list of fruits as intimidating and fail to display these fruits because, as did the Galatians, we try to do these things on our own, making the list of fruits that we are supposed to exhibit and the acts of the sinful nature that we are not to exhibit into a new law that we have to drum up the strength to obey.

This is not Paul's message at all. Galatians 5 ends with Paul telling his readers that they must "keep in step with the Spirit" (Gal 5:25, NIV). Paul emphasizes that the negative behaviors come from being out of step with the Spirit, while love, joy, peace, patience, etc. are fruits of the Christian's cooperation with the Spirit, who joins them to Christ. Apart from Christ and his empowering Spirit, they will not be able to live as God has directed. When Christians ask God for God's Spirit, however, they are enabled through cooperation with the Spirit to let the light of their good works shine before others so that the world will give glory to God (Matt 5:16).

A Pastoral Need

What does a "spiritual" life look like? Some Christians describe their lives in rather other-worldly terms. More than once I have been in the company of Christians who, although very earnest, find it difficult to locate God in the ordinary and so instead tell stories indicating that eye-popping miracles happen to them on a fairly regular basis. They claim that God routinely sends them personalized spiritual messages while they sip orange juice at breakfast. Life for them seems to be a long series of wondrous acts or clarion words from God. It can make the average Christian feel pretty shabby by comparison.

Now let's grant that God does extraordinary things in our world. But let's also grant that God works in the ordinary, non-miraculous moments of our lives as well. Christ is found "among the pots and pans" (to riff on Teresa of Avila) and in all those quiet places where Christian people manage to let spiritual fruits like kindness and gentleness shine through.

When Jesus set out for Jerusalem, his path took him through many ordinary circumstances, even as he sometimes encountered frustrations and unfriendly folks. Jesus' mission did not remove him from this world, but then that makes sense: after all, becoming a flesh-and-blood person with hair and fingernails was the first step in God's redemption of all things. It's no surprise, then, to discover that we live out our faith today in the throes of the real world, finding ways to let Jesus shine in even the most mundane of circumstances in and through which we do our best to "keep step with the Spirit" in all the walking-around normalness of life.

Ethical Implications

Cheeky bumper stickers sometimes say, "I Love Jesus: It's His Followers I Can't Stand." But since Christianity is an incarnational religion, it goes without saying that no one can really get to know Jesus without acquaintance with his flesh-and-blood followers. It can never do, then, to pretend that spiritual truths can get through to the world even if the actual followers of Jesus are a turn-off. As Paul knew when writing to the Galatians, our faith needs to emerge smack in the middle of a world that tempts us with sex, drugs, booze, and the whole carnival of pleasures that exist here.

Instead of giving in to such temptation, our lives display control where others display wanton abandon; our lives display kindness and gentleness where others display only brutal self-interest; our lives display love and peace where others spew venomous words of hatred that divide persons from one another. What's more, this all happens not behind stained glass on Sundays but in corporate board rooms on Tuesday afternoons and in shopping malls on Friday mornings and while driving down jammed highways on Saturdays. Elijah may have been picked up in a chariot of fire, but what the company of the prophets needed to know was that God was going to keep up with the work here *on earth*.

The world needs to know that, too. Cults are the place to go to hear about escape from the world. The church should be the place to go to hear the gospel's transformative message proclaimed in words that have traction for all we do during all those moments when we are not sitting in a pew.

Gospel Implications

My comments above focus on the need to be spiritual in the hurly-burly world of the everyday and not to pretend that spirituality cuts us off from life. Yet near the end of Luke 9, Jesus encounters people with some real-world concerns but tells them that if *that* is all they are concerned with, then they cannot follow him. So which is it: does following Jesus allow us to engage in life, or are we to become austere people who exist slightly "above it all"?

Jesus came to redeem the whole of human life and to restore us to shalom, to the full flourishing of life in *all* of our relationships. But we also know that Jesus and his apostles had no patience with anything that would hinder a person's embrace of the kingdom of God. In Luke 9 Jesus was on his way to death. His mission was "all or nothing." Salvation could not come through a different route. Jesus had to walk to the cross unhindered and without second thoughts. Those who follow him to that cross must likewise acknowledge its utter necessity. Jesus' mission was clear to him. When it comes to the cross, that mission needs to be equally clear to us.

Scott Hoezee

Mary Vanden Berg

PROPER 9 [14]

THE LESSONS IN PRÉCIS

2 Kings 5:1-14. Naaman, a Gentile, will do anything to cure his leprosy, even if it means following the advice of his servant, traveling to Israel, and accepting the help of the prophet Elisha. After resistance to human directions, the great general does as he is told and is cured.

Psalm 30. We hear the song of one who cried out to God for help and healing, and found restoration. Only God can turn our "mourning into dancing" (vs. 11) and grief into joy.

Galatians 6:(1-6) 7-16. To be a "new creation" (vs. 15) in Christ is not about the state of our bodies, circumcision, or our own success. Rather, it is about working for the good of all and boasting in the cross.

Luke 10:1-11, 16-20. Jesus sends out seventy who are carrying only the good news of the nearness of God's reign. In the name of Jesus they could cure the sick and cast out demons.

THEME SENTENCE

God heals. Working with and through human agents, God brings healing and wholeness. Elisha and the seventy are given a mandate to cure the sick. The challenge for people is to focus on God rather than the human agent.

A KEY THEOLOGICAL QUESTION

God heals.

These texts invite us to reflect on the nature of healing and God's purposes for us in the good creation.

We have a fundamental desire for health and wholeness. Whenever we experience a wound or a breakdown in the way in which our body normally functions, we take measures to treat the wound or restore normal function to the body. Whenever our lives become disordered by imbalance because we are overextended in our obligations, we take steps to facilitate more balance, if we are wise.

The psalmist in Psalm 30 suggests that it is natural to seek healing. In the book of James, the writer exhorts us to pray for healing of those who are sick (Jas 5:14). There are many examples of healing in the Old and New Testaments, which indicate that God desires our healing and wholeness. The text from 2 Kings reflects that while we can and should pray for healing, we cannot dictate the terms and methods of that healing (2 Kgs 5:11-13).

In our texts, the agents of God's healing vary. In 2 Kings, the agent of healing was Elisha the prophet. In Luke 10, Jesus sent out seventy disciples who were empowered to cure the sick and cast out demons. Throughout the Bible, people were healed in many different ways. All three Synoptic Gospels record the story of the woman who suffered for years from an uncontrollable hemorrhage and received healing when she touched the hem of Jesus' garment in a crowd (Matt 9:20-22; Mark 5:25-34; Luke 8:43-48). In Acts 3:6, a disabled man was reduced to begging, and Peter told him to rise and walk in the name of Jesus Christ. Immediately, the ankles and feet of the man were strengthened and he was able to follow Peter and John into the temple. Regardless of the agent, healing is a work of God.

Today, in the West, we no longer go to prophets or holy men or women for healing. We seek healing through modern medicine. We go to medical specialists. But people do not have to be medical specialists to be agents of healing. An encouraging word spoken to a discouraged person, an embrace to a distraught parishioner, or a lending hand to an overwhelmed single mother are simple yet meaningful ways in which we facilitate movement toward healing and wholeness within our communities of faith.

There is no prescribed method of prayer that can guarantee that all who are sick will be cured of every disease. We are painfully aware that there are times when we pray for ourselves and seek recommended medical attention but are not healed. This happens also to friends and loved ones for whom we pray. Some may be forced to manage a chronic illness like the Apostle Paul, who bore with patience and forbearance an unidentified "thorn in the flesh" (2 Cor 12:7, KJV). Others may be called upon to prepare for imminent death because their illness is terminal. At such times we may be led to question whether God answers prayers. Our heartache may lead us to agonize over the presence of suffering in the world, if God is indeed all-powerful and all-good. In those times, the prayers and support of the faith community may mean the difference between despair and hope. When illness lingers for years or death comes despite extraordinary measures, we confront the truth that there is a deeply mysterious aspect to healing.

The need for healing extends beyond the physical. A marriage has been broken through domestic violence. Siblings who fought through childhood continue to fight as adults. A long-term friendship is destroyed through a betrayal of confidence. To limit our understanding of healing is to limit our understanding of the depths of wholeness that God desires for us. We miss the areas in which disorder and *dis*-ease can mar our existence.

Not only do human beings need healing, but so also do communities and nations. Those with wealth and greater access to political power can abandon those who are economically deprived and lacking in the kind of social and political capital that can enable them to secure the resources that can transform their communities into safe and vibrant places in which to raise their children. Relationships between racial/ethnic groups can lead to ongoing conflict that can erupt into war. Those with the lowest status and the least amount of power are left with few defenses.

Healing is a sign that the reign of God is near. Thus healing should be understood in terms of our relationship with God. Health and wholeness are gifts that come from God. They can enhance our lives before God and in relation to others. All that we have belongs to God and this knowledge should remind us from whom all blessings flow. Healing is connected to kingdom living. We have been granted the privilege as sons and daughters of God to be agents of healing in our communities through faithful discipleship.

A PASTORAL NEED

I suspect you will not have to look far or think for long before you can identify someone in your congregation who, like Naaman, is longing for some kind of healing. They may seek healing from some physical ailment, or perhaps a mental or spiritual ailment. These stories invite us to reflect upon not only the ways that God heals but also how God calls us to be agents, with God, in the healing of our sisters and brothers.

Naaman was healed of his leprosy through God's gracious intervention—but there were several people involved as well: the young slave girl, Elisha and his messenger, and Naaman's own servants. Each pointed Naaman to God, the source of healing. Likewise, when Jesus sent the seventy out into the harvest, he told them the first thing they were to do was to "cure the sick" (Luke 10:9, NRSV). Some in the congregation may be part of a health care team—nurse, doctor, or first responder. Do they think of what they do as ministry?

A challenge in reflecting on the theme of God's healing is the difference between being healed and being cured. Naaman was cured and healed of his leprosy, but you may know many people who have been healed, that is, brought to wholeness, who still suffer from their illness or ailment. A wonderful example of this is the story of Helen Keller. Through the gift of her teacher, Anne Sullivan, Helen, who went blind and deaf at 19 months when she contracted scarlet fever, was able to learn and communicate through hand signing.

In the 1962 film, *The Miracle Worker*, there is a wonderful scene when the young Helen finally begins to make the connection between what her teacher is doing when signing in her hand and the world around her. Like Naaman, Helen was led to water as her teacher pumped fresh water over her small hand while spelling the word "water." In that moment Helen was healed. She was still blind and deaf, but she was brought back into connection with the world around her.

ETHICAL IMPLICATIONS

I recently experienced pains in my chest. I was sure these pains indicated merely a virus, but my husband, who is a physician, was like Naaman's servants; he would not take no for an answer. He insisted that he drive me to the emergency room where I spent the next 16 hours. Fortunately nothing was wrong, but it took a number of very expensive tests and conversations with many doctors to confirm that.

I was fortunate in many ways. First, there was a hospital only minutes away, and I had a loving husband who made sure I got there. The hospital had the staff and equipment to evaluate me. And perhaps most importantly, I had insurance that would cover the cost for all of the tests and physicians that I saw. I did not lie in the emergency room worrying about how I would pay for everything.

We are all anxious to answer Christ's call to bring help and care for people in our congregations and local communities. Many churches have groups who prepare meals for families in crisis. There are those who drive people to doctor's appointments. And many churches now have parish nursing programs to help people navigate the challenging health care system.

But I believe these stories also challenge us to take great risks when it comes to caring for others. The slave girl of Naaman's wife took a risk in telling her mistress that the general would find healing in her country. We are challenged to think beyond the healing of individuals. The cost and availability of health care are a need not only for individuals in our congregations but also for our nation as a whole. Think of how many hospitals were started by religious bodies. In Washington, D.C., there is a facility called Christ House, where homeless men and women both receive health care and are able to stay in residence as they recover from their illness if they have been discharged from the hospital.

How can we educate ourselves and our congregations to become active participants in this important debate? How can we become involved in finding ways to provide health care for those in need? As disciples, we are called to reach out to all who are in need. Jesus reminds us, "The size of the harvest is bigger than you can imagine" (Matt 9:37). I recall an observation by a Roman Catholic cardinal talking about his church's health care facilities, "We don't help people because they are Christian. We help people because we are Christian."

GOSPEL IMPLICATIONS
The gospel stories are filled with stories of healings: the blind see, the lame walk, the dead are raised. But we have very narrow vision if we think these are the only ways people are healed. To be healed is to be made whole. To be healed is to be welcomed back into the community. We are surrounded by God's healing moments. As disciples we are called to recognize those moments and to lead people to the healing waters.

Lucy Lind Hogan

Beverly E. Mitchell

PROPER 10 [15]

THE LESSONS IN PRÉCIS

Amos 7:7-17. Called by God, Amos has gone from herding sheep and goats to challenging King Jeroboam and the people of Israel. God has held up a plumb line, Amos tells them, and found the nation warped.

Psalm 82. God confronts the nations of the earth with their sins and misdeeds. They have ignored the poor, favoring the wealthy. The divine judge declares they must give justice to the weak and orphans and rescue the needy.

Colossians 1:1-14. Paul praises the saints in Colossae for their faithfulness to the gospel and their love of God. They are "producing fruit in every good work" (vs. 10). He prays they will be strong and, with God's help, able to endure the challenges that may lie ahead.

Luke 10:25-37. Jesus and a lawyer match wits. Jesus agrees that the lawyer gives the right answers but questions whether he really understands the heart of God's law. Jesus tells him the story of a man beaten and left for dead. Who was the neighbor—the priest or Levite? Neither, as instead it was the Samaritan; "the one who demonstrated mercy" (vs. 37).

THEME SENTENCE

God's way is justice and mercy. Are our lives judged by a plumb line? Absolutely. Each of these texts elucidates God's plumb line. We are to love our neighbor, to extend justice and mercy to the least among us just as God does.

Key Theological Question

God's way is justice and mercy.
These texts serve as a warning that justice and mercy toward others are the measure of our faithfulness to God.

The parable of the Good Samaritan in Luke 10 illustrates vividly that the fulfillment of the double commandment to love God and love our neighbor is the ethical standard by which our righteousness is determined in God's eyes. This theme is even more explicitly made clear in Matt 25:31-46, where Christ identifies himself with the hungry, thirsty, imprisoned, naked, sick, or otherwise needy. In this parable of the final judgment, the ones who are saved are the ones who cared for those in need. In the Bible, justice to the oppressed and mercy to those who need loving kindness are never considered optional.

Sometimes we are diverted from the practice of the law of love by a focus on external practices that give the appearance of holiness. We can be like the Pharisee Jesus spoke of in Luke 18:11, who boasted of his outwardly pious acts. His pride deluded him about his true spiritual condition, and his vanity betrayed his ignorance about what truly pleases God. Of course pious living, private devotions, and regular corporate worship have their place in the life of our communities of faith. However, if these worship practices fail to match the ethical commitment required of God's people to love our neighbors as ourselves, then they are repugnant in God's sight. This can be seen in Isa 58:1-5, where God's people are condemned for exhibiting the practices of holiness while refusing to practice justice and mercy within the community. The kind of sacrifice that pleases God is that in which we bring relief to the oppressed, give bread to the hungry, and make a home for the homeless (Isa 58:6-7).

The prophets in the Bible do not leave us guessing as to what they believe is the will of God. Though Amos was not from a normal prophetic lineage, he brought a word of judgment that exposed the ways the Israelites had failed to live according to the law of love. Prophets of God may not always come through "normal" channels. The homeless who confront us by their presence in our urban areas might not strike us as "normal" prophets. However, they, too, bear witness against callous policies that foster indifference toward those who lack the economic, social, and political means to safeguard their own interests. Though like Amos, they are not descendants of the normal prophetic line, they are modern-day truth-tellers whose very presence in the midst of affluence is an indictment of unfaithfulness to the God of love. We are told clearly what God requires (Mic 6:8). Doing justice and loving mercy top the list. Living faithfully to these requirements is the essence of kingdom living, and both must be understood within the context of divine love.

The first epistle of John informs us that God is love (1 John 4:8). Within the sacred circle of the communion of love between the Father, Son, and Holy Spirit, God freely chose to extend that love outward in the act of creation. God's desire for all of creation is to experience *shalom*, a Hebrew word often translated as "wholeness." Shalom encompasses harmony and right relationship between God, humans, and the remainder of creation. If God's desire is that the good creation experience wholeness, then anything that threatens *shalom* evokes God's wrath and calls forth a return to right relationship. The restoration of right relationship within the created order constitutes justice. Unfortunately, the web of sin that has entangled humankind in history continually distorts the harmony of relations such that it is difficult for us to practice justice or show mercy. The divine will for creation is for mutuality and reciprocity, which mirror the communion of love in the very life of God.

Without justice there is no chance of right relationships. Without mercy we cannot know wholeness. The redeeming work of Christ reconciled the world to God. By the transformative work of the Holy Spirit, we have been empowered to act as agents of reconciliation in the world.

A Pastoral Need

A friend tells a convicting story. He was part of a group of inner city clergy who were participating in a meeting at a church located in the heart of a depressed and violent part of the city. The church was involved in offering programs for its neighbors, the poorest of the poor. The meeting was held on a very cold winter morning. As the participants arrived for the meeting, which was being held in the parish hall next to the church, they had to pass the front doors of the church. Each saw that a homeless man was still bundled in blankets, sleeping on the front steps of the church. During the meeting, thinking about the ways that the church is called to live into the gospel command to love our neighbor and show mercy, many spoke of the man they had seen on the steps.

Their hearts went out to the homeless man. His presence encouraged them in their work, and they busied themselves with developing programs to aid the least among them. We might even speculate that they were inwardly congratulating themselves for not being like the priest or Levite. Unfortunately, while they were not entirely like those who passed by on the other side, they also were not like the Samaritan, who was moved with pity and bandaged the traveler's wounds. During the meeting one of the church staff came to tell them disturbing news—the man on the church steps had actually died of hypothermia.

To love our neighbor means that we will have to stop and take risks.

ETHICAL IMPLICATIONS

When Mary anointed Jesus' feet with oil, Judas scolded her for squandering money that could have been used to help the poor. Jesus said, "You will always have the poor among you" (John 12:8). Mary was preparing Jesus' body for the passion that lay ahead, and for that she was to be honored. In this moment it was alright, he was telling them, to spend their money this way.

Unfortunately, all too often we turn to this scripture to justify not helping the poor. We have a rather fatalist approach to justice, "What can we do? There are so many things wrong in our world, so many people who are poor. And didn't Jesus tell us that they would always be with us?" We are overwhelmed by the enormity of the problems. We give up on helping before we even begin.

There is a plumb line held against all of our actions, great and small, global and intimate. Are there people we pass by? Are there times when we are tempted to say, "That's not my problem?" We ought not do that because our God does not. Everyone—family, friend, neighbor, stranger, enemy—is a beloved child of God, created in God's image.

A home across the street was recently sold. Many of the neighbors were very upset, having found out that the home will now serve as a halfway home for people who are suffering from bipolar schizophrenia. They are fighting the home in every way they can. If I am to answer Jesus' question, "Who was neighbor to the man," what should be my response? I don't think Jesus would want me to fight the house. But I also don't think he merely wants me to either tolerate or simply accept its presence in my neighborhood. I think that to be neighbor means to reach out to those who are my new neighbors. I cannot pass by on the other side of the street.

Gospel Implications

How we understand ourselves as disciples of God's justice and mercy may depend on our image of God. Do we picture God as distant and judgmental? The book of Job ends with a provocative portrait of God. This is a God more like Amos' image of the divine being who holds a plumb line against our uneven lives. This is the God who spoke out of the whirlwind, the God who laid the very foundations of our earth. This is the awesome, transcendent God who can flood the earth and who commands snow, rain, ice, and every living creature. What is the quality of this justice, this mercy?

Perhaps it will help if we think of a different picture of our God. Jesus reminded us that we have a God who feeds the ravens, cares for the tiniest sparrows, and "dresses grass in the field so beautifully" (Luke 12:28). This is the image of an immanent, tender God who is able to count the very hairs on our heads. Jesus cared not only for the crowds that followed him, but also for individuals: the blind man, the lepers, and the bent-over woman. This is a God who is involved in the most intimate moments of each person's life and challenges us to be equally involved.

Lucy Lind Hogan
Beverly E. Mitchell

PROPER 11 [16]

THE LESSONS IN PRÉCIS

Amos 8:1-12. God shows Amos a basket of summer fruit as a visual image of Israel's end. Songs will be turned into wailing and feasts into mourning because the people have ignored God and oppressed the poor and needy. They are to prepare for famine of God's word.

Psalm 52. The psalmist reminds the wicked who are trusting only their wealth, their lying, and their love of evil that they will be subject to God's judgment. Our trust should be in the love of God.

Colossians 1:15-28. All that we know—whether it is the church or the entire creation itself—comes through Christ who has shown us God. Central to this is the knowledge that we have been forgiven by and reconciled to God through the "blood of his cross" (vs. 20).

Luke 10:38-42. Jesus' friend Martha complains that her sister, Mary, has chosen to study at his feet rather than helping her in the kitchen. What is the "better part" (vs. 42)? It is not to worry about worldly chores, but to focus on the word of God.

THEME SENTENCE

Our trust is in God. We are presented with several images of those who do and do not trust in God. If we focus on worldly concerns or wealth, we will be frustrated in the end. If we trust in ourselves, our wealth, and our work alone, it will be our downfall. Paul reminds us that Christ is the firstborn of all creation and, like Mary, we are to sit at his feet and trust in his reconciling love.

A KEY THEOLOGICAL QUESTION
Our trust is in God.
These texts warn us of the futility of placing our faith in things other than God.

From cradle to grave our finitude stands as a reminder that we cannot navigate this life without dependence upon others. As infants we are completely dependent upon the care of adults who will nurture us, protect us from harm, and help us to reach our potential. As we mature, we lose the utter helplessness characteristic of infancy, but we never lose the need for the help and support of others. Our natural interdependence with others can lead us to place undue trust in people and things that will ultimately disappoint us.

If our well-being is tied to the character of the object of our trust, then we need have no fear of placing our trust in God. God, who is love, is committed to our welfare, and desires that we experience life more abundantly. We should not be fixated on material needs, for God already knows our need of these things (Matt 6:31-48). Rather, our focus is to be directed on participation in God's commonwealth. We are exhorted to trust in God. If we do, God will direct our paths (Prov 3:5). Because of God's utter faithfulness, we can place ourselves unreservedly in the care of the divine. Unfortunately, in the history of God's people, many have chosen not to place their trust in God alone.

Today's biblical texts warn us about the significant ways we can squander our trust. The psalmist speaks of those who trust only in wealth. Likewise, the prophet Amos charged the Israelites with feasting and merry-making at the expense of the poor and needy. Undoubtedly they trusted their riches to supply all their needs, even as they overlooked the needs of those in their midst. The overindulgence of the Israelites led them to ignore the living God who faithfully provided for them. Their misplaced trust led to God's wrath and judgment. Although in our day we are reluctant to reflect upon the wrath of God, that wrath is generally evoked when the welfare of the community is at stake. If some are consumed with their own wealth at the expense of those in need, the welfare of the community is in jeopardy. In such cases, the wrath and judgment of God are designed to wake us up, to help us realize that our ways and actions rupture the peace of the community because we are unable or unwilling to see how we adversely affect others.

We lose an opportunity to learn from the mistakes of the Israelites if we fail to see the connection between their conduct and ours. In some of our more affluent communities, our attention may be consumed by the things we have acquired. We may share out of our largesse here and there, but remain oblivious to the ways our lifestyle commitments, habits of consumption, or political allegiances contribute to the oppressive suffering of those who are powerless. When, like the Israelites, our attention is overly focused on activities that have no lasting value, our attention is diverted not only from those who need our help, but it is also diverted from the source of our life. There is no room within us to receive the nourishment that only God can offer. When that happens, we, too, will be subject to famine—the famine of the word.

We might also invite spiritual famine in our lives by being overly busy. In contemporary life, the demands of our jobs, the over-scheduling of our children, and the constant temptation of various media distractions make it extremely difficult to attend to the kind of spiritual practices that keep us attuned to the Spirit's transformative work in our lives. Like overworked Martha in Luke 10, who placed her focus on chores rather than on hearing Jesus teach, we may miss what is most needful. When we focus attention on activities that have no lasting value, or depend upon the things that money can buy for our well-being, we exhibit a lack of trust in the God who has created us, redeemed us through Christ, and now sustains us through the power of the Holy Spirit. We also set ourselves up for deep disappointment.

The passage in Colossians reminds Christians of even greater reasons to trust in God. By faith in Christ we have the knowledge that God has forgiven us for our sins and has given us new life through the death and resurrection of Christ. In the divine life, God models community, where the Father, Son, and Holy Spirit work together in unity of purpose for the good of the created order. Through the reconciliation accomplished in the life, ministry, death, and resurrection of Christ, we become part of the new creation. By the power of the Holy Spirit we experience the birth pangs of transformation that will draw us into the very life of God.

A Pastoral Need

For several years, people in the United States put their trust in real estate. They trusted that the price of homes was going to continue to rise dramatically. They trusted that they could buy a home that cost more than they could actually afford, because they believed that home would increase in value. They trusted that home prices would never go down and that banks would always be there to lend them more and more money. Unfortunately, those potential real estate feasts were soon turned into mourning, and there were (and continue to be) songs of lamentation. Many Americans have faced foreclosure, and others worry each month about whether or not they will be able to pay their mortgages.

We have limited vision when it comes to trust; we prefer to put our trust in things that we can touch, feel, or count. You or others in your congregation may have done trust falls as a trust-building game. The rules are quite simple: one person stands on a table or platform three feet above the ground, arms folded, eyes shut, facing away from a group of people who are standing on the ground below and behind that person. The person is then asked to fall backwards into the waiting arms of the group below. Is that person able to trust that the group will be there to catch her or him?

Trust is difficult. We have to learn that it is not always appropriate to trust in banks or mortgages. Likewise many people are not trustworthy. But the good news of the gospel is that we can always trust in God.

Ethical Implications

A challenge of preaching on this set of lectionary texts is the apparent disconnect between Amos' harsh words of famine and ruin, and Luke's story of the faithful Mary and overworked Martha. Many preachers will be drawn to preach a sermon about sitting at the feet of Jesus and choosing the "better part" (Luke 10:42), such as reading scripture, praying, and gathering in worship. But can we put these two images together?

I would argue that both are about trust. Amos and the psalmist bring words of judgment on people who "didn't make God their refuge. Instead they trusted in their own great wealth. They sought refuge in it—to their own destruction" (Ps 52:7). Likewise, Martha took refuge in her many tasks—she trusted in herself and her ability to get things done. Who was going to prepare the meal if she didn't do it?

These are texts that make us uncomfortable, which is the point. We are more willing to take our refuge in our bank accounts and retirement saving plans than we are to take refuge in God's graciousness. And we are surrounded by people who are willing to lie in order to feather their own nests. Even as I write this, the news is coming out that the companies who built the off-shore drilling rig that exploded in the Gulf of Mexico knew that the cement they used would not stand up to the pressure and would eventually fail. This went way beyond simple mischief. They did, indeed, plot destruction (Ps 52:2).

To sit at the feet of Jesus means to come in an attitude of humility and penitence. We must confess those times when we have trampled on the needy and brought ruin to the poor (Amos 8:4). We must take an honest look at the way we live our lives.

Gospel Implications

The question of trust, or perhaps our lack of trust in God, is a recurring theme throughout the scriptures. When the people of God find themselves in difficult positions our first thoughts are, "Where are you God? Why is this happening to us? Aren't you going to help us?" These were the cries of the children in the wilderness. In fact, they were so insecure they longed for a return to slavery in Egypt. I think that we can take comfort in Jesus' cry from the cross, "My God, my God, why have you left me?" (Mark 15:34). Even Jesus wondered if God was there.

Therefore, an important message of this and every sermon is to remind us that we have a God who has been, is, and always will be trustworthy. We have a God who will always be there for us, and in whom we can place our lives. A second theme throughout the scriptures is God's continuing care and love. God was there for the children in the wilderness. God was there with Jesus on the cross. God is here with us in our good times and our bad times. And God will be with us not only throughout our lives, but also through our deaths. To Martha, Jesus declared, "I am the resurrection and the life. Whoever believes in me will live, even though they die. Everyone who lives and believes in me will never die. Do you believe this? " (John 11:25-26).

Lucy Lind Hogan

Beverly E. Mitchell

Proper 12 [17]

The Lessons in Précis

Hosea 1:2-10. Hosea develops the analogy between his marriage to a prostitute and Israel's marriage to God. Israel has been unfaithful, and God declares that Israel's children are not God's children. God will not save them in the onslaught that is to come.

Psalm 85. God is angry, and the people ask to return to God's favor. They remind God of all the good things God has done in the past and pray that those times will come again.

Colossians 2:6-15. Through his death, Christ cleansed us from our sins. Paul reminds us that through our baptism we have been raised with Christ. But he is concerned that the Colossians are being lured away by human philosophy and traditions, and he urges them to remain faithful to the one true God.

Luke 11:1-13. Jesus teaches the disciples to pray to God, who forgives us our sins and gives us all we need. He then encourages them to keep praying, for God will always listen and give us the good gift of the Holy Spirit.

Theme Sentence

We are to be faithful to God alone. The scriptures are filled with stories of people being lured away by other gods. God has created us, loves us, and desires that we remain a faithful and loving people. God reminds us that if we stray, there can be disastrous consequences. The good news is that God will always be more faithful than we are.

A Key Theological Question

These texts affirm that God, the source of every blessing, requires *our* faithfulness in return.

God, who freely chose to enter into covenant with the children of Israel, and who extended that covenant to the world through Jesus Christ, seeks our faithful allegiance. Yet, like the Israelites in Hosea, we are incapable of perfect fidelity to God. The first commandment emphatically states that we are to have no other gods before God. Yet, as the sixteenth century reformer John Calvin observed, our minds are "factories of idol-making" (*Institutes* I.XI.8). Thus, we are constantly vulnerable to the temptation of inordinate desire of things that cannot satisfy the deepest, innermost desire of our heart: to know and love the one true God. Of course, our idols are not fashioned as brazenly as the golden calf, which the Hebrews made and worshiped during the absence of Moses, who had gone to Mount Sinai to receive the Ten Commandments from God (Exod 32:4). But although our symbolic gods of wealth, power, prestige, and social acceptance may be less concrete, they are, perhaps, even more insidious. Our faithlessness hounds us despite the fact that the everlasting mercies of God are "renewed every morning" (Lam 3:23). Despite God's goodness to us, we resonate with the sentiments of Robert Robinson, writer of the hymn, "Come, Thou Fount of Every Blessing." The following line captures so well our devastating existential reality:

> *Prone to wander, Lord, I feel it,*
> *Prone to leave the God I love.*

This propensity to stray, to bend away from rather than toward God, is the lingering legacy of original sin. Because we do not have the natural inclination for perfect faithfulness, we must constantly seek and rely upon the grace of God for strength to resist the myriad of temptations that divide our loyalties and rob us of the affection that rightly belongs solely to God.

Our lack of faithfulness leaves us vulnerable to enslavement to the things to which we give our hearts. If our god is wealth, we can become like the rich man, often given the name Dives, in Luke 16:19-31. This man amassed a fortune but was indifferent to the suffering and misery of the impoverished and diseased Lazarus, who begged for a pittance outside the gates of the rich man's mansion. If we crave power, it distorts our personality and leaves us vulnerable to the temptation to dominate those we perceive as weak. If we pursue prestige or social acceptance at any price, we may sell our souls to the highest bidder.

Our ultimate allegiance must be to God alone. The way of Jesus Christ our Savior reveals the nature of the faithfulness we are called to emulate. What is it to be faithful to God? It is to love God with our soul, heart, mind, and body, such that we love what God loves. In concrete terms, then, how do we begin this practice of faithfulness? Being faithful to God requires a commitment to heed the Apostle Paul's exhortation to pray without ceasing (1 Thess 5:17). It demands diligence in tempering our insatiable desire to acquire things and to love the things in creation more than we love God our creator. It involves the commitment to cultivate an appetite for the stillness of mind and body to wait quietly in the presence of God. It includes consistent study and meditation on the word of God. It demands that we monitor the attention we give to genuine worship of God. Finally, faithfulness to God requires the adoption of a spirit of mindfulness about how we spend our resources, time, and energy. It seems very difficult to practice this kind of faithfulness. In fact, it is *impossible* to be completely consistent in such practice on our own. However, the Colossians text reminds us that through the saving work of Jesus Christ we are released from the *power* of sin. In turn, through the Holy Spirit's work of sanctification, we can begin to exhibit the fruit of the Spirit: love, joy, peace, patience, kindness, goodness, *faithfulness*, gentleness, and self-control (Gal 5:22-23). Though we may stumble, we are not left to wallow helplessly in our failures. God is ever more faithful than we are. Because of this, we have the assurance of God's steadfast love toward us—even when we fail. This assurance is never an occasion to take divine faithfulness for granted, but is an enormous encouragement to persevere in faith when we do fall.

A Pastoral Need

What are the outward and visible signs of our faithfulness? Do our lives bear fruits that witness to the fact that we are children of the living God?

A number of years ago a popular motion picture explored the theme of faithfulness and what someone was willing to give up in order to follow God's commandments. The 1981 movie *Chariots of Fire* recounts a true story from the 1924 Summer Olympic Games, held in Paris. A member of the British team, Eric Liddell, was a devout Christian. When he discovered that his race, the 100 meters, was to be held on Sunday, he withdrew. To be faithful to God would mean that he could not race on Sunday. It meant more to him to live a life rooted in God, as Paul writes, than to compete and potentially win an Olympic medal. One of his teammates, who had already won a medal, offered his spot in the 400-meter race to Liddell. The race was to be held on Thursday. Liddell ran that race instead, and much to everyone's surprise he won a gold medal. Eric Liddell went on to serve as a missionary in China and was killed in World War II.

Our congregations are filled with people who pray daily. Unfortunately, they do not pray for God's reign. Rather, they pray for success at work, entrance into an outstanding college, material worth, and gold medals, instead of daily bread. Through our preaching can we help people find the right door on which to knock? Can we encourage people to be faithful day by day?

ETHICAL IMPLICATIONS

We are, indeed, "factories of idol-making." For what are we willing to sell our souls? While most of us will probably never be in the running for an Olympic gold medal, we will be frequently confronted with occasions that challenge our allegiance. God has declared that we should have no other gods, yet our lives seem to be filled with many idols—materialism, the accumulation of wealth, and just plain business. I am often reminded that there are two places I can look to reflect on my faithfulness to God: my checkbook and my calendar. How do I spend my money? How do I spend my time?

If we reflect on Mr. Liddell's faithfulness, we are reminded that the fourth commandment declares, "Remember the Sabbath day and treat it as holy. Six days you may work and do all your tasks, but the seventh day is a Sabbath to the LORD your God. Do not do any work on it" (Exod 20:8-10). How many of us set aside a day to God? How many of us keep the Sabbath? I would add that this is a particular problem for clergy. We all have seven-day work weeks.

When I was a child, it was much easier to keep the Sabbath. No stores were open. In fact, department stores even put drapes over their windows so that people would not be tempted even to window shop. Today, many stores are open not only seven days a week but also twenty-four hours each day. And these are just the brick and mortar stores. If a store is actually closed at some point, we can go online to shop any time of day or night. Shopping has become a god for many.

Our lives are filled with things that can draw us away from God. It might be shopping, work, or sports. Many parents are weekly faced with the choice of taking their family to church or allowing their children to take the field with one of the many soccer, baseball, and football teams that now practice and play on Sunday mornings. Facing these kinds of choices, how can we remain faithful to the one true God?

GOSPEL IMPLICATIONS

The disciples watched Jesus as he went away, taking time from his busy ministry to pray and reconnect with God. Only when Jesus was finished did they approach him and ask him to teach them to pray. He taught them not only the words that we rightfully call the Lord's Prayer, but he also taught them through his actions. Jesus took time to pray. He knew that his ministry, his teaching, his preaching, and his healing ability all depended upon being in a right relationship with God. That meant that he needed to pray, to listen to God.

Faithfulness is about having our priorities straight. It is about knowing that God comes first, before all else. Only through the grace of God do we have the power to put God first. And when we ask, when we seek God and knock on God's door, God will answer. "If you who are evil [ouch] know how to give good gifts to your children, how much more will the heavenly Father give the Holy Spirit to those who ask him?" (Luke 11:13).

LUCY LIND HOGAN

BEVERLY E. MITCHELL

PROPER 13 [18]

THE LESSONS IN PRÉCIS

Hosea 11:1-11. God recalls the punishment visited on peoples in the past (the destruction of Admah and Zeboiim) and realizes that, in spite of Israel's disobedience, God cannot destroy again. Using wonderful images, God reminds us that God is our loving, long-suffering, faithful parent.

Psalm 107:1-9, 43. Salvation history is the recurring story of God's people wandering away and God's rescuing and reviving. We have every reason to give thanks to God.

Colossians 3:1-11. Paul places before us contrasting images— old and new, earthly and heavenly—to help us understand what it means to be raised with Christ. We are challenged to put aside the way we were and live into our new being. Can we strip off our anger and greed?

Luke 12:13-21. Greed continues to be the theme as Jesus rejects the request of a man to help him gain his inheritance. Jesus recounts the story of a man whose crops far exceeded his expectations. But the man had no time to party, because death came and bigger barns would do the man no good in heaven.

THEME SENTENCE
We are to remember that good things come from God and not from ourselves. We are self-centered, selfish individuals who think only of ourselves. To live in Christ is to live a life of thanksgiving, gratitude, and caring for others.

A Key Theological Question

These texts offer a contrast in the quality of life between those who go their own way and those who live mindful of the goodness of God.

One of the saddest things in life is the inability to appreciate the goodness of God. Those who are wise are able to discern the ways God has been faithful. Recognizing the goodness of God requires the habit of recalling the ways in which God has blessed and continues to bless. In African-American prayer services it is not uncommon for someone to offer a prayer or testimony that expresses thanksgiving because he or she awoke that morning with the "activity of my limbs" and was "clothed in my right mind." In such colorful expressions, the worshipper of God takes nothing for granted, for it could just as easily have been otherwise. The habit of gratitude for not only the special, extraordinary, or inspiring events in our lives but also for the simple, ordinary, or mundane rhythms of life arises out of our keen awareness of the need for dependence upon God. This awareness, in turn, grows out of personal and communal experiences of difficult times when God "made a way out of no way." Perhaps it might be easier for those from historically oppressed communities to live with a certain awareness of God as provider, but living with such an awareness is available to all of us.

Those of us who enjoy economic, educational, and other forms of privilege are often lulled into complacency about the extraordinariness of the ordinariness of daily existence. If we enjoy a measure of relief from the struggle to put food on the table because we earn enough to meet not only our basic needs but also many of our wants, we can easily forget that the good things we have ultimately come from the hand of God. We can fall prey to the "pride of life," where we not only take for granted our ability to provide for our basic needs, but we also succumb to the illusion that *our* industriousness, intellectual ability, and superior talents are the ultimate source of our success (1 John 2:16).

The more affluent among us are also tempted by the inordinate desire to acquire more than what we have or need. We may become enamored with the latest tools of technology, thirst for the latest fashions, or hunger for prestige and power. Because we are enticed to serve the god of acquisition, we may eventually find that we have confused the abundant life, which Christ came to offer (John 10:10), with the accumulation of an abundance of *things*, which can never truly satisfy us.

When we are not anchored in God, we are left to drift in ways that can lead to our own destruction. Despite our lack of steadfastness, God remains constant. God woos and pursues us despite our repeated forays on paths of our own making. One of the most critical ways we dethrone God is by focusing on ourselves. When we ourselves become the measure of all things, we can neither see the abundance we already have nor give thought to the needs of others.

The saving work of Christ breaks the bond of sin—that which distorts our natural desire for God. Through Christ we can be freed from bondage to whatever enslaves us. Alive in Christ, we are empowered to resist and then to yield to what truly satisfies. This empowerment leaves us more room to be mindful of the goodness of God. Mindfulness evokes thanksgiving and gratitude. It is also an avenue to the generosity that enables us to perceive the needs of those around us, and guides us to respond in freedom to the command to love our neighbors. The deepest consolation we have is that, even as we fail in love and faithfulness, we need not give way to despair. Thanks be to God that divine faithfulness is not predicated on our own!

A PASTORAL NEED

I suspect God gets very frustrated with our inability to be thankful for all that God does for us. I remember a story from Sunday school in which a person was being shown around God's workshop. In one large room angels were bustling about, receiving basket after basket and stacking them everywhere. "This," the tour guide explained, "is where prayer requests are received." They then continued down the long hallway, finally coming to a small, quiet room. In the room sat one angel with a small in-box on the desk. "And this room is where we receive prayers of thanksgiving." We are much more eager to ask God for help than we are to say thank you.

Hosea reminds us how quickly the Israelites forgot what God had done for them. The successful farmer in Luke's Gospel thought he himself was responsible for his good fortune. Thanksgiving and gratitude depend upon being aware of all that God has done for us.

In Montreal there is a beautiful church, St. Joseph's Oratory. It sits on a large hill, and to reach the church one must climb a block-long staircase, which many of the faithful do on their knees. But what captures one's attention is the very large crypt chapel. The walls are covered from floor to ceiling with the crutches and canes of people who have come to give thanks for their healing.

Ethical Implications

When I baptized my granddaughter she wore the same baptismal gown that her father had worn and that I also had worn many years before. Made by my godmother, that gown is very special. But more important than family memories, the white garment of baptism is, as Paul reminds us, a sign of the new self we receive when we have been "raised with Christ" (Col 3:1).

Do we know what it means to be a new being? Turn on almost any cable channel, and you will be able to watch a program about people trying to become new beings: to lose weight, undergo plastic surgery, or find a new way of dressing. We are invited to follow these people as they take on a new self. But they do not come close to the new selves Paul describes. They are making external changes. Paul reminds us that when we have been raised with Christ, we become new beings inside.

We live in a self-centered, egotistical, ungrateful world. As new beings we are to live drastically different lives, giving up the ways of the world—evil desire and greed, anger and wrath. The ways of the world also include taking our very lives for granted. To be raised with Christ is to know that in both this world and the next, we owe our existence to the God who created and sustains us.

Following the traumatic, devastating earthquake in Haiti in 2010, many of the people who went to help the residents were stunned by what they saw. These people had lost everything. Their city lay in rubble. Many of them had lost their families. And many had lost limbs to the crush of rock. Yet volunteers did not see people who were depressed and angry. Rather, over and over again they heard joyful singing. The people were singing praises to God in thanks for being saved. They were grateful God had spared them and they were still alive. The volunteers could not understand. Having lost everything, how could they sing? The people could sing because they knew what is important—not big houses or the abundance of things. They knew they were rich in God's love and grace. They gave "thanks to the LORD because he is good, because his faithful love lasts forever" (Ps 107:1).

GOSPEL IMPLICATIONS

Over and over again I am grateful that God is not a parent like me. I know that when my children forgot to say thank you, when they were ungrateful and rude, I lost my temper. I was angry and frustrated and was likely to remember this slight for some time to come. Years later I still remember the time that my young son (who is now a father himself) looked up from the pile of birthday presents that sat before him and asked, "Is that all there is?" Needless to say, his father and I were not pleased.

But Hosea paints a very different portrait. It is the portrait of a parent who cannot imagine being angry at the child he taught to walk. The message of the prophets and of Jesus is that we follow a God who will never give up on us. Ours is a God whose "heart winces within" and whose "compassion grows warm and tender" (Hos 11:8), even though those children turn away.

Lucy Lind Hogan

Beverly E. Mitchell

Proper 14 [19]

The Lessons in Précis

Isaiah 1:1, 10-20. The opening message of the prophet Isaiah is quite clear: God is most angry. While holding out the possibility of forgiveness, God sees a people whose violent and unjust actions give the lie to their empty worship.

Psalm 50:1-8. God, the mighty one, is our judge, and no other. And it is God who testifies against us.

Hebrews 11:1-3, 8-16. What does it mean to live by faith? After presenting us with a definition of faith—things hoped for but not seen—the author presents us with portraits of those who lived faithful lives: Abraham, Sarah, Isaac, and Jacob. They stepped out in faith but did not see the promise fulfilled.

Luke 12:32-40. We are given two dimensions of living as faithful disciples. First, we are encouraged to focus on heavenly rather than earthly treasures. Second, we are always to be ready for our redeemer to return, "dressed for action, . . .lamps lit" (vs. 35, nrsv).

Theme Sentence

God looks into our hearts and recognizes true faithfulness. God is neither fooled nor placated by empty worship. We cannot go through the motions, for we have a God who loves us but also sees if our lives, our actions, the very depth of our hearts are focused on the God we follow. We are asked, "Where is your treasure?"

A KEY THEOLOGICAL QUESTION

These texts contrast the folly of self-centeredness with the wisdom of faithfulness to God.

The word *faith* forms the root of both of the words *faithfulness* and *faithlessness*. A crucial aspect of the biblical understanding of faith is trust. Faith involves a wholehearted trust in the One whom we love and worship. In our biblical texts, faithfulness to God is linked to concrete expressions of obedience to the commandment to love our neighbors as ourselves (Mark 12:31). For God, signs of genuine faithfulness are concern for the poor and needy and a commitment to justice.

The prophetic critique of the Israelites in Isa 1:10-20 is similar in tone and content to that of Isa 58:1-5. In both texts, the people of God were engaged in showy acts of worship involving elaborate burnt offerings of bulls, lambs, and goats. They observed days of fasting that called attention to their acts of piety. To the untrained eye, such acts would have suggested that they were completely devoted to the divine, but God knew otherwise. The prophet Isaiah charged God's people with lacking the spirit of humility that would enable them to discern true worship. They engaged in empty rituals with fanfare, ostentation, and pride but failed to actually do what the Lord requires: "to do justice, embrace faithful love, and walk humbly with your God" (Mic 6:8).

In our day we do not offer burnt offerings, but we may compose elaborate liturgies with printed prayers, give polished musical performances in worship, or conduct highly choreographed services that outwardly suggest a desire to please God. Yet at the same time we chase the homeless away from the doorways of our churches in time for worship services on Sunday mornings. Some of us may contribute a modest amount of our earnings to the benevolence fund or even serve a meal to the hungry every now and then. In such cases, we may give out of our surplus (and benefit from a tax write-off) or make a modest sacrifice of our time but then consistently support government policies which maintain socio-economic structures that keep the poor from rising from the pit of intergenerational poverty.

Elaborate expressions of worship that fail to reflect a commitment to advocate for the least among us are offensive to God. Our merciful, gracious God, who judges our hearts and knows our true motives and intentions, desires the kind of worship that reflects transformed lives. If the process of maturing in the faith through the work of the Holy Spirit is designed to conform our way of thinking, acting, and being to that of Jesus Christ (Rom 8:29), then our manner of relating to others should become increasingly consistent with the way of Jesus of Nazareth. This involves a complete surrender of the "right" to determine how we live our lives and what we do with our talents, resources, and time. Those who would follow Jesus Christ must realize that our lives belong to God. If we truly believe the greatness of God's faithfulness, we will surrender the impulse to govern our lives according to what makes us most comfortable.

Selfishness and faithfulness cannot coexist. With selfishness, undue concern for our own well-being becomes the operating principle of our lives. In genuine faithfulness, our loyalties remain undivided. Our attachment to God must be greater than our attachment to anything or anyone else. When we are not focused on acquiring things for ourselves or pursuing "the good life," then we are free to consider the needs of others. We no longer see giving assistance to others as engendering loss for ourselves. Because faithfulness frees us, we, like Abraham and Sarah, do not fear moving forward in God's call on our lives. We trust that we will be fine if God leads us.

What does it mean to live by faith? It means to continue on the path to which God calls us, whether or not we can see good accrue to us. Living by faith means that we remain steadfast in obedience, whether or not it is obvious that such obedience will lead to what we desire. Living a faith-filled life means doing what God calls us to do without undue worry about our future. Living by that caliber of faith is possible only when we have complete trust in the fundamental goodness of the one true God. Faith in any other "treasure" will be our downfall.

A Pastoral Need

As many of our congregations struggle with a drop in attendance, worship is one of the first places identified as the cause or source of the problem. The suggestions for ways to fix the problem are many. Animal sacrifice and burnt offerings are not the usual suggestions. Rather, consultants and pastors of mega-churches encourage adding a praise band, getting rid of the organ, and installing projectors and screens so that people no longer need hymnals—all in the name of making the worship service more entertaining and attractive. The end goal is to draw in more people by making the community's worship accessible, welcoming, and less intimidating for those unfamiliar with more traditional forms of worship. Isaiah prophesied God's displeasure with the people's empty worship. Is this how we engage in empty worship? How might we be better "dressed for service and keep [our] lamps lit" (Luke 12:35)?

In *Teaching a Stone to Talk,* author Annie Dillard (1982) reflects on people and worship. She suggests that we are clueless when it comes to understanding the immensity and depth of what we are doing when we come before the presence of the living God. We are, she suggests, like children mixing up TNT with our home chemistry set. Worship is not about entertainment or gathering for coffee and doughnuts. Worship is about meeting the creator of the world. We should, she declares, be wearing crash helmets, and "ushers should issue life preservers and signal flares; they should lash us to our pews" (p. 40).

Aren't discipleship and worship about taking a risk? Aren't they more about listening to the teachings of God than to marketing consultants? How can we be servants who are waiting for our master to return at any moment? How can we "put an end to such evil" and "learn to do good" (Isa 1:16-17)? How can we help the widow and the orphan? These are the questions we the church should be asking ourselves.

Ethical Implications

What are the possible reasons for today's empty worship? Could it be that our attendance numbers are lower not because of our worship styles or the music we do or don't sing but because we have found our treasure in the wrong places? Are we chasing after church growth rather than justice and mercy? Are we servants who have grown complacent, thinking more about worldly success than the second coming?

One of the earliest crises in the life of the church was the fact that Jesus had not returned. Jesus had challenged his disciples to be like servants awaiting the imminent return of their absent master. They were to keep their lamps lit. They were to be ready at any moment. Therefore, the first generations of Christians did just that. They sold all of their possessions; they weren't going to need them anymore. Many stopped working and devoted themselves to prayer while they waited for Jesus to return in the clouds and judge the world. They waited, and they waited, and they waited. But he did not return. They then began to worry. Some of their sisters and brothers in Christ had died. What happened to them? Were they saved? We see that Paul had to write words of comfort in his early letters. He wanted to remind them that Christ would eventually return and that those who had died were indeed in the arms of God. But with each passing year it became more and more difficult to maintain that sense of anticipation. The people turned their attention from the master who was to return from the wedding banquet, and focused again on the cares and concerns of this world.

Our "master" has been away for a long time. But Jesus told us, "You also must be ready, because the Human One is coming at a time when you don't expect him" (Luke 12:40). How are we to be watchful servants? What is the opposite of empty worship? Is it full worship? How do we worship God in the beauty of holiness? As we wait we must be dressed for action and carry our lamps. And these texts would suggest that we accomplish these things by going out into the world and caring for the least and the lost.

A church located in the heart of Washington, D.C. has come to understand that an important part of their worship is not only to help the homeless in their neighborhood but also to invite them in to be a part of their community. They worship together, eat together, and listen to the word of God through Bible study together. That is "full" worship.

Gospel Implications

We live in a permissive age when parents are reluctant to scold or place boundaries on their children for fear that their children will not love them. But the scriptures present us with the portrait of a God who places boundaries and judges us, not out of anger but out of love.

The good news of these more difficult passages is that God loves us. God cares for us. God is concerned when we wander away and become more interested in ourselves than in God or our sisters and brothers.

We also hear in these texts that God has not abandoned us. God is ready to welcome us and forgive us. God's love for us and our love for God are treasures that cannot be stolen from us and cannot be destroyed.

Notes

Annie Dillard, *Teaching a Stone to Talk Expeditions and Encounters*, 1982.

_____

Lucy Lind Hogan

Beverly E. Mitchell

PROPER 15 [20]

THE LESSONS IN PRÉCIS

God is committed to having a people of justice and righteousness. To this end, God sends Jesus to set us on fire.

> *Isaiah 5:1-5.* The prophet sings of the Lord as a dedicated vintner whose vineyard, Israel, has failed to produce justice and righteousness and will now receive judgment: its destruction.

> *Psalm 80.* The psalmist laments at God's turning away and asks God to restore and care once more for the vine that was so carefully planted and tended but has now been burned and cut down.

> *Hebrews 11:29–12:2.* The preacher encourages listeners to persevere in the race, keeping their eyes fixed on Christ, faith's pioneer and perfecter, enduring whatever suffering comes for the joy that awaits us.

> *Luke 12:49-56.* Jesus comes as a cleansing and purifying fire, winnowing wheat from chaff, and even creating division within families whenever blood ties block commitment to him and his mission.

THEME SENTENCE

God calls us to harvest justice. Just as God called Israel to be fruitful by acting justly, Jesus fulfills his Father's agenda and demands his followers commit to this same work. While this may cause division in families, the fire Jesus brings purifies all hearts and minds committed to him.

A Key Theological Question

God cultivates a people for justice. How does God do this? Today's readings touch on justice in God's relationship with us, our relationship with God, and our relationships with one another and with God's creation.

Our philosophical and theological traditions have offered several understandings of justice. Sometimes it is based on merit, on the contribution that a person has made to a community or society. Another notion suggests that justice consists in the equal distribution of goods. We also speak of justice in terms of retribution, punishing persons in proportion to their offense. Each of these captures an aspect of justice, but none is sufficiently broad to include them all. Further, each suggests that one can fulfill completely the demands of justice on the basis of the criteria stated: merit, equality, or punishment.

A scriptural notion of justice is clear and simply stated, yet much more demanding. Justice means being in right relationship with God, with one another, with ourselves, and with the created world. We find a theological foundation for this notion of justice in the harmony and mutuality among the persons of the Trinity. As people created in the image and the likeness of God, we live justly to fulfill this more fundamental call to live in a communion of love with God and others.

Practically speaking, living justly might be framed in terms of keeping the commandments and thereby guarding against serious offenses against God and neighbor. This approach to justice is laudable and necessary for harmony in society. However, it fails to capture fully the virtue of justice.

Virtue implies not simply performing a particular action, but doing so with a virtuous heart. Some authors distinguish between justice and righteousness precisely on this account, suggesting that a just action meets the criteria of justice, while righteousness describes moral character, having an upright heart. There is no unanimous agreement on the validity of this distinction between justice and righteousness, but the substance of the argument captures a truth. A truly just act flows from a righteous heart. For example, one might help out at a soup kitchen out of genuine compassion for the poor and the needy, or one might do so to impress a newfound friend. The actions appear to be the same, but the former is truly an act of justice. Just actions flow from just persons. So, as helpful as the commandments are to direct us toward just lives, they are insufficient in and of themselves. Cultivated for justice, we are called to do more in our relationships with God, others, and ourselves.

Isaiah's text speaks of the tender care with which God nurtures his people, his vineyard. Each vine is precious and requires special attention. Yet the Divine Vintner does not force his vines to produce good grapes. God does not coerce humanity but invites us to a similar, tender love for God as well as care and mercy toward one another. This is the justice for which we have been created. Yet too often, as Israel did in its day, we do not care but curse; we yield not justice and righteousness but bloodshed and wailing.

The psalmist views Israel not as perpetrators of injustice, as Isaiah does, but as victims calling out to God to save them. In their shaky faith, they call and count on their refuge, their rock, their stronghold, their just God whom they have come to know to be still in right relationship with them, even if they turn their backs to God time and again.

The preacher of Hebrews responds to a question about the fruits of living justly in our own lifetime. It is common to suggest that people who love God, pray, and entrust their lives to God experience blessing. How often do we hear, "God was with me," or, "God spared me." Yet while some name God as the font of their blessing, others curse God as the source of their suffering. Does God always bless the faithful and curse the sinner? Hardly. Hebrews suggests that living justly will bring a reward, but in God's time, not ours. Just as our forefathers and fore-mothers experienced blessing as well as torment and suffering, so we do today. Living justly—living in right relationship with God and with one another—does not guarantee a suffering-free life for us. It does, however, promise a place before the throne of God.

The basis of that promise is Jesus, "faith's pioneer and perfecter" (Heb 12:2). Jesus is the Justice of God in our world. His life and minis-try show us concretely what it is to live in right relationship with God, with one another, and with oneself. Future readings will make this point more specifically. As Luke's Gospel suggests, however, just persons and their message are not always well received, and they give rise to tensions in the very relationships that ought to characterize us as people created by God for justice.

In terms of our relationship with God, some people speak and act as if questions of justice are distinct from a love for God. Politics doesn't belong in the pulpit, they say. But although political endorsements do not belong there, surely God's concern for his vineyard must be addressed when we see bloodshed and hear the cries of today's victims.

Receiving the gospel message and its implications for justice also strain relationships within civic communities, families, and even religious communities. Consider how discussions about the just treatment of immigrants continue to divide people in our own day.

Finally, receiving the call to justice frequently causes division within our own hearts as we struggle to let go of habits of comfort and ways of seeing the world, to follow Jesus more faithfully, and to live in the same faith and trust of our forefathers and foremothers.

A Pastoral Need

The opening of the television series *Raising Hope* begins with a young man quitting his job as a swimming pool cleaner and going home. As he is nearing the front door, his mother is leaving for work. "What are you doing home?" she asks. "There's got to be more to life than cleaning the same pool over and over," he answers. "There isn't," she says, sailing past.

The desire for something more in life is rooted deep within us. Years ago Studs Terkel went around the country talking to people about their jobs and compiled his findings in a book titled *Working*. His main conclusion was that most people's jobs were not big enough for them. We have more to give, to share, and to invest. So much in us remains untapped.

We have been created in the image of God, whose work was—and is—the work of creation, redemption, and sanctification. This work now involves our helping to bring about the kingdom of God, a rule of justice and righteousness. We have been invited to take part in it. From the beginning, God enlisted his creatures in caring for creation. Right after his baptism, Jesus went out preaching and teaching that the kingdom was at hand, and he called others to join him in this work. When the Holy Spirit descended on those gathered in the upper room, they were propelled out into the world to spread the gospel and call others to participate in the life of the kingdom. Worthy work, indeed, that fulfills a life!

ETHICAL IMPLICATIONS

The work of conversion involves living just lives and working to bring about God's justice in the world. This justice calls for engagement on the four levels noted: living in right relationship with God, with oneself, with each other, and with the earth. Such just living will bring new life to our world. Jesus came to fire us up to live such fruitful and worthwhile lives. When Jesus speaks of bringing fire on the earth, we can understand this fire working in different ways: it judges our actions, purifies our hearts, and signals the presence of God's passionate love for us.

This fire that can both cleanse and consume reminds us that, while God has given us the freedom to choose, we remain accountable for our choices. When God chose Israel as God's people, God's beloved bride, and God's very possession, Israel was asked to make a reciprocal choice, thereby entering into a covenant with God. But the promise had been barely uttered before Israel began to turn away, setting up a golden calf to worship in God's place. The fire of God's judgment blazed up in the desert, as it would throughout Israel's history. Jesus came to offer a new covenant, in his own blood. And we have been baptized into that covenant. Each day is an opportunity to renew our covenant by working for a more just world.

Now is the time of God's judgment on how we are bearing fruit. Jesus' words have no consoling conclusion—he will be the basis for division between those who accept him and those who do not. God in Christ calls us to choose. We do this when we live lives of justice and righteousness.

GOSPEL IMPLICATIONS

God can restore the vine, as God has in the past restored both Israel and the church. God brought Israel out of the desert, then again out of exile. The risen Lord brought peace to those who had deserted and denied him, and continues to bring a fire that purifies and perfects our faith. This cleansing fire reveals the working of the Holy Spirit, bringing about the transformation of the world.

Our world continues to thirst for justice. There is no place on earth where God's plan for justice has come to completion. Look at the twentieth century alone, with its record of world wars and genocide on almost all continents. But God does not give up on us. Again and again we are invited to read the signs of the times, revealing that God is near to each generation. We cling to Jesus as our hope, trying to walk in his way. He is with us, protecting the vine God's right hand has planted. We are the branches of the vine, capable of producing worthy fruit.

Notes

Studs Terkel, *Working: People Talk about What They Do All Day and How They Feel About It*, 1972.

JAMES A. WALLACE

KEVIN J. O'NEIL

PROPER 16 [21]

THE LESSONS IN PRÉCIS
The human capacity to make a mess of things is always at hand, but, thank God, we have God. God raises up prophets and sends them into lives that need to be straightened out and put back in order.

> *Jeremiah 1:4-10.* Despite Jeremiah's resistance, God commissions him to be a prophet to the nations. This task involves both pulling down and building up. "I'm with you," promises the Lord (vs. 8).

> *Psalm 71:1-6.* The psalmist prays for refuge and protection, praising God who has been with him from his mother's womb.

> *Hebrews 12:18-29.* The author reminds listeners that they have access to Mount Zion, the presence of the living God, the heavenly Jerusalem, and to Jesus, mediator of the new covenant.

> *Luke 13:10-17.* On a Sabbath, Jesus liberates a woman from eighteen years of being bent over under Satan's bondage. When others protest, Jesus calls them to recognize that God was working to set free a daughter of Abraham.

THEME SENTENCE
God comes to straighten up. God rescues from the grasp of the unjust and cruel. Jeremiah is not to be weighed down under fear, for God is with him. Jesus brings a daughter of Abraham to her full stature. At his touch, she straightens up to praise God and move freely into a new day.

A KEY THEOLOGICAL QUESTION
A God Who Straightens Up

Not known for having a spotless desk and office, I have heard with some frequency, "Why don't you just straighten things up a bit?" I have always taken some consolation in the remark, "If a cluttered desk is the sign of a cluttered mind, what's an empty desk the sign of?" Nonetheless, a straightened desk and office do help to keep things in order. By setting the theme that God comes to straighten up, we suggest that God hopes to put some things in order.

The woman in today's Gospel reading needs to be straightened up. Interestingly, Jesus speaks of her being in Satan's bondage for eighteen years. The precise cause of her affliction is not known. Is she at fault in some way, or has she been overtaken by a power greater than she is? Either way, she needs healing. Her condition calls to mind one of the words from the Old Testament associated with sin: *awon* (Gen 4:13; Job 13:23, 26; Dan 9:13). The word itself means "to be twisted or bent over because of sin." Forgiveness and healing straighten one up. We see this dynamic clearly in Luke's Gospel.

Although God is capable of approaching us directly, God chooses to do so through people like ourselves, through ones like Jeremiah, Jesus, and all those who reveal to us the authentic, life-giving presence of God. The similarities between the prophet Jeremiah and the prophet Jesus are most striking in today's readings. Jeremiah is known and called by God before he even takes flesh. Being known by God not only denotes the choosing of Jeremiah to be God's prophet but also promises God's protection and support. This type of knowing calls to mind the beautiful Psalm 139, depicting a God who knows us through and through and who is so near to us that we cannot escape God's gaze or care. The simple yet profound text of John 3:16, "God so loved the world that he gave his only Son," speaks of God's action in Christ, drawing near to us to save us, straighten us up, and bring us eternal life. Furthermore, Jeremiah and Jesus are God's prophets who were sent ultimately to all peoples. While their immediate destiny was the children of Abraham, they ultimately bring the word and presence of God to all peoples (Jer 1:10; Luke 2:31). Through them, God straightens out any misconceptions.

God is not selective in choosing only certain people to receive God's gift of life and healing. Rather God draws near to all, awaiting their response in faith. Jeremiah and Jesus are prophets who denounce and straighten out religious leaders of their day regarding who God is and who they ought to be. In today's passage from Luke's Gospel, Jesus rebukes the Pharisees for suggesting that fidelity to the Sabbath could include ignoring the need a daughter of Abraham has for God's healing touch. The Pharisees are not coldhearted, since they suggest that the healing might occur on another day. But Jesus' words shake them out of their legalistic blindness and call them to common sense. If we would rush to rescue our animals that are in need, even if it is the Sabbath, so much more ought we rush to rescue, restore, and heal a daughter of Abraham.

In this Gospel passage, as elsewhere (see, for example, Luke 6:6-11 and 14:1-6), Jesus reveals a God who straightens us up. Two chapters later, we read the stories of the lost sheep and the lost coin. As in today's scripture passage where Jesus approaches the ailing woman, these parables depict a God who draws near to those who are lost, in order to heal them so they might stand up straight in righteousness.

The preacher of today's readings must grapple with his or her own image of God. Conflicting spiritualities in the Christian tradition have depicted a God who is distant and waits for us, saints and sinners alike, to approach God. Several years ago while attending a meeting, I overheard a conversation between two participants who were chatting before the session. One said that she had just finished a thirty-day silent retreat. The other responded, "I don't know if I'd want to spend thirty days with my God." Who is the God we believe in and preach?

Preachers will also want to be cautious when dealing with the text from Hebrews, because it could easily be interpreted as a dismissal of the Old Covenant. While the contrast between the God of Sinai, a distant God, and the God of Mount Zion, revealed in the person of Jesus, is quite strong, we need to be careful not to suggest that it was a different God at work in the past. The same God who worked through Jeremiah works and is revealed in Jesus, and works through us. Similarly, we must be responsible in our portrayal of the law. While a Gospel passage like today's lends itself to rants against legalism, it is important to remember Jesus' putting the law in context, reminding that the law attempts to articulate the demands of a relationship with God and others. The purpose of the law is to promote justice in our relationships. When the fulfillment of the law, as in today's Gospel passage, would harm rather than heal, burdening people and causing them to stoop rather than to stand upright, the law must be challenged because it is not true to the God of life, the very one who gave the law.

A PASTORAL NEED

"Don't get all bent out of shape over it"—words of advice that encourage us to stand up straight, take a deep breath, and calm down. They are usually spoken when something we strongly believe in has been questioned or denied. Our deepest beliefs can take on an authority that seems irrefutable. And we become rigid under the weight of our beliefs. We don't see any other possible way of "reading the situation."

The leader in the synagogue was likely a man who considered it his responsibility to monitor what was happening there, to see to it that nothing occurred that would be contrary in any way to the law of the Lord. When Jesus cured this woman on the Sabbath, he saw this as a violation against Sabbath rest. But he could not bring himself to address Jesus directly, so instead he turned on the woman. And Jesus reacted strongly to everyone there who had remained silent: "[You] hypocrites!" (Luke 13:15).

Sometimes our convictions about how things should be become weights that bear down upon us, and, as with the synagogue leader, our inner vision becomes restricted. Sometimes we become aware of this, but are frightened to change, or even to talk about the need for change. This is when we need the God in today's scriptures.

ETHICAL IMPLICATIONS

We know from experience that laws and regulations established for the common good can also limit people unnecessarily, and sometimes even do harm. Laws can lock us in, rather than protect and secure. New York Times columnist David Brooks has written about "the responsibility deficit" (*The New York Times*, Op Ed, 9.23.2010), pointing to a thicket of rules and regulations that defy common sense and prevent not only the president and his or her cabinet members, but also teachers, doctors, and local officials from acting responsibly for the common good. Presidents find their budgets precommitted to entitlement programs, while teachers are constricted by educational mandates on everything from discipline to methodology. And federal rules limit both cabinet secretaries as well as local town officials from carrying out necessary innovations.

Another area in need of reform is our immigration laws that presently have such a destructive impact on families. There have been instances where parents were suddenly seized and deported back to their native country, thereby separated from their young children who were left behind, at best to be cared for by friends.

Today's Gospel reminds us how even the law of the Sabbath could be used as a basis for preventing healing of a daughter of Abraham. A law meant to call the people to turn from their usual daily work and allow God to be present to them and touch their hearts and minds was used to prevent God from liberating a woman from Satan's bondage.

Jesus came preaching that the kingdom of God is at hand even now in the lives of his people, revealing God's healing power at work in him. This healing power was fulfilling the words of the prophet Isaiah about the blind seeing, the deaf hearing, the mute speaking, and the lame walking (Isa 29:18). In him the law of love was given full expression. We might examine our lives to see what role this law has both in our judgments on how others are to be treated and our own actions, especially in relation to those most in need.

GOSPEL IMPLICATIONS

True religion is honoring God as a God of creation, liberation, redemption, salvation, and sanctification. In Jesus we see Israel's God fully embodied. He came to usher in the kingdom of God, proclaiming, "God's kingdom is already among you" (Luke 17:21). This is clearly seen in today's Gospel when Jesus liberates a woman bound by Satan for eighteen years. We know, too, that Jesus came not only to liberate bodies from sickness but also to liberate minds and spirits held captive by the power of sin and evil. Today, Jesus is successful on the first account, but we don't know how he fared in opening the hearts of his listeners to how God was at work in him and his deeds.

God, who formed us in our mother's womb, continues to come to deliver and save us, to be our rock and our fortress where we can find safe shelter from the storms that threaten to overwhelm us. Let us give thanks for the new world God continues to usher in through the power of the spirit of the risen Christ, a kingdom that will not be shaken, a kingdom of sons and daughters who stand upright in virtue and grace before their God.

JAMES A. WALLACE

KEVIN J. O'NEIL

PROPER 17 [22]

THE LESSONS IN PRÉCIS

God cares for the people by providing them with food and drink. In return, those who gather at the table are to care for each other, showing humility and hospitality.

> *Jeremiah 2:4-13.* After bringing Israel to a new land to eat its fruits, God finds that all have turned away, even the kings, lawyers, priests, and prophets. They have replaced God, the living water, with leaky cisterns.

> *Psalm 81:1, 10-16.* God laments Israel's refusal to listen and walk in his ways. Even so, God offers to feed them with wheat and honey.

> *Hebrews 13:1-8, 15-16.* The Christian community is to be a living sacrifice of praise, revealed in lives of mutual love, hospitality, and care, especially for those usually excluded.

> *Luke 14:1, 7-14.* Jesus sets out the kingdom's table etiquette, emphasizing humility and hospitality. Sure signs the kingdom has come are when hosts invite the least and those typically considered most important take the last seats.

THEME SENTENCE

God sets a table for all. God has been feeding people since Eden. God fed Israel in the desert, and led the people to a land "to eat its fruits" (Jer 2:7, nrsv). Jesus, who fed the multitudes in a deserted place, now calls for a radical hospitality in return, asking both hosts and guests to move from self-absorption to other-centeredness.

A KEY THEOLOGICAL QUESTION
A Humble and Hospitable God

"Work your way from the outside in," we are advised when trying to figure out which utensils to use at a rather elaborate table setting. That is good practical advice for table etiquette. However, it does nothing to direct our attitudes toward those who sit at the table with us and, even more so, to those who are not at the table. Today's scripture passages talk of eating and drinking; of living water and cracked wells; and of "A-list" guests, "B-list" guests, and those not invited. The texts remind us of two virtues that are essential to the table of life, reminding us of who we are before God and before one another: the virtues of humility and hospitality, evidenced in truthfulness and generosity.

Humility has often been misrepresented in the spiritual tradition as self-humiliation or self-demeaning behavior. For example, one might go to a dinner and take a lower seat because one is self-conscious or almost embarrassed about oneself. One shirks off genuine compliments as if they are not deserved. This behavior does not reflect humility. Authentic humility is marked by truth about ourselves before God and one another.

We stand before God as finite creatures, completely dependent upon God, recipients of countless gifts, including life itself. Yet salvation history and today's readings remind us of the numerous times when our ancestors in faith forgot who they were before God. They failed to call out to the very God who had rescued them and constantly nurtured them. Thirsty, they turned from living water to cracked and dry wells. The belief that they, and we, are self-sufficient, or that some "worthless things" (Jer 2:5, NRSV) will ultimately satisfy us, denies who we are before God and what God has done for us (Ps 81). What was true of our ancestors is true of us when we turn from Jesus, the life-giving water (John 4:7-15), and love our own "worthless things." We come to the table of life hungry and thirsty. The only one who will ultimately satisfy these needs is God. Relying on ourselves, we forget who we are and do not listen to God or call out to God (Ps 81).

What does it mean to stand in humility and truthfulness before one another? Contemporary moral philosopher Alasdair MacIntyre (1999) proposes two qualities that mark all human beings: vulnerability and dependence. We might readily recognize the vulnerability and dependence of the young, the elderly, the sick, and the disabled, but we might not recognize our own ongoing vulnerability as finite human beings, living and dependent upon other vulnerable, dependent human beings. Humility before one another requires recognition of these universal qualities of humanity. We fail in humility when we exalt ourselves, that is, when we presume that we are better than others or deserve more from others, forgetting that all is gift from the outset. The humbled and exalted wedding guests are alike in their vulnerability and dependence, in their inability to satisfy every longing and need on their own. The failure of those who take the better seat is that they consider themselves more than they are; they refuse to see themselves truthfully. Those who humble themselves do so with a clear sense of where they stand before God and others.

MacIntyre suggests that the virtues corresponding to these qualities of vulnerability and dependence are truthfulness—what I am here calling humility—and generosity to fellow human beings—here expressed in hospitality—acknowledging that we too are beneficiaries of the generosity and hospitality of God and others.

God's constancy toward Israel, despite its rejection of God, shows us the truth of who God is and God's generosity, which is not dependent on human behavior. Paul reminds us in the letter to the Romans that even if we are unfaithful, God will still remain faithful (Rom 3:1-8). We might say we have a standing invitation to the table of the Lord, an expression of the truth of God and God's hospitality toward us.

Made in God's image, we have been created to live in that same truth and generosity. Hebrews invites us to share what we have (Heb 13:16); this concept is characteristic of the early Christian community (Acts 4:32-37), and breaches were challenged within the community (Acts 5:1-11). The reference in Hebrews to welcoming the stranger might well refer to Abraham and Sarah's welcome of the angels of God (Gen 18:1ff). Might we not think as well of Matthew 25, where the "sheep," unknowingly, had ministered to Christ in the hungry they fed, the naked they clothed, the prisoners they visited, and so on. In seemingly unilateral acts of generosity, however, the "sheep" received the gift of the kingdom. In nourishing others, we are fed.

Ultimately this "mutual love" that should mark the disciples of the Lord as they gather around a constantly larger table replaces the table of sacrifice of the Old Testament as a genuine act of worship to God. Hungry and thirsty, we are fed and we worship as we gather humbly and hospitably around the table of the Lord.

A Pastoral Need

We live in a hungry world, marked by hungers of the body and the soul. The former are more easily met than the latter, even though so many still go through their days malnourished and go to bed hungry. Efforts to meet the physical hunger of the world are closely tied to meeting the hungers of the soul. To do this, the words of Jesus offer guidance. When Jesus calls for humility and hospitality at the table, he is setting the agenda for meeting some of the most pressing human needs in our modern world.

The story of humankind is one of nations that come to power and are then overcome by a more powerful nation. The lust for control of the world's resources always leads to a world at war. In the biblical world, Israel was under the thumb of Mesopotamia, Babylon, Persia, Greece, and Rome. Since then the story of Christianity has been marked by either persecution or war, with Christians sometimes taking the lead in both. To gather people to live in peace can be seen as an effort to gather them around the table of life. Here is where humility and hospitality can change the rules of the game. When we begin to compete within these two realms, the world will have a chance of becoming a place marked by familial love, where brothers and sisters try to outdo each other in generosity and service.

Ethical Implications

Consider the Salwens. Nicholas Kristof, a regular columnist for *The New York Times*, wrote about them on January 23, 2010. Kevin Salwen and his daughter Hannah had stopped at a traffic light. On one side was a black Mercedes coupe, on the other side a homeless man begging for food. Hannah turned to her father and said, "If that man had a less nice car, that man over there could have a meal." When the light changed, Kevin drove on but part of Hannah stayed back at that stoplight. She began to talk about this to her parents, and about other instances of economic disparity between people.

Finally, in exasperation, her mother asked, "What do you want to do? Sell the house?" Wrong question for an idealistic teenager. The proverbial bone tossed and snatched up immediately. And guess what? They sold the house. With the money they got, half was donated and half went towards another house. The family found that having a smaller house brought them together more often, since it was not as easy to escape into private spaces. The new house became more of a home, and its occupants became more of a family.

The half they gave away went to the Hunger Project to sponsor health care, microfinancing, food, and other programs for about forty villages in Ghana. Hannah and her father wrote a book about this called *The Power of Half.* Not everyone applauded. They never do. Some people accused them of showing off. Others asked, "Why didn't they help people in this country?" But Kevin said that this was just something they had decided on. It may not be for everyone, but everyone can do something. The last line belongs to Hannah, who said, "Everyone has too much of something, whether it's time, talent, or treasure. Everyone does have their own half, you just have to find it."

GOSPEL IMPLICATIONS

It seems to be the case that God hardwired our brains so that being generous to others gives us pleasure—the same kind of gratification that comes from food and sexual activity. Selflessness is really something to be sought. And why not? We are made in the image of God, to do what God does and to have a taste for looking and acting like our Father. Can anything nicer be said of us than, "You are just like your Father/Mother!" when the object of that remark is our Creator?

God sets not only the table but also the agenda for those coming there. Not everyone buys into it, to be sure, but for those who do, there is the satisfaction of knowing that we can define ourselves more by what we share than by what we accumulate, that we can recognize God at work in us when we follow the way of Jesus Christ and love each other as he loved us. It has been said that you are what you eat; in the case of the Eucharist, that is certainly to be hoped for—to grow ever more and more into being the body of Christ. But it can also be said that you are most who you are meant to be when you share all you have. Being fed should lead to feeding the hungers of others.

Notes

Alasair MacIntyre. *Dependent Rational Animals: Why Human Beings Need the Virtues*, 1999

Hannah Salwen and Kevin Salwen, *The Power of Half: One Family's Decision to Stop Taking and Start Giving Back*, 2010.

JAMES A. WALLACE

KEVIN J. O'NEIL

PROPER 18 [23]

THE LESSONS IN PRÉCIS

Every life is subject to being shaped by forces within and without, constructive and destructive. We freely decide whether God is one of them.

> *Jeremiah 18:1-11.* God is like a potter, shaping and forming Israel, the clay in his hands. Israel's decision to turn away from God determines its future.

> *Psalm 139:1-6, 13-18.* God's intimate knowledge of each person is poetically praised in this witness to God's loving artistry.

> *Philemon 1-21.* Paul's letter witnesses to his effort to shape a forgiving and reconciling Christian community, here calling on Philemon to accept a runaway slave back as a "dearly loved brother" (vs. 16).

> *Luke 14:25-33.* Jesus' words aim at shaping the hearts of his disciples to be totally committed to him by willingly accepting the cross. This effort includes an honest estimation of what discipleship costs.

THEME SENTENCE

God's plan is to shape us in the image of the Crucified. God's activity in shaping a people through an intimate, covenantal relationship reaches its fulfillment in the saving death of Jesus. Whether we are shaped by Jesus' words and the Spirit's action to be a people of mercy, justice, and reconciliation is up to us.

A KEY THEOLOGICAL QUESTION
God may be our maker, but is God our shaper?

Analogies like that of God as a potter, offered to us by Jeremiah, often help us to understand concepts, relationships, and divine dynamics while, at the same time, give us images to understand better what God is doing and what our response ought to be. The image of God as a potter suggests how God might destroy a work of pottery because it is deformed, just as God might destroy an unfaithful nation; or that God might reshape a work of clay that holds promise, as God might renew a nation that has repented. The reading itself mixes metaphors and speaks of a God who builds and plants as well as breaks down and destroys. Moving the analogy to the level of individuals, we could suggest the idea of the divine artisan shaping each of us, individually, according to God's will for us. It suggests rightly the individual attention that God gives to each of God's creatures, particularly God's beloved sons and daughters.

However, analogies are incomplete descriptions of what is going on, precisely because they are used to compare, not to define. So, while this image from Jeremiah gives us a helpful insight into God's action in the lives of the Israelites and also in our lives, it does not account sufficiently for the human response to God's activity. One might suggest that clay "responds" to the potter, but, once again, we would be speaking analogously. The analogy of God as divine potter and us as clay fails to take into account human freedom as a response to God's activity. A key theme of the readings today is not that God shapes passive creatures. Rather, it is humanity's response to God's activity and to the divine call through the use of freedom. To suggest either extreme—that is, only God shapes us or only we shape ourselves, apart from God—fails to capture the relationship between God's grace and human freedom. In fact, God shapes us through the gift of freedom entrusted to us. Are all our choices, however, necessarily reflections of the divine potter's design for us? No, they are not. This is the reason the prophet speaks of a potter breaking clay that has become deformed. We deform ourselves through sinful choices or in choices for things that compromise our relationship with God in Jesus Christ.

Today's readings direct Christian human freedom toward its proper end, that is, toward union with God through discipleship in Christ. We deform ourselves when our choices get in the way of being genuine followers of Jesus Christ. In the Gospel, Jesus points to the challenges that family might pose to following Christ, going so far as to speak of hating father, mother, wife, children, brothers, and sisters. Similarly, choosing to save our lives rather than to witness to Christ also abuses freedom. Temptations to believers to deny Christ in order to save themselves occurred frequently in the early Christian community and throughout the history of Christianity, and they occur even today. Choosing life over Christ distorts us as disciples of Christ. Finally, Jesus speaks of the danger of attachment to possessions. In each of the cases presented, we would become enslaved and unable to exercise freedom in Christ as we should.

The emphasis on the cross raises the question of our stance toward suffering. Are we to choose the cross, choose suffering, even pursue suffering? It is not true that Christ pursued suffering. Rather, because he was faithful to the Father's will, he faced and accepted the suffering that came his way. It was in his love, in fidelity, that he accepted the cross that came to him. Similarly, the cross will come into our lives and should be freely chosen, as it accompanies our fidelity to Jesus Christ. In other words, suffering and the cross are not saving in themselves; rather, by choosing to love even in the face of suffering, God shapes us into the image of the Crucified.

In light of the second reading, we might offer another image of God. Just as Paul desired freedom for the slave Onesimus and did not force Philemon to release Onesimus, so too God wants us to be free from whatever enslaves us and whatever prevents us from being faithful disciples of God's son. But God does not force us anymore than Paul forced Philemon to release Onesimus; God does not shape us against our wills. God desires that we be free.

Paul offers one more image that seemingly contradicts our whole notion of freedom. He describes himself as a "prisoner for the cause of Christ" (Phlm 1). This phrase may be taken simply as descriptive of a man in prison. However, a more profound interpretation highlights the consequences of Paul's free choice for Christ. It has been a choice away from those things that could prevent faithful discipleship (family, life itself, possessions) and a freedom for radical discipleship and its consequences, including both imprisonment and, eventually, martyrdom. Paul is indeed enslaved to Christ and uses his freedom only for that end. By placing himself wholly at the service of the gospel, Paul allowed himself to be shaped by God, the divine potter, into the image of the Crucified. Not pursuing the cross, but accepting it as a consequence of our discipleship, we, too, become more and more enslaved to Christ and free from what compromises our fidelity. Simply put, we cooperate with the grace of God as we freely choose to be molded in the image of the Crucified.

A Pastoral Need

The image of the potter and his clay continues to remind us that God is at work on our world and on us. And is there anything that is not in need of being shaped for the better these days? But the question is: to what do we surrender ourselves? What or whom do we allow to fashion our spirit and form our heart? What forces influence or even direct our thinking, values, and choices?

In *Hamlet's Blackberry,* author William Powers (2010) considers the effect digital technology is having on us. Today's digital world shapes us into a "connected" people. And who could be against connection? Yet, while this technology allows us to connect via Internet with resources for every sphere of knowledge, to events across the globe, to hook-ups with the most current analysis of topics of interest and import, and while we are able through e-mail and Skype to contact people across the world, there is also a downside to all this connectedness. Powers points to a loss of focus in our lives as we are continually checking our screens, our e-mail, our voice mail, our links on Facebook and LinkedIn, the latest videos on YouTube and Hulu, and all other forms of incessant requests for our attention. He writes, "We're losing something of great value, a way of thinking and moving through time that can be summed up in a single word: depth. Depth of thought and feeling, a depth in our relationships, our work and everything we do" (p. 4). In the end, we might ask: Do they increase our freedom or diminish it?

Ethical Implications

We like to think we are the shapers and makers of our souls, but this no longer appears to be the case. Powers argues that while there has always been a struggle to maintain a balance between the outer, social self and the inner, private self, we are directed more and more by voices other than our own. We are increasingly taking our cues from voices that surround us, ignoring our inner voice. The question for believers is whether we allow God's voice to register in any deep way. Does our digital connectedness work against any chance of God "having a word" with us? Can God get any hearing in our digital world, with its constant clamoring for attention, with its incessant beeping that signals the most recent inpouring of messages?

Jesus' call to discipleship invites us to commit ourselves to a relationship with him that will shape our lives not just on Sundays but through all the days and all the years that lie ahead. He invites us to a lifelong connection through the working of the Holy Spirit that will effect a transformation at the deepest level of our being. But does he stand a chance? Can our craving for connectedness with all the world offers us yield to God's purposeful plan to penetrate and shape us in the pattern of the Son's self-giving love and surrender? All our relationships, whether with people or possessions, all our plans, causes, interests, and preoccupations, are meant to be taken up and subjected to the saving power brought about by the death and resurrection of Christ.

Christ's word continues to knock on the door of our hearts, awaiting a response: "Happy rather are those who hear God's word and put it into practice" (Luke 11:28).

GOSPEL IMPLICATIONS

God continues shaping a people into the image of God's self-emptying Son. God does not give up on us but continues to work out the flaws. And God's love serves as the furnace strengthening us through adversity into a lasting masterpiece.

Paul recognized God at work in a runaway slave willing to return to his master. Paul the potter had completed his work, and now he invited Philemon to witness what God had achieved through him. Paul presents Onesimus as "my child" and says that sending him is like "sending you my own heart" (Phlm 10, 12). Paul invites Philemon to see Onesimus "no longer as a slave but more than a slave—that is a dearly loved brother . . . personally and spriritually in the Lord" (Phlm 16). Philemon was being asked to die to the world he lived in, one of masters and slaves. Did he yield to being shaped into the image of the Crucified? We don't know. Nor does it matter now. What matters is whether we respond to God's outstretched hand.

Notes

William Powers, *Hamlet's Blackberry: A Practical Philosophy for Building a Good Life in the Digital Age*, 2010.

JAMES A. WALLACE

KEVIN J. O'NEIL

PROPER 19 [24]

THE LESSONS IN PRÉCIS

At creation, God's first act was to roll back the darkness and bring light to the world. This pattern of divine behavior has not ended.

> *Jeremiah 4:11-12, 22-28.* A sirocco signals God's judgment on a people whose evil has produced a land that is desolate, barren, and lifeless. Creation is rolled back; the heavens have no light.

> *Psalm 14.* The psalmist sings a song of sorrow, lamenting human corruption and alienation from God. Yet, lament yields to hope for God's deliverance and the restoration of Israel's fortunes.

> *1 Timothy 1:12-17.* Paul voices his basic kerygma and personal witness: "'Christ Jesus came into the world to save sinners'—and I'm the biggest sinner of all" (vs. 16), proclaiming God's mercy and grace in Christ.

> *Luke 15:1-10.* A shepherd wandering in the wind and rain for one lost sheep, and a woman turning the house upside down for one small coin are images of God's persistence in seeking sinners.

THEME SENTENCE

God's mercy trumps human darkness. Fools say, "There is no God" (Ps 14:1) denying God's presence and power in their world, even acting to make it a desolate place. Jesus did not deny that people are sinners, but neither was he content with letting them wander in the dark. He went out to bring them home.

A KEY THEOLOGICAL QUESTION

Comedian Steve Martin is known for a joke about a popular ad for orange juice. The advertisement said, "A day without orange juice is like a day without sunshine." Martin quipped: "A day without sunshine is like, you know, NIGHT." The word of God today would suggest that "a day without God is like, you know, NIGHT." It is darkness. Jeremiah imagines a world plunged back into pre-creation darkness and chaos because the people have chosen to live in darkness rather than in the light of God, a theme dominant in the Gospel of John as well. They have ceased to call upon God, acting as if God does not even exist. Interestingly, in this reading, cosmic darkness and chaos follow sin. One might say that the cosmos reflects the souls of the people, now darkened in sin. In their darkness they wandered from God.

One of the Hebrew words associated with sin is *hattah*, sometimes described as "losing one's way" or "missing the mark." Proverbs 19:2 states: "Ignorant desire isn't good; rushing feet make mistakes." And Psalm 14:3 says: "All of them have turned bad. . . . No one does good— not even one person!" When people stay on the way, when they hit the mark, human life flourishes and their relationship with God, others, creation, and themselves are harmonious; when people stray from the way or miss the mark, they walk in darkness. Remaining in darkness only increases the probability of further stumbling and getting hopelessly lost, as the Israelites appear to be in the text from Jeremiah. The parables of Luke 15 of the lost coin and the lost sheep both call to mind losing one's way in the darkness of sin and then, wonderfully, being found.

Although the text of Jeremiah seems to suggest that God has determined Israel is to be dismantled forever, God says "I will not destroy it completely" (Jer 4:27). Destruction will not be total. Despite sin and darkness, God will not abandon God's people, because God's mercy trumps the deepest darkness.

This truth is borne out in both the Gospel of Luke and in Paul's letter to Timothy. Despite sin, God remains faithful. God remains merciful. *Hesed* is the Hebrew term often translated as "mercy," "loving kindness," or "covenantal love." A characteristic of covenantal love, *hesed*, was that it be mutual. This term was used for God's covenant with Israel. It expected fidelity on the part of God to Israel and also from Israel to God. This fidelity was not just to each other but also to oneself. In other words, it was God's nature to be loving toward Israel; it was Israel's nature to love and worship God. And this was where Israel failed. If the covenantal love were something akin to a legal contract, one would reasonably expect that one party's infidelity or betrayal was legitimate grounds for the other party to break off the covenant. Yet, this is precisely where God's *hesed* goes beyond what justice requires. Even in the face of the darkness and infidelity of Israel, and here we could include all of us, God remains faithful. Although *hesed* presumes mutuality, it is evident, time and again, that God remains faithful even if we do not. God's mercy endures forever.

A contemporary author has described mercy as "entering into the chaos of another" (Keenan, 2005, p. 3). Commentators on scripture highlight that mercy is a noun, not a verb. One *does* mercy. And mercy is what God has done. From Adam and Eve, to Paul, "a blasphemer, a persecutor, and a man of violence" (1 Tim 1:13, NRSV), to us in our day, God is not passive but seeks us out to enter into the darkness of our chaos and to invite us to come home. God's response to human chaos is Jesus Christ, who is mercy incarnate, God's mercy in the flesh.

God's *hesed*, God's seeking us out, God's invitation to us in Christ, expects a response. As with Israel, the covenant expects mutual fidelity, not one-sided fidelity. But God leaves us free to accept the invitation to fullness of life. Jeremiah's text recounts the judgment of God on those who prefer to walk in darkness, as "fools" who say, "There is no God" (Ps 14:1). One wonders if mercy is lost in this reading from Jeremiah. Does God give up? God does not, but issues a judgment about the choices Israel has made. One may consider the judgment of God as indicative of righteous anger, at the sight of Israel's and our behavior. That is, repeatedly given a chance to repent, we do not do so, and God says, finally, "To hell with you." But God cannot desire that for us, not a God who is mercy. Rather, we may so completely reject the covenant that God finally acknowledges this choice and, sadly, lets us go. Years ago Pope John Paul II (1999) described this dynamic of judgment: "[E]ternal damnation or hell . . . is not a punishment imposed externally by God but a development of premises already set by people in this life."

Mercy trumps the deepest darkness when those in darkness are willing to be found and to be led out of chaos into the light, when they are willing to enter again into covenantal love. When this happens, when we once lost are found, we experience how amazing is God's grace and mercy.

A PASTORAL NEED

I remember as a boy the comfort of having a nightlight near my bed that I could easily reach out and turn on, especially after waking from a bad dream. A dark room's shadows were an invitation for the imagination to take over and create chaos in a small boy's soul, hinting at all kinds of possible intruders concealed by the shadows. The slightest noise in the darkness became magnified into movement approaching the bed.

Darkness can put fear into a human heart, no matter how far away childhood has receded. This is especially true when you are in unfamiliar surroundings—walking down a street whose streetlights are out. But it also occurs when your world has turned dark by the loss of a loved one. Some occasions bring darkness to a community. Remember those thirty-three Chilean miners caught two thousand feet under the earth when their coal mine collapsed? On being rescued, Mario Sepúlveda, the second one to return to the surface, said: "I've been near God, but I've also been near the devil. God won." Into that darkness came a light that comforted many. Nineteen-year-old Jimmy Sanchez sent up a note two days before his rescue, saying, "There are actually thirty-four of us because God has never left us down here."

ETHICAL IMPLICATIONS

We are called to be children of the light by bringing light into the threatening darkness. It doesn't always take a grand gesture to bring light into someone's life. It can be as simple as entering their space and telling a story, like Jesus did.

The movie *In the Valley of Elah* has a touching scene when Tommy Lee Jones, portraying a man facing the darkness of his son's murder, goes to the home of a policewoman who is trying to help him. He shares a meal with her and her young son, David, whom the viewer knows has a fear of the dark. David needs a light on at night to sleep. After dinner, when Jones asks the woman if he can do anything to help, he finds himself in the boy's bedroom perplexedly staring into the *Chronicles of Narnia*.

Instead, he decides to tell David the story of his namesake, David, and his battle with Goliath. The boy becomes caught up in it. Finishing the story, Jones tells him that the biblical David first had to face his own inner fears before he could kill Goliath. When Jones gets up to leave, he turns off the boy's nightlight and shuts the door. The mother, standing nearby, starts to say, "He likes the door . . . " But Jones cuts her off, saying, "He'll be all right." A few seconds later the boy yells out, "DOOR!" But when the mother goes to his room and begins to open it completely, he says, "No, not that much, just a little." A kind stranger comes into a little boy's life, and, through the gift of a story, helps him overcome his fear of the dark. God's mercy can appear in many guises.

Gospel Implications

Stories about bringing light into darkness abound, both on the individual and community levels. They are one of the ways we witness and confirm that we are truly made in the image of a loving God, the creator and source of all light. It is one of the ways we remind ourselves that we are brothers and sisters of Jesus, the mercy of God, the light who has and who continues to come into the world. I believe that most often God chooses to work through us, so we come to know ourselves as children of the light. As Bishop Quintana of Chile said when various religious leaders were making special claims on how God was working through *them*: "What matters is that God is acting through human ingenuity to rescue these men."

In John's Gospel, Jesus proclaims, "I am the light of the world. Whoever follows me won't walk in darkness but will have the light of life" (John 8:12). And in Matthew he goes up onto a mountain and there teaches his disciples, "You are the light of the world . . . Let your light shine before people, so they can see the good things you do and praise your Father who is in heaven" (Matt 5:14-16). This light that is the gift of the Father and Son we name Holy Spirit.

Notes

James Keenan, *The Works of Mercy*, 2005.

Pope John Paul II, "Hell is the state of those who reject God," Wednesday Papal Audience, July 28, 1999, # 1.

James A. Wallace

Kevin J. O'Neil

PROPER 20 [25]

THE LESSONS IN PRÉCIS

Prayers petitioning God for salvation and a peaceable life are one way to participate in God's will to save us.

> *Jeremiah 8:18-9:1.* The voices of Jeremiah and God are intertwined in this duet professing grief and heart sickness at the condition of Israel. Jeremiah's anguish is God's anguish.

> *Psalm 79:1-9.* The psalmist petitions for help and deliverance for a people whom the nations have devoured, begging God to turn away his wrath and forgive.

> *1 Timothy 2:1-7.* The author urges all to pray for their leaders and everyone else, so they might "lead a quiet and peaceable life in all godliness and dignity" (vs. 2, nrsv). Such prayer joins us with our saving God.

> *Luke 16:1-13.* Perhaps the most elusive—and allusive—parable in the Gospels. An unjust servant is commended because of his ingenuity in making friends for the future, signaling God's expectation that we do all we can to be saved, by hook or crook!

THEME SENTENCE

God's salvation includes our participation. The grief Jeremiah expresses in both his own name and in God's name is provoked by Israel's turning to other gods. God's salvation, always available as gift, requires that some human initiative be taken in attaining the kingdom. Prayer and good works are both necessary.

A KEY THEOLOGICAL QUESTION
A God who invites collaboration

I remember hearing a preacher who started his homily after a Gospel passage on the end times with the words, "God is selective." He proceeded to suggest that God chooses who will go to heaven and who will go to hell. Although the preacher's intentions were good in terms of encouraging people to live faithfully, his suggestion that God, rather than we, selects heaven or hell for us mistakenly implies that God might actually desire our damnation and inflict it on us.

Yet twice, in seven short verses in Paul's first letter to Timothy, we hear God's genuine wish: "[God] wants all people to be saved and to come to a knowledge of the truth" (1 Tim 2:4). Two verses later we read of Jesus who "gave himself as a payment to set all people free" (1 Tim 2:6). These passages voice God's desire for universal salvation.

The fact is that salvation has already been accomplished in Christ. We are saved. Yet, we live in the "in between" time where we "carry out [our] own salvation" (Phil 2:12), where we live so as to receive this gratuitous gift from God.

Any talk of working out our salvation or suggesting that God requires our participation in salvation raises questions and perhaps fears of misunderstanding the relationship between faith and works. Scholars see a tension between Paul and James on this point. It was a chief concern at the time of the Reformation and was recently a topic of dialogue between the World Lutheran Federation and the Catholic Church, resulting in a "Joint Declaration on the Doctrine of Justification."

The doctrine, briefly, is that salvation is pure gift from God and that we do nothing to earn it. We do not "work out [our] salvation" (Phil 2:12, NRSV) if that suggests in any way that our actions force God's grace to work. However, our works demonstrate the authenticity of our faith. We live in such a way that the salvation, the wholeness, won for us by Jesus Christ is experienced in our lives. Even though God desires salvation for everyone, God does not thrust it upon us. It is a gift. We receive that gift partially now in the "in between" times when we live the life of the kingdom of God, but our response itself is the work of God. The text from Phil 2:12-13 goes on to say: "Carry out your own salvation with fear and trembling. God is the one who enables you both to want and to actually live out his good purposes." It is God who justifies us in Christ and God who graces us to live the renewed life in Christ. This divine activity opens us to receive the free gift of salvation.

Another parable from Luke's Gospel might shed light on this point and help us to understand today's readings better. In the parable of the prodigal son (Luke 15:11-32), we have a story of a gift received and a gift refused. We hear the father speak to his elder son words that capture the gratuitousness of the gift: "Everything I have is yours" (vs. 31). It is the younger son, however, who, after "proving" that he was a sinner, returned thinking that he had lost "everything." In fact, it was still there for him. It was a gift all along, but he had not been ready to receive it. Upon his return he finds that the gift is still offered and he is now in a position to receive it. The elder son actually hears the words "Everything I have is yours," but does nothing, apparently, to receive that gift.

For all the righteous anger that precedes today's passage from the prophet Jeremiah, the principal image that comes to mind in this text is that of a weeping parent, or a heartbroken, grieving loved one. "No healing, only grief; my heart is broken . . . Because my people are crushed, I am crushed; darkness and despair overwhelm me" (Jer 8:18-21). God has offered everything to God's people, yet they have chosen "foreign gods" (Jer 8:19). The gift is offered, but God's people do not live so as to receive the gift. It is clear from the reading of the full chapter of Jeremiah that the people of Israel understand that the destruction they are experiencing comes from God, because of their sins. Yet, they do nothing. They lament that God has not saved them and wonder about his providential care but do nothing to connect with their God. God, on the other hand, sees an unfaithful people who will not even call out to him for help but who continue to engage in self-destructive behavior. Apparently they see the way out of their misery but do nothing to return to God. Although they claim a faith in God, nothing in their actions demonstrates that relationship.

We contrast the people of Israel with the shrewd manager of Luke's Gospel. Jesus praises the man because he sees what is going on and acts so as to make his life easier. He actually works with the goods of his master and manages to work out a plan to avoid devastation in his own life. While the passage may seem like an endorsement for crime, the man's master (Jesus?) praises him and implicitly criticizes the children of the light. Why? Perhaps the children of the light, like the Israelites, are failing to act so as to work out their salvation.

We may miss or seize the moments of grace and conversion that God offers. In the end, God's salvation requires our participation not because God needs us but because we must receive the gift offered from the One who desires that we be saved.

A Pastoral Need

Today's readings allow us to consider the greatest pastoral need of all—the need to be saved. The first struggle may be to admit that we have this need at all. Spiritual author Michael Casey, OCSO, says that while in theory salvation seems desirable, at the level of feeling it is different because most of us find it humiliating to be saved. Even people who are drowning will often resist the efforts of their rescuers. And this same dynamic can be operative in our spiritual life. We like doing things for ourselves. And we are clever and creative enough to come up with many alternative ways to save ourselves. Some of the more popular ones are an endless pursuit of power and possessions, and the cultivation of pride in our achievements. This is what Israel did as we witness in today's reading, isolating herself from God.

But, as the author of 1 Timothy reminds us today, "There is one God and one mediator between God and humanity, the human Christ Jesus, who gave himself as a payment to set all people free" (1:5). God alone saves, and God has done this through Jesus Christ. In Luke's Gospel, the title Savior is given to Jesus from the beginning (2:11). In coming to grips with the fact that we need God's intervention in our salvation, we also must recognize that God has called us to play a part. We do this by being both recipients and activists, as today's texts indicate, in a life of prayer.

Ethical Implications

One of the ways we participate in our salvation is through prayer. We hear the prayer of the psalmist today, petitioning: "God of our salvation, help us for the glory of your name! Deliver us and cover our sins for the sake of your name!" (Ps 79:8-9). First Timothy urges that "requests, prayers, petitions, and thanksgiving be made for all people," especially for all in positions of power, "so that we can live a quiet and peaceful life in complete godliness and dignity" (1:1-2). We do this because God our

Savior desires that all be saved and come to know the truth. The importance of prayer is rooted in the Gospels themselves, where Jesus teaches his disciples both about the importance of prayer and how to pray.

Alphonsus de Liguori (1696-1787), recognized as a saint and a great spiritual author and moral theologian in the Roman Catholic tradition, wrote a spiritual classic called *Prayer, the Great Means of Salvation*, in which he boldly stated that the person who prays will be saved, and the one who does not will not be saved. Alphonsus saw the prayer of petition as essential to the Christian life and at the heart of the spiritual life. It is not a matter of our informing God about things God doesn't know or may have missed, but such prayer marks the beginning of the redeemed life, of living in the awareness that God is the One who saves us in Christ through the power of the Holy Spirit. We recognize this when we engage in prayer and turn to God as God who can change human hearts and who wills that all be saved. From this awareness come our actions in the world, flowing from our fundamental choice of God over Mammon, and our dedication for working for the coming of the kingdom.

Gospel Implications

One of the ways God saves us from ourselves is by drawing us into a life of prayer. One of the prefaces that begins the Eucharistic prayer in the Roman Catholic rite places our prayer of praising God as part of the gift of salvation when it proclaims: "You have no need of our praise, yet our desire to thank you is itself your gift. Our prayer of thanksgiving adds nothing to your greatness, but makes us grow in your grace, through Jesus Christ our Lord" (Weekday Preface IV, *The Sacramentary*, 453).

We do not pray alone. Paul reminds us, "We don't know what we should pray, but the Spirit himself pleads our case with unexpressed groans. The one who searches hearts knows how the Spirit thinks, because he pleads for the saints, consistent with God's will" (Rom 8:26-27).

James A. Wallace

Kevin J. O'Neil

PROPER 21 [26]

THE LESSONS IN PRÉCIS

The theme for these readings is assurance, its substance and, perhaps, its limits?

Jeremiah 32:1-3a, 6-15. God calls Jeremiah to act out a sign of hope for Israel's future in the midst of a foreign siege. He buys a field, pays for it, and receives a deed that is to be preserved as a reminder of future hope in present calamity. The drama and specificity of the details of the purchase underscore God's determination and reliability.

Psalm 91:1-6, 14-16. The psalmist offers an assurance of God's protection to those who live in the shelter of the Most High (vs. 1), who have made the Lord their refuge (vs. 9) and who love him and know his name (vs. 14). How are we to interpret a blanket assurance of God's protection for some and God's seeming indifference to the fate of others?

1 Timothy 6:6-19. This passage is directed at those who have resources and are in danger of not sharing them with others. The author offers the assurance that when we live a life of generosity, the benefits far exceed the passing pleasures of self-indulgence.

Luke 16:19-31. This odd parable is unique to Luke. It warns readers that the messengers of God will come to them in the form of the poor in their path (Lazarus in the parable). If they ignore them, as did the rich man, there will come a time when they will recognize their error, but it will be too late.

239

THEME SENTENCE

God stands by us in adversity and holds us accountable in prosperity. Our texts from Jeremiah and the Psalter assure us of God's faithfulness to God's promise to preserve the faithful in adversity. Our texts from 1 Timothy and Luke challenge listeners to exchange lives of unthinking comfort for habits of radical generosity. Taken together, the message is that God's persistent challenge to the comfortable from generation to generation is an integral part of God's faithfulness.

A KEY THEOLOGICAL QUESTION

Power is one of the attributes that Christians assign to God. Nevertheless, as the various texts of the lectionary talk about power, some surprising reversals take place. Luke's well-known parable of Lazarus recalls the repeated proclamation of Jesus in the Synoptic Gospels that the last will be the first and the first will be the last (Mark 10:31; Matt 20:16; etc.), noting that "a great crevasse has been fixed" (Luke 16:26) that cannot be crossed. Moreover, God is not impartial in this reversal but is to be found on one side rather than the other.

Many Judeo-Christian traditions, in both the Old and New Testaments, tell of a distinct reversal of power. God is not on the side of the great empires, be they of Babylonian or Roman provenience. And neither is God on the side of the wealthy, whose wealth and power are linked to the exploits of the ruling empires of their day. This comes as a shock, both then and now, especially when we have gotten used to the idea that God is on "our side," and that great political and financial success is God-given.

This reversal of power does not mean, however, that God abdicates power. The point is simply that God represents a different power than the power of the status quo. God's power is manifest in the resistance against the Babylonian Empire, in the ongoing struggle against oppressors, by providing alternatives to an economy that values capital above all else (1 Tim 6:10), and in the vindication of poor Lazarus, who appears to have died before his time of starvation and untreated sores (Luke 16:20-21). God's power is at work not only in resistance to the powers that be but also by providing the sort of alternatives that empire—the dominant powers that expect our allegiance not only in politics and economics but also in our everyday lives—tells us do not exist. One of the key characteristics of empire in all ages is the mantra, "There is no alternative" (Rieger, 2007).

If God's power differs from the power of the status quo, what about those who share in the power of the status quo? The parable of Lazarus appears to end on a negative note. Abraham responds to the request of the rich man that Lazarus should return from the dead and warn his brothers: "If they don't listen to Moses and the Prophets, then neither will they be persuaded if someone rises from the dead" (Luke 16:31). Still, the possibility remains that some might listen to Moses and the Prophets, as well as other texts such as 1 Timothy.

What would it mean for the rich "not to become egotistical and not to place their hope on their finances, which are uncertain [but to] hope in God, who richly provides everything for our enjoyment" (1 Tim 6:17); and what would it mean "to do good, to be rich in the good things they do, to be generous, and to share with others" (1 Tim 6:18)? In a world of top-down power, this might be taken to mean that God guarantees power, success, and the smug security of those who are home free. Here, God is the ultimate warrant of the status quo, even more so than large amounts of wealth and power. In a world where God's reversal of power is at work, however, things are different.

"Not to become egotistical" and to "hope in God" means that God's power will prevail, that the last shall be the first and the first shall be the last. To "be generous and to share with others" is a reminder that the power of solidarity will prevail over the power of competition, which is at the heart of our current world not only in economics and politics but also in religion. To "do good" and "be rich in the good things they do" in this context is not about the giving of alms but about the reversal of power that God embodies in the most literal sense of the word in the incarnation, life, ministry, death, and resurrection of Jesus Christ.

In the tradition of the church, the Nicene Creed can help us deepen these insights. Constantine, the first Roman emperor to convert to Christianity, might have hoped to domesticate Jesus Christ by declaring him "of the same substance" with a God that was characterized by the traits of the empire. The declaration of Jesus as one with God who rules from the top down, whose power mirrors the power of the Roman emperors, had the effect of, and, indeed, was designed to co-opt Jesus for the empire. The good news is, however, that there is another way of interpreting this creed, which brushes against the grain of the empire.

The power of the empire is challenged when God is understood in light of the ministry of Jesus, who was raised in a family of day laborers and construction workers, who rejected the temptation to rule from the top down (Matt 4:8-10), and who remained in solidarity with "the least of these" (Matt 25:45) all his life and continues this pattern in his risen life among us.

Instead of the power of the empire, another power is manifest in Jesus that reminds us of the power that the prophets proclaimed: God has taken the side of the marginalized and invites all to join him. Fighting "the good fight of faith" (1 Tim 6:12) only makes sense if it takes us to the root of the problem. Our Judeo-Christian traditions present us with a rather clear-cut choice: Will we serve God or wealth? (Matt 6:24; Luke 16:13) Will we serve the God of Jeremiah, the psalmist, Timothy, and Luke, or will we serve the status-quo God of top-down power? Our problem, as theologian Karl Barth recognized several decades ago, is not the struggle between faith and atheism but between the true faith and a distorted faith, both of which claim to be Christian. At stake is nothing less than the question of the true God, which is also the question of true power. As we become clearer about this, the "great crevasse" of which Luke speaks loses its threat, and there is hope that the rich man can be saved after all.

A PASTORAL NEED

These texts assure us of God's reliability and determination (Jer 32:1-3a, 6-15) and of God's protection for those who live in the shelter of the Most High. There are those in our congregation who need hope and may wonder, based on their current circumstances, "What is God determined to do? All I see is a downward spiral." They may wonder, "Toward what end is God reliable? I see no signs of hope in the midst of my siege as Jeremiah did." When the psalmist assures us of God's protection, they may sit with arms folded, thinking, "God certainly hasn't protected me and my people from harm." Or, if they are materially comfortable and facing no crises at the moment, they may attribute their favorable conditions to God's protection and go no deeper.

In our preaching we need to point people to signs of God's hope in the midst of their own misfortunes. We may need to point others to ways they can be signs of hope out of their own good fortune, not just by charitable giving but by living in ways that undercut the injustices charity alone is inadequate to resolve. Today's texts from 1 Timothy and Luke warn against the danger of making wealth our aim and ignoring the needs of the poor at our doorstep. We need to be careful that we don't preach these texts in ways that offer false promises of protection from harm or salvation by philanthropy. The gospel has power, but it is not the power of material prosperity as a sign of divine protection and approval. The gospel has power, but it is not the power of reward for our philanthropy. The power of God informs our lives as we live, not by cheap grace or works righteousness but by participation in resistance to the abuse of power in the name of God.

Ethical Implications

It is all too common in preaching these days to focus on the personal realm—on health, finances, and relationships. Too often, the message prizes the accumulation of personal power, which it labels "positive thinking." Can we preach *God's* power and *God's* hope instead of this distortion of the Christian faith? Can we preach participation in a hope that is public as well as personal? Can we flesh out what it would look like for our congregation to embody God's power by embodying hope for those in the neighborhood, community, and world who are experiencing the siege of poverty, discrimination, or homelessness but who are not experiencing the assurance of hope in the form of food, shelter, or an advocate?

A church started a ministry called Apt G, which has nothing to do with apartments, but stands for "A Place to Go." It is a ministry for special needs adults and their caregivers. The church provides a meal and activities for the special needs folks and a field trip to a movie or bowling or dinner off-site for their caregivers. It is a weekly sign of hope to both groups. There is power in these gatherings, but not top-down power.

A church in State College, Pennsylvania, burned to the ground several years ago. Shards of its beautiful stained glass window (Jesus praying in Gethsemane) remained. The pastors gathered them up and had crosses made for the congregation to hold or wear around their necks. They were signs of hope in the debris. In some sense this church is every church—in shambles but with the opportunity to rebuild by the power of God. What would that look like? It might look like one of the rich man's brothers, peering out his door and noticing who is on his doorstep.

Gospel Implications

In reflecting on Psalm 91, we remember that Satan steals some lines from this psalm in trying to tempt Jesus. Satan urges Jesus to jump from the pinnacle of the temple, saying to him "Since you are God's Son, throw yourself down" (Matt 4:6). He then quotes Psalm 91:11-12 ("Because he will order his messengers to help you, to protect you wherever you go. They will carry you with their own hands so you don't bruise your foot on a stone.") Jesus refuses to put God to the test. He refuses to define God's protection in superficial terms. He refuses to define God's power in terms of empire. Out of this refusal comes the eventual fulfillment of the promise of this psalm in the resurrection. As Jeremiah affirmed that God was the people's hope amid their siege, so Jesus becomes our hope in the midst of our siege and gives us courage to embody hope to others in the midst of theirs. He empowers us to notice the poor on our doorsteps.

Notes

Jeorg Rieger, *Christ and Empire: From Paul to Postcolonial Times*, 2007.

Alyce M. McKenzie

Joerg Rieger

Proper 22 [27]

The Lessons in Précis

The theme for these readings is the power of remembering and holding fast to our hope in God's saving faithfulness. Doing so will enable us to persevere and prevail in times of adversity that threaten the community's faith.

Lamentations 1:1-6; 3:19-26. The first part of this reading (from chapter 1) is a lament for Jerusalem in the wake of its destruction at the hands of the Babylonians in 586 BCE. It personifies the city as a bereaved, abandoned widow. The reading from chapter 3 shines a ray of hope into the darkness as the writer calls to mind the steadfast love of God that will abide with the city in the future as it has in the past.

2 Timothy 1:1-14. Paul encourages Timothy to persevere in faith and leadership by remembering and holding fast to the faith in a God who can be trusted to fulfill what God has promised, a faith kindled in him by his mother and grandmother and by Paul, through the power of the Holy Spirit.

Luke 17:5-10. Jesus reminds his disciples that if they had faith the size of a mustard seed, they could do greater things than they can imagine.

Theme Sentence

God is faithful to God's promises. The people of Jerusalem, Timothy, and the disciples in Luke's Gospel all needed a reminder that what God has promised remains in effect in times of testing. Affluence and privilege can be times of testing as surely as poverty and exile. It is the Holy Spirit who helps us activate our small grain of faith, or, as the text puts it, "protect this good thing that has been placed in [our] trust" (2 Tim 1:14).

245

A KEY THEOLOGICAL QUESTION

Religion is often a stabilizing force. As such, it stabilizes society, communities, and families, and promotes the values that hold these entities together. In Western civilization, Christianity has taken on a stabilizing role for centuries, to such a degree that many theologians assume a deep unity between the two.

The texts of this week, however, present a different picture. Here, religion becomes a destabilizing force that poses substantial challenges to the way things are, yet it is precisely in this destabilization that hope is found. Common sense would have suggested that the Babylonian exile, of which Lamentations speaks, should be accepted as the status quo, the way things are. Babylon, one of the great empires of the ancient world, would not easily be destabilized. The same was true for the Roman Empire, in power at the time when the letter to Timothy was written. For those who lived under the rule of the Babylonian Empire as well as for those who lived under the rule of Rome, adaptation seemed to be the only option.

When religion becomes a destabilizing force in these contexts, consequences are inevitable. The author of Timothy experienced this firsthand: "I was appointed a messenger, apostle, and teacher of this good news. This is also why I'm suffering the way I do" (2 Tim 1:11-12). The Roman Empire, faced with the threat of destabilization, was prepared to strike back, thus causing suffering. The problem was not religion in general but a religion that challenges the way things are. The Roman Empire would not have opposed other religions in general, as the Romans were hospitable to a great variety of religions, to the point of including foreign gods in their pantheon.

Jesus presented his own destabilizations. In Luke 17:6 he describes the destabilizing power of one of the smallest seeds of all, the mustard seed. What is destabilized is the sort of thing that everyone else considers impossible to move: a mulberry tree, which without pruning can reach 80 feet in height. And not only will this tree be moved, but it will also be planted in the sea, upright. (In Matt 17:20, the point is made even more boldly: a mountain will be moved.) All this leads us to wonder, of course, whether we are dealing with just wishful thinking. Large trees and mountains are as hard to move as empires, both ancient and modern. The way things are, we are usually told, is here to stay, which was the famous pronouncement that former British Prime Minister Margaret Thatcher used to make about capitalism.

Oddly, however, there is hope in the midst of suffering and defeat. The people in the Babylonian exile did not despair, but developed new trust in God. It is in this situation that the biblical creation stories emerge, as a reminder that God is not just the God of Israel but the God of the whole world (von Rad, 1962, 1965). The theological horizons broadened in one of the darkest hours of the nation. New hope and the destabilization of the way things are go together.

Timothy was called to embark on his mission not in the context of a mountaintop experience but with the reminder of the suffering that the proclamation of the gospel has caused his mentor. In the midst of a life-and-death struggle with the Roman Empire, God gives not "a spirit that is timid," for which we could hardly blame our forefathers and foremothers, but a spirit "that is powerful, loving, and self-controlled" (2 Tim 1:7).

The hope that emerges in the midst of suffering and defeat is not the hope of empire. Just the opposite, this hope destabilizes the hopes and dreams of the empire. Perhaps one of the most typical hopes of empires is the hope for the strong man, the hero who will set things straight. The hope of the mustard seed that Jesus proclaims is not the hope of the hero. It is the hope of the service workers who know they are not in control and who are reminded every day that they are merely "worthless slaves" (Luke 17:10, NRSV). The fact that the work ultimately gets done not by the rulers but by the workers is what is striking here. Unlike the rulers, workers have known for a long time that this is how large trees get moved.

John Wesley (1764) once wrote in his journal that "religion must not go from the greatest to the least, or the power would appear to be of men" (p. 178). Religion that goes from the greatest to the least appears to be able to do whatever it sets its sight upon, and this is no miracle. If the wealthy decide to build a cathedral or a mega church, they will do it. If the wealthy decide to fix up whole neighborhoods, they will do it. Yet much of the power here does indeed "appear to be of men." This is the sort of religion that promotes stabilization.

What happens when religion goes the other way around, from the least to the greatest, is more interesting and exciting, as these dynamics cannot as easily be explained away as purely human work. There is something miraculous in the fact that the religion of a defeated people and of service workers has the power to move large obstacles, just like faith as small as a mustard seed can move a mulberry tree. The defeated people living in exile in Babylon gave the Judeo-Christian traditions their distinctive creation stories, and ultimately they got to return home. The early Christians were not wiped out by the Roman Empire but developed powerful traditions and alternative ways of life that continue long after that empire has fallen.

Confessing the power of God from a position of strength is easy, and it is never quite clear whether the power of God confessed in these situations is a projection of our own strength. Confessing the power of God in the midst of the Babylonian exile, the Roman Empire, and the lives of service workers is a different story altogether.

Pastoral Implications

The lament from Lamentations may resonate with those who feel bereaved or hopeless. In the text the entire city is personified as a grieving, abandoned widow (Lam 1:2). How might our church, our community, our nation identify with this metaphor? Are there people and communities that feel abandoned by God? To them the Lamentations text expresses not only their despair but also a ray of hope that God will be in the future the steadfast God of the past. Says 2 Timothy, "I know the one in whom I've placed my trust" (1:12). Says Lamentations, "Certainly the faithful love of the Lord hasn't ended; certainly God's compassion isn't through! They are renewed every morning" (3:22-23). We address this homiletically by giving examples of how God has shown steadfast love in the past in our lives. Then, we encourage our listeners to move beyond their own experiences to those of others where the God who is a steady presence in times of sorrow also shakes up times and places of complacency.

We invite them to consider that one way God shows that love is in strengthening the poor, the disadvantaged, and the left out, to stand up to the wealthy, the advantaged, and the let in. God showed God's steadfast love through Catherine Booth's determination to preach despite opposition, Mahatma Gandhi's commitment to nonviolent revolution, Martin Luther King, Jr.'s burning passion for racial and economic equality, and Harvey Milk's commitment to end discrimination on the basis of sexual orientation. Their lives testify to the fact that the large tree will not be moved without suffering. We are invited to view the status quo as the huge tree and the faith of the "worthless slaves" as the mustard seed. Isn't it amazing that in this showdown, it is the tree that is moved and not the mustard seed?

ETHICAL IMPLICATIONS

Like the author of 2 Timothy, we ought not be ashamed of this subversive, unimpressive gospel. It is our treasure. In the Old Testament, the superpowers Assyria and Babylonia are pictured as grand cedar trees (Ezek 31:6; Dan 4:12). The mustard seed, by contrast, seems a paltry, pathetic image for our faith. As 2 Tim 1:8 reminds us, those whose lives don't have the cultural "curb appeal" of brains, bucks, and beauty, need not be ashamed of this faith in a crucified Messiah. We are, instead, to embrace lives of perseverance in small acts of subversive devotion, without flash or flamboyance.

The mustard seed life is one in which we hold fast to our faith in the mercy of God in the midst of exile. (Just as the creation stories of the Old Testament came from a time of exile, so incidences of new creation can come out of our own exiles and the lessons we learn from others' experiences.) The mustard seed life is one in which we do not allow suffering to negate our faith; nor do we allow our faith to negate our responsibility to respond to others' suffering. The mustard seed life is one in which we are not fooled by appearances. Large trees with big roots are more vulnerable than they appear to the effects of mustard seed faith. The status quo is not the way things are supposed to be or how they must remain. The gospel is power, not weakness. The gospel is a source of joy, not shame.

GOSPEL IMPLICATIONS

The Lamentations text speaks of human despair and points to hope provided by God. It affirms "Certainly the faithful love of the LORD hasn't ended; certainly God's compassion isn't through!" (3:22). God's mercies are "renewed every morning" (3:23). Because of the character of God and God's dealings with us, we hope in the Lord (3:24).

Second Timothy 1:1-14 speaks of God as saving and calling us for a purpose. God empowers us to respond to this call by the grace God gives us in Christ. Christ abolished death and brought life and immortality to light through the gospel. Faith and love are in Christ Jesus, and he is in us.

Maybe it's not so surprising after all that a mustard seed sized portion of this faith can move large trees. Look who's behind it! Jesus himself is a mustard seed. He was small and insignificant in the eyes of the religious, political, and economic power brokers of his day. They both hoped for and feared a cedars of Lebanon lord. They got a mustard seed Messiah. He seems easy to destroy with one small cross on a hill. And yet faith the size of a mustard seed can move a tree, and one tree the size of a cross can move the boundary of God's mercy to infinite measure. The power of God works through the vulnerable, through the crucified one, through the one who is transparent to the purposes and the compassion of God whose mercy never ends, even at death.

Notes

Gerhard von Rad, *Old Testament Theology*, trans. D.M.G. Walker, 2 vols. (Edinburgh: Oliver and Boyd, 1962, 1965).

John Wesley, Journal Entry of May 21, 1764, *The Works of the Rev. John Wesley*, 3rd ed., Vol. III, ed. Thomas Jackson, 1872, reprinted 1986.

Alyce M. McKenzie

Joerg Rieger

PROPER 23 [28]

THE LESSONS IN PRÉCIS

These texts have to do with the importance of remembering and being grateful for what God has done. This is the only sure foundation for the community's future.

Jeremiah 29:1, 4-7. This text describes Jeremiah's letter to the people Nebuchadnezzar took into exile from Jerusalem to Babylon. The Lord instructs them through his letter to bloom where they are planted, to seek and pray for the welfare of the city that must now become their home, rather than listen to the pipe dreams of false prophets not sent by God.

Psalm 66:1-12. This psalm is a song of praise to God, who has delivered the people from adversity and enemies. The psalmist rejoices that, though he believes God has tested the people (66:10), God has not allowed the people to decrease and decline.

2 Timothy 2:8-15. This passage underscores the importance of remembering to whom we owe our lives. By enduring we will be rewarded, and God will be faithful no matter what, so we are not to battle "over words" (14).

Luke 17:11-19. Jesus marvels that, though he healed ten lepers, only one, and that a Samaritan, came back to praise God. He does not praise the one grateful leper as much as he chastises the thoughtless nine.

THEME SENTENCE

God guides the community's future. The exiles were in danger of listening to false prophets. Timothy's community was in danger of losing their focus on Jesus' saving death and life and "wrangling over words"

251

(2 Tim 2:14, NRSV). The nine lepers did not direct their gratitude toward the source of their healing, but dispersed thoughtlessly in nine different directions.

A KEY THEOLOGICAL QUESTION

It may be hard for us to understand what it means to do theology in exile, but this is a persistent theme in the Bible. How does theology change when it develops not from a position of power and control but from a position of pressure and stress? This question is important not because of some generic concern for political correctness but because many of the deepest theological insights of our traditions have been developed under pressure. A large number of our biblical texts have their origins in situations of pressure, including all of the texts of this week. The psalmist talks about oppressive situations that the people had to endure. The author of Timothy is involved in struggles where the existence of his community is at stake. Even Jesus works in a situation where the cards are stacked against him. Many of our later Christian traditions have shaped up in similar contexts of pressure, including the early monastic movements, mysticism in the Middle Ages, the radical wings of the Reformation in the sixteenth century, Methodism (Rieger, 2011), and the diverse theological liberation traditions of recent memory.

The theological insights produced from positions of pressure and stress are remarkably different from insights produced from positions of power and control, although they may look similar on the surface. God calling us to, "Promote the welfare of the city where I have sent you into exile" (Jer 29:7), differs from a triumphalist perspective where religion and dominant politics go hand in hand. The perspective of the exile reminds us that there is always a difference between God and the powers that be. As a result, the concern for the welfare of the city is not a matter of seeking to preserve the status quo but of obedience to God, which often puts those who seek true welfare in conflict with the self-centeredness of the status quo, which seeks welfare in order to perpetuate its power.

Psalm 66:6 talks about the liberation from Egypt, which serves as a constant reminder that the beginning of Israel's history is tied to an encounter with God in an act of liberation from enslavement and forced labor. The old story of God talking to Moses out of the burning bush (Exod 3) is not a generic story of someone encountering God in miraculous ways, but a story of God calling Moses to participate in a particular instance of God's work of liberation. For this reason, celebrating the power of God, who has brought the people "through fire and water . . . out to freedom" (Ps 66:12), can never turn into a celebration of the sort of power that oppresses and enslaves other people and exploits their labor, although this is a constant temptation even in some of the biblical traditions.

The author of 2 Timothy notes that he is "in prison like a common criminal" (2:9) for proclaiming the good news of Jesus Christ, who was executed like a political criminal by the Roman Empire. Clearly, there is something in the Christian message that puts it in tension with the powers that be. The promise of living and reigning with Christ (2:11-12), therefore, cannot be modeled after living and ruling in the Roman Empire. Christ's lordship is diametrically opposed to the lordship of Caesar, as scholars as diverse as John Dominic Crossan, Richard Horsley, and N.T. Wright have shown. Living and reigning with Christ is grounded in a bottom-up movement that begins with the subversive power of the cross and suffering.

These non-triumphalist readings suggest a fresh take on an ancient theological theme at the heart of the Judeo-Christian traditions: the theme of grace. Grace, God's invitation to share in God's power and love, begins as grace under pressure. It is most powerfully at work in situations of exile and resistance. Its trajectory is opposed to the works righteousness of the status quo that goes hand in hand with top-down power. Works righteousness, the effort to take things into one's own hand and to earn merit with God, is not the affliction of the powerless but the affliction of those who are in control and are used to being in charge. Rather than tying us into the powers that be, God's grace provides alternative ways of life that are sustainable because God has proven time and again that a new thing is possible even in situations of great adversity and oppression. This is the theme that our texts demonstrate in various ways.

Jesus' experience of healing lepers in the border region between Samaria and Galilee reflects a similar dynamic: the only one who gets it is the one who suffers from multiple layers of pressure, not only from his disease but also from his stigma of being a "foreigner" (Jesus' word in Luke 17:18). The experience of grace under situations of extreme pressure results in thinking theologically under pressure and in realizing who is the true God. The point is not to lay blame on the nine who did not return but to point out the extraordinary thing that they missed. Time and again, the surprising and life-giving power of God is experienced in situations of pressure where we least expect it. As theologians, we might read this as an invitation to do our work more consistently and systematically from below, so as not to miss the powerful manifestations of God's grace under pressure in our time.

A PASTORAL NEED

Many people feel they are outsiders, in exile in our congregations. Whatever their economic level, circumstances in people's lives can lead to this sense of being "in between," lacking direction, perhaps with their faith faltering. Circumstances that produce a desire for release include health challenges, bereavement, the loss of relationships and jobs, and even the process of aging that can make people feel exiled from the youth and energy worshipped by our culture. Such a purely personal application doesn't do justice to the power of the good news, to the "grace under pressure" that pervades the prison cell in which the author of 2 Timothy resides, or to the breadth and depth of the acts of social resistance in his preaching and teaching, or to the miracles that led Jesus to be executed as a political rebel.

Jeremiah's word of hope speaks to communities who are struggling and discouraged in pressure cooker situations. They need to experience not works righteousness, but grace. When I interviewed pastors serving congregations of various ethnicities about five years ago, a number of Korean American and African American pastors said the various experiences of exile in scripture form a framework for their congregation's life experience. Living with this experience as a central metaphor for their own lives, their congregations find hope and stamina. This text from Jeremiah, an exhortation to do good in whatever condition we find ourselves, offers a word of hope for exiles in Babylon, both with regard to personal and communal life. That good may mean working against an injustice that mars the lives of those around us. For this text reminds us that we cannot separate our individual well-being from the well-being of our society, no matter how deeply ingrained in our American psyche such a separation may be. Those who suggest a single focus on the personal are the false prophets to which Jeremiah and 2 Timothy refer. Preachers need to remind congregations of the good news that God desires justice for the land we inhabit and that Christ's resurrected power is activated not in heroic human victories but in grace under pressure (Rieger, 2011).

Ethical Implications

These texts speak to the identity of the church in the various communities in which it finds itself. Jeremiah encourages us to regard the welfare of our community as integrally connected with our own. A billboard recently pictured a luxury home and bore the caption, "Live the Dream!" Jeremiah's message of actualizing our own welfare through seeing to the welfare of our community is a countercultural message when it says that "the good life" cannot be limited to financial prosperity. According to Jeremiah, limiting our dreams for the future to our own material security is the work of false prophets and diviners (Jer 29:8).

There are plenty of congregations that find themselves in neighborhoods they no longer recognize as their own, but who believe that the neighborhood needs them. Jeremiah would point out that they also need the neighborhood. In planting gardens, building houses, and forming relationships in the neighborhood, the church becomes itself. The church learns from its neighborhood how to be the church. Psalm 66:1-12 praises God as the one who "turned the sea into dry land" (vs. 6) so the people could pass through. The church needs to be a path-clearer for those in the community and beyond who live in places of pain, isolation, and abuse, for those who struggle to get by. The church ought to be the tenth leper, expressing gratitude to God for Jesus' resurrected life and for our calling to participate in Jesus' suffering, overcoming presence in the world.

Gospel Implications

The original authors of Old Testament texts were not specifically thinking of Jesus when they spoke of God's character and actions. Still, as Christians, when we read certain Old Testament texts, we experience fresh ways to understand God working through Jesus. Several powerful images arise from these texts. We might think of Jesus incarnationally as a letter sent from God as we contemplate the Jeremiah text. We might think, when reading Jer 29:3-7, that Jesus himself is an alien in our world/city who makes himself at home and through the Spirit seeks our welfare. Jesus is our path to freedom from oppression and sin (Ps 66), and Jesus is the one who breaks our chains (2 Tim). Jesus ought to be the recipient of our gratitude for making us whole (Luke 17:11-19).

Jesus is a letter sent from God to people in exile. Jesus is the Word made flesh who dwelt among us. He took to heart the advice of Jeremiah to make himself at home in a foreign land. Jesus is our path through the waters of death into the embrace of God in this life and in the next. God guides the community's future. These texts point to a hope of future glory (2 Tim 2:10), but also to a present reality. Jesus is the now unchained Word of God who empowers us, in the particular cities in which we find ourselves, to learn from him how to live for the welfare of the community that surrounds us.

Notes

Joerg Rieger, *Grace under Pressure: Negotiating the Heart of the Methodist Traditions*, 2011.

ALYCE M. MCKENZIE

JOERG RIEGER

Proper 24 [29]

The Lessons in Précis

A theme that ties these texts together is the accessibility of God's law and the practical resource it is for daily life.

> *Jeremiah 31:27-34.* Jeremiah asserts the old adage that the descendants will suffer the consequences of the sins of their forbearers. Then he overturns it by proclaiming a new covenant in which God's law will be in our hearts and God's forgiveness will wipe the slate clean.

> *Psalm 119:97-104.* The psalmist sings a song of praise to God's law, as he meditates on its role in providing understanding, self-discipline, and joy in his life.

> *2 Timothy 3:14-4:5.* God's word is useful for teaching and training in righteousness. We need to proclaim it in both favorable and unfavorable times and settings.

> *Luke 18:1-8.* The parable of the widow and the unjust judge cuts two ways. It points to our need to be persistent in petitioning God for justice. It also points to the need for those in authority to act on behalf of the poor because it is in keeping with God's will for justice.

Theme Sentence

God helps us to fulfill the law. The law, by its accessibility, removes our excuses for not responding. God's law is written on our hearts (Jer 31:33), sweeter than honey to our mouth (Ps 119:103), and useful for teaching, correction, and training character (2 Tim 3:16). Our persistence in seeking justice is energized by God who, unlike human authorities, makes justice for all people a priority.

A KEY THEOLOGICAL QUESTION

While theologians have at times played law and grace against each other, there is something powerful about God's law. It has grace-like qualities in that it not only makes demands but also encourages, empowers, and motivates. The visions that God's law puts before us provide new perspectives and sustain the hope that a new world is possible.

There is a deep tension addressed by the topic of the law that is often overlooked. While the opposition of God's law and God's grace may not be as stark as we once thought, God's law is in constant opposition to the laws of the status quo. The texts of this week share an awareness of this particular tension, as they realize in their own ways that there is something countercultural about God's law. The texts in Jeremiah and Psalms remind us that there are enemies and even wise people who have no understanding of God's law. As a result, those who follow God's law live in tension with the status quo, as they are wiser than the wise and more insightful than their well-trained teachers.

This opposition of God's law and the laws of the world results in constant tensions and distortions. Due to the allures of the dominant culture, which determines the lives of the majority of people, turning away from God's law and rejecting sound teaching is always an option. To complicate matters even further, sometimes it is not so easy to distinguish God's law from the laws of the status quo or to distinguish sound doctrine from myth. And even the teachers of the church can be bought, as 2 Tim 4:3-4 reminds us. While one of the marks of God's law is that it is at work through grace, the dominant state of affairs offers another sort of dynamic that is not only powerful but that also sometimes disguises itself as God's grace.

One of the most profound problems for theologians has to do with the fact that even our most cherished traditions and doctrines are influenced by the powers that be. From the earliest beginnings, for example, our images of Christ have been shaped by the powers of empire. While the early Christians emphasized the difference between the top-down power of the empire and the bottom-up power of Christ, it is not hard to see the temptation to interpret the power of Jesus in terms of the power of the status quo. The challenge was to understand the myths of the Roman Empire about Caesar as Son of God, Savior, and object of faith in tension with Christian understandings of Jesus as Son of God, Savior, and object of faith. The good news is that the powers that be never managed to take over the Christian faith completely and that Christianity was able to give birth to alternatives to the empire (Rieger, 2007).

The counter-cultural message of Christianity in the context of the Roman Empire is that God's law is very different from Roman law. It respects the "least of these" and the last, rather than those who put themselves first. The justice of God's law is available freely through grace, the grace of God. The justice of the law of the Roman Empire, on the other hand, is available only through a system of merit, privilege, and wealth. God's law is accessible to the poor, but Roman law is accessible primarily to the educated or wealthy elite.

God's law as grace turns the tables on status quo law, not only in the ancient world. In our own time, being able to afford a good lawyer, to influence the elections of judges to the bench, and to hire lobbyists that negotiate with lawmakers, provides clear advantages. These are some of the methods currently used to maintain the status quo, which allows the rich not only to maintain their wealth but also to get richer as the poor grow poorer. That this status quo is often endorsed as the law of God demonstrates the depth of the tensions discussed above and the timeliness of our theological discussion.

In this context, the story of the widow and the unjust judge gains new power. Perhaps the most surprising thing in this story is the persistence of the widow. The law appears to be on her side, but in a system where the law is in the hand of unjust judges, there is little hope that justice will prevail. What is it, therefore, that inspires her to go on insisting that justice be done?

There seems to be something in the law itself that inspires the widow not to give up, to keep fighting. This dynamic consistently unfolds when people understand that justice is on their side and that the way things are is not right. There are many examples of this dynamic in U.S. history, from the struggles for voting rights by women and African Americans who understood that democracy could never be restricted to the privileged, to the struggles for eight-hour workdays and pension and health benefits by labor unions that understood that the wealth produced by people's work needs to be distributed in ways that benefit everyone.

Although this is often forgotten today, Christianity was involved in the particular struggles for justice listed here and in many others, as

God's law has repeatedly inspired people to work for equality, the fair distribution of resources, and the general appreciation for the contributions made by those who are often overlooked.

A PASTORAL NEED

There is good news in this text for those who feel trapped in patterns they did not create—the "law of the status quo." Our text from Jeremiah sounds on the surface like bad news. We are all responsible for our own sins. But there is good news within this text that carries a liberating message. The patterns and conditions of those who have gone before us, those who have shaped our context, do not hold our fate in their hands. God's grace and law working together can break the hold of the law of the status quo. There is a chance that people can break free of cycles of poverty and abuse. Just because the fathers have eaten sour grapes doesn't mean the children's teeth have to be set on edge. The covenant God made with Moses and the Israelites was a gift to them to show them wisdom and justice. The new covenant Jeremiah describes will convey God's forgiveness to their hearts, the seat of both emotion and decision-making. It will be freely offered to everyone. Jeremiah eloquently described God's forgiveness and the fresh start God was offering to the people.

As Christians we affirm that in Jesus's life, death, and resurrection, God offers us forgiveness and empowerment to live lives devoted to the welfare of others. It will not be necessary to pester God for this gift, as the widow pestered the judge. God will empower us to create anew. The experience will not be one of eating sour grapes and having our teeth set on edge, but one in which, as 2 Timothy describes, we teach our children the message of salvation through faith in Jesus Christ mediated through scripture, and they receive it and believe it from generation to generation (2 Tim 3:14,15).

ETHICAL IMPLICATIONS

It is helpful, up to a point, to be told that we need to replace negative habits of thought and life (eating sour grapes) with a focus on the commandments and law of God. It's helpful up to a point to hear that if we change our thoughts we can change our future and our outward circumstances, as Jeremiah tells his people that they are now responsible for their own sins (Jer 31:30). But not everyone has the luxury of changing their circumstances by simply changing their thoughts. We are all influenced by our contexts. The more resources one has, the more influence one has to shape one's circumstances.

Many people live lives that are severely limited by poverty and the accompanying lack of health, resources, and opportunities. How would we preach the value of an inward covenant to them? Psalm 119:103 says, "Your word is so pleasing to my taste buds—it's sweeter than honey in my mouth!" How would that text be good news to someone who is physically hungry?

Our texts from Luke (widow and the unjust judge) and 2 Timothy (instructions for young preachers) offer some encouragement to people whose teeth are still set on edge by the sins of others. They hold out the hope that God, unlike the judge in the parable, will respond because God is just, not because God is pestered. They encourage integrity, patience and commitment in one's ministry. John Wesley believed that there is no personal holiness that is not also social holiness. So the inward covenant flows outward to affect our manner of living in the world. Abiding by God's law written in our inward beings means fostering opportunities for education, work, adequate food, housing, and health care for those whose teeth tingle from sour grapes they have not eaten.

Gospel Implications

These texts offer us images for the human condition and images for the liberating actions of God. Images for the human condition include the sound of the munching of sour grapes (Jer 31:29), the sound of the stone tablets breaking as they fell from Moses' hands (Jer 31:32), the feel of one's teeth on edge after eating sour grapes, and the feeling of itching ears (2 Tim 4:3).

Images for God's liberating actions include the psalmist's feet being held back from evil (Ps 119:101), the words of God's law as honey to the psalmist's mouth (119:103), the visual of words written on our hearts (Jer 31:33), the sound of the widow's feet trudging back and forth to the judge's door and her incessant knocking (Luke 18:3), and the vision of God's word useful for training in justice and righteousness (2 Tim 3:16).

As a preacher, I appreciate the sensory imagery for our human condition. These images express that there is something radically askew with human nature. It takes different forms in individuals and groups. Some need help restraining destructive behavior. Others need courage and confidence to oppose mistreatment. Still others need incentive for good behavior and encouragement in difficult times.

Sensory imagery is used to convey the character and actions of God in these texts. God is, in these passages, both our judge and our savior. Jesus Christ is God's Word placed in our hearts, sweeter than honey, on whom we "meditate day and night," whose guidance equips us "for every good work" (2 Tim 3:17, NRSV).

Notes

Joerg Rieger, *Christianity and Empire*, 2007.

ALYCE M. MCKENZIE

JOERG RIEGER

Proper 25 [29]

The Lessons in Précis

The common theme running through these texts is deliverance, whether from transgressions (Ps 65:3), plagues and military destruction (Joel 2:25), or the lion's mouth (2 Tim 4: 17).

> *Joel 2:23-32.* God promises to repay the people for all their sufferings, never allowing them to be put to shame again, and pouring out God's spirit on them (vv. 28-29).

> *Psalm 65.* Psalm 65 is a song of praise and thanksgiving to God for forgiveness of the nation's iniquity (v. 3), for acts of deliverance (v. 5), and for acts of creation (v. 6 ff.). Verses nine through thirteen describe God's blessings in terms of the flourishing of nature's bounty.

> *2 Timothy 4:6-8, 16-18.* Paul speaks of being deserted by everyone but God, who rescued him from the lion's mouth.

> *Luke 18:9-14.* This text is the parable of the Pharisee and the tax collector. One cannot receive God's deliverance unless one is willing to divest oneself of the arrogance of the Pharisee and stand with those who, though not valued by society, are valued and welcomed by God.

Theme Sentence

God delivers the persecuted. All of these texts make this affirmation in the face of definite appearances to the contrary: a nation's exile in Joel and an unjust trial in 2 Timothy. It's not enough to stand on the sidelines talking God up. God calls us to be agents of divine deliverance by divesting ourselves of arrogance and espousing the identity of those viewed as "children" in our societies.

A KEY THEOLOGICAL QUESTION

The message of deliverance proclaimed by these texts constitutes an important building block of the Judeo-Christian traditions. This fact is well-known, and few would contest it. What is less well-known and more contested, however, is how broad and deep this message of deliverance is.

God's deliverance is proclaimed not only in the dynamic of the person and work of Jesus in the New Testament but also in many of the dynamics of the Old Testament. Joel's vision of God pouring out God's spirit on the people describes an act of deliverance. Nevertheless, this act of deliverance benefits not only the insiders but also the outsiders; even the slaves, located at the very bottom of society, are included (Joel 2:28-29). This was unheard of in the ancient world. Even today, when contemporary theologians tend to celebrate equality, the radical nature of this promise is easily missed. When God's spirit is poured out on the "least of these," the privileges on which many of our communities are grounded are deconstructed.

Commonplace assumptions about leadership and the organization of the church will have to be rethought. Pouring out God's Spirit in this way is bound to lead to the deliverance of those to whom we habitually fail to pay attention. When this deliverance happens, the shape of our communities and the world will be renewed.

Moreover, God's deliverance does not stop with familiar communities but reaches and awes "those who dwell on the far edges" (Ps 65:8). Instilling awe in those who live far off can, of course, be accomplished in various ways. Empires throughout history have sought to instill awe in people. The Romans attempted to extend their empire to the ends of the earth. A recent military doctrine developed in the U.S. in 1996 is titled "shock and awe" and is based on the use of overwhelming power on the battlefield in order to destroy the enemy's will to resist. Dominant models of globalization follow similar trajectories, while using soft economic and cultural power, rather than hard military power, to awe people (Rieger, 2010).

While all empires promise deliverance and peace, God's deliverance is different. God's deliverance promises genuine hope for those on the periphery, who often do not benefit from the gains of the center. Following the psalmist, what would it mean to say that God's deliverance is "the security of all the far edges of the earth, even the distant seas" (Ps 65:5)? Unlike the deliverance promised by empires, God's deliverance is effective even for the "least of these," who have rarely benefited from the schemes of the powerful, not only in the world but also in the church. While God's deliverance would not necessarily end the churches' outreach programs and missionary efforts, it challenges us to rethink them from the bottom up.

One difference between the messengers of God's deliverance and the messengers of the deliverance of the powers that be is that God's messengers often stand alone, deserted, as the author of 2 Timothy notes. Unlike the false prophets who are celebrated and revered in every age because they support the dominant flow of power, true prophets are recognized by their courage to proclaim God's deliverance from the dominant flows of power that keep people down. True prophets can be recognized because they do not stand above the struggles for deliverance but proclaim their message in the midst of them. Thus they are frequently in need of being "rescued from the lion's mouth" (2 Tim 4:17). False prophets, on the other hand, hardly experience substantial challenges because their message proclaims the things that the powerful want to hear. This dynamic can be found in many places in both the Old and the New Testaments and throughout the history of the church.

How broad and deep God's message of deliverance is can finally be seen in the parable of the Pharisee and the tax collector (Luke 18:9-14). Neither Pharisees nor tax collectors were the heroes of the messianic deliverance preached by the Jesus movement. Pharisees were part of the religious status quo that resented Jesus' good news of deliverance and attempted to stop him. Tax collectors were collaborators with the Roman Empire, increasing the burdens on people in their own ways rather than exemplifying deliverance. The good news of this parable is that even those who are the representatives of the empire can be delivered from their bondage to the status quo and become agents of change. The tax collector recognizes his sinfulness and that his life falls short of what it might be, which is remarkable, as those in power rarely see so clearly what is going on. Nevertheless, the power of God's deliverance is at work even in this seemingly hopeless case. If even tax collectors can be delivered, begin to work for justice (Luke 18:14), and follow Jesus, then perhaps it is not too late for Pharisees either.

Realizing the breadth and depth of God's deliverance finally brings us back home into our own communities. If God's Spirit is poured out on the least of these, if it reaches the ends of the earth, if it rescues prophets from destruction, and if it is at work even in the representatives of the status quo, we should never give up the expectation that God can also make a difference in our churches.

A PASTORAL NEED

The authors of our four texts this week all witness to God's deliverance. God's deliverance takes several forms: forgiveness of the nation's sins (Ps 65), a future outpouring of the Spirit (Joel 2), rescue from the lion's mouth (2 Tim 4) and mercy for the sinner (Luke 18).

The author of Psalm 65 has written a psalm of praise that is grateful and joyful. He seems to be in a place of consolation in happy circumstances, "How happy is the one you choose to bring close, the one who lives in your courtyards!" (v. 4). What about those not chosen and brought? Is God's deliverance for everyone, or just those who have the right clothes to come to church? Some in the congregation might have a hard time hearing this unremittingly happy psalm. At least it does imply that there have been other times when the psalmist prayed and wasn't certain there would be a response (v. 2).

Likewise, the author of Joel seems to be in a spiritual state of consolation. And yet it is somewhat precarious. He has a sense that the present good times are to pay them back for past suffering. And the future outpouring of the Spirit will be the preface to the day of the Lord, a day of vindication for some but of judgment for others. The good news is that God's deliverance benefits those who have, up to now, been on the edges; God's Spirit will be poured out on those whom some might not expect to receive it.

The author of 2 Tim 4:6-8, 16-18 is at the end of his earthly life. His mood is a mixed one. He feels contentment at having fought the good fight. He is confident that God will vindicate him for his life of sacrifice. He is sad that his friends deserted him at his trial (v. 16), and he is certain that God will rescue him and allow him to enter God's heavenly kingdom (v. 18). He seems to be in a place of spiritual consolation in threatening circumstances.

In each case there is gratitude but also acknowledgement that deliverance is subversive of the status quo, a sense that deliverance discombobulates tidy worldviews. God chooses on whom to pour out God's spirit and whom to forgive. There is a sense that deliverance always faces fresh challenges; the statement, "The Lord will rescue me from every evil action" (2 Tim 4:18), sounds like there are more troubles to come. God's deliverance comes in dangerous situations. It is daring. It is undaunted. It is not over.

ETHICAL IMPLICATIONS

We are to call upon the name of the Lord. We are to be grateful for God's bounty. We are to expect God's Spirit to be poured out on everyone, not just the usual suspects. The daughters, not just the sons; the old men, not just the young men; the slaves, not just the free. We are to give God the praise that is due (Ps 65:1). We are to join creation in praise of God. Like the tax collector in the parable from Luke, we are to be humble and realize our need to repent. We are to assume that God can be at work in a group of people on whom we normally look down. In Jesus' day, people looked down upon, in fact detested tax collectors, and with good reason. They respected the Pharisees, again, in some respects, with good reason.

The original listeners to this parable would have been very surprised to observe in it a Pharisee, a respected, well-intentioned leader of the day, portrayed so negatively. Yale professor emeritus and preacher William Muehl (1994) once preached a sermon on the parable of the Pharisee and the tax collector entitled, "The Cult of the Publican." In it he observed that the tax collector's abject, head-bowed posture was just the first step in the pilgrimage of faith. If that is as far as the tax collector ever got, we'd quickly tire of him. Getting stuck in the "Lord, be merciful to me a sinner," doesn't lead to fighting the good fight, keeping the faith, and finishing the race. We are delivered to do something. By the grace of God, we are empowered to do something, to move beyond the prayer of confession to the life of action.

GOSPEL IMPLICATIONS

Testimony to the liberating acts of God abounds in these texts. In Psalm 65, God chooses us and brings us into God's courts. But God also speaks and reveals Godself to those beyond the divine courts. To me, perhaps the most joyful line in the psalm is this: "Those who dwell on the far edges stand in awe of your acts. You make the gateways of morning and evening sing for joy" (v. 8).

The reader of Joel is reminded of Pentecost in reading the prophecy that God will pour out God's spirit on all flesh (Joel 2:28). In 2 Tim 4:6-8 and 16-18, the author recounts, with obvious pain, how his friends deserted him at his trial. He tells of his forgiveness of them and affirms his faith in God. He claims for himself the identity of one who has fought the good fight, finished the race, and kept the faith (v. 7). God speaks to the ends of the earth; God pours out God's Spirit on everyone, not just a few. And, in the fullness of time, God comes to teach and to heal.

Notes

Joerg Rieger, *Globalization and Theology*, 2010.

William Muehl, "The Cult of the Publican," in *A Chorus of Witnesses: Model Sermons for Today's Preacher*, 1994.

ALYCE M. MCKENZIE

JOERG RIEGER

PROPER 26 [31]

THE LESSONS IN PRÉCIS
The theme of these texts is the need to approach present sufferings and afflictions from a standpoint of faith in the hopeful future God offers communities.

> *Habakkuk 1:1-4; 2:1-4.* Though times may seem hopeless, the righteous stand at their watchpost and work for and await a hope-filled future, since God has promised that "there is still a vision for the appointed time" (2:3).

> *Psalm 119:137-144.* In the midst of troubles and anguish, God's reliable promises and guiding commandments are our delight.

> *2 Thessalonians 1:1-4, 11-12.* The author praises the Thessalonians for their steadfastness and faith during their persecutions and afflictions.

> *Luke 19:1-10.* In Habakkuk God tells the prophet to station himself on the rampart, so Zacchaeus, a wealthy social outcast, stationed himself where he could see Jesus. Zacchaeus' response to Jesus' inviting himself to dinner was to divest himself of wealth gained at the expense of others.

THEME SENTENCE
Christ restores true life. God's saving action in Jesus Christ is our beacon of hope. In times when our community suffers from a lack of vision and hope, God calls us to the watchpost to work and wait for the deliverance we proclaim in the cross and resurrection of Jesus Christ. We are called to climb the tree with Zacchaeus, to see the face of Jesus Christ, and to hear his voice calling us to repentance and discipleship.

A KEY THEOLOGICAL QUESTION

Unlike contemporary theologians of the bubble, the ancient theologians at work in these texts know that trouble is real. It is precisely within these troubles, however, that they find God at work. This awareness of trouble changes their theological approach, since there are no easy solutions and there is no easy way out. Bubble theologians work the other way around: blissfully unaware of the real world of trouble at work outside their safety zones because they never leave the protective structures that shelter them. It is easy for them to proclaim that God is in charge.

The so-called Prosperity Gospel in its various forms is a case in point: unaware of the real-life struggles of working people, the unemployed, and the homeless, it is not hard to proclaim that God has things under control and wants to make everybody rich beyond their wildest dreams. Mainline theologies often operate in such bubbles as well, since mainline communities tend to constitute fairly homogeneous bubbles and allow for diversity only in so far as it does not challenge the dominant perspective. In this context, severe trouble remains the trouble of others, and it never gets to touch directly the heart of one's own work.

Hope in this latter model is grounded in pride (Hab 2:4): the insiders have made it to wealth and power, and so they assume that everyone can do the same. Moreover, if there are some who do not attain these things, it is quickly assumed that this is their own fault. Blaming the victim and seeking fault with those who struggle and suffer is an often overlooked, theologically significant consequence of bubble theology. How many people in our churches would agree that the poor are just not working hard enough, that they are inherently lazy, and that they have caused their own problems? The solutions in this model are always simplistic and are mostly developed on the backs of those on the underside, while the work of God is seen as upholding the status quo.

Hope in the earlier model, where theologians have gotten to know the depth of real trouble, is different. It is grounded not in pride but in patience that waits for God (Hab 2:3). In this context, the victims are not blamed; instead, their struggles and sufferings become the point of reference for observing the work of God. Rather than seeking God in the status quo, these theologies seek God in terms of the difference divine action makes in people's lives. "What difference does God make?" is an appropriate question here. At that point, even the most theoretical systematic theologies will have to become specific and talk about what

God is doing in actual situations of suffering and distress, or they lose any value.

In this context a different understanding of God's work can emerge. Aware of suffering and distress, the psalmist notes the particular character of God's righteousness. Not surprisingly, bubble theology has co-opted terms like "righteousness" and interpreted them in narrow religious categories. When viewed from the perspective of trouble, however, God's righteousness cannot be compartmentalized any more: either it makes a difference in all of reality and in all of life, economics and politics included, or it is not worthy of God.

Both the Greek and the Hebrew terms for *righteousness* are better translated as *justice*. God's justice is holistic, as it keeps running up against the justice of the status quo. The psalmist, in the midst of "stress and strain" (Ps 119:143), understands this, and so does the Apostle Paul, who notes the persecutions and afflictions of the earliest Christian communities (2 Thess 1:4). The justice of God that becomes visible in the steadfastness and faithfulness of the Thessalonians rubs up against the justice of the Roman Empire. That the Romans persecute Christians and even decry them as atheists is no accident or mistake. After all, the Romans had no problem with the deities of many other religions. The Christian God was different, as this God challenged their notions of god and therefore their notions of justice.

The Zacchaeus narrative illustrates what is at stake in these tensions between two very different theologies, and it shows us what God's justice looks like. Keep in mind that this story plays out in the real-life tensions between the privileged and the underprivileged, the elites and the common people, and there is no easy reconciliation. The encounter of Jesus and Zacchaeus does not play down these tensions. Neither does this encounter end in an endorsement of wealth and privilege and in blaming the victims, which is what the crowd might have feared (Luke 19:7) and what has unfortunately often happened in the history of the church as religious leaders have met with the elites. Rather, the encounter of Jesus and Zacchaeus begins with a stunning commitment by Zacchaeus that points out and at the same time deconstructs elite status: "Look, Lord, I give half of my possessions to the poor. And if I have cheated anyone, I repay them four times as much" (v. 8.).

The Zacchaeus narrative shows how God's justice becomes real in the real-life tensions between the privileged and the underprivileged, which mark the sites of real trouble. Salvation is the difference that God makes in this context, and this is the reality that is missed by bubble theology. While this latter theology is constantly struggling to prove its relevance, a battle that is often lost then and now, the relevance of theology that seeks to identify God's work in the midst of trouble is never an issue.

A Pastoral Need

How do we approach sufferings from the standpoint of faith? How can we believe in a hopeful future in the midst of a world filled with injustice? In a Sunday school class studying the Life of Paul, I brought up the affirmation of Acts and Galatians that God has a plan for the redemption of the world through the church. "Well, that's a pretty tough sell these days," said one class member. "There are a lot of things that contradict that belief." And she is right. It is. Appearances certainly seem to be to the contrary.

That's why it's good that the biblical canon contains a persistent prophet like Habakkuk. We need a prophet who is willing to stand at his watchpost until God gives him an answer to his complaint. He reminds me of Job. And, like Job, he gets his answer. In the readings from Psalm 119, 2 Thessalonians, and Luke 19, I can picture the psalmist, the author of Thessalonians, and Zacchaeus joining Habbakuk as he stands at his watchpost. They each have a concern about their futures. They are all praying for something, and God answers each prayer.

The author of Psalm 119 speaks out of a situation of anguish. He says that, while God is righteous, he himself is "insignificant and unpopular" (v. 141). And then he affirms God's promises to guide and to save.

The author of 2 Thessalonians prays that God will make the Thessalonians "worthy of [God's] calling" (1:11), and then he praises the Thessalonians for keeping the faith in tough times.

Zacchaeus, short of stature and short on friends, climbs a tree to see Jesus. And then Jesus invites him home to dinner, which prompts him to make a very generous annual pledge.

Each of these people is asking, in their own way, what to do with their futures. The answer is trust in God's future. To do that, they must first deconstruct false notions of God's future (bubble theology). God's future is not the Prosperity Gospel's idolatry of financial wealth or some magical promise of protection from all misfortune.

ETHICAL IMPLICATIONS

The message of these texts seems to have something to do with perseverance, with persistence in seeking the vision. Habakkuk makes his complaint and refuses to take silence for an answer. He stands at his watchpost, stations himself on his rampart. Finally, the Lord assures him that he has a vision that involves the vindication of the righteous and the receiving of just deserts by the arrogant wealthy who oppress others. This text is about persistent prophetic witness to God's work for justice in the world and to that which is not just in the world. It has to do with keeping the vision before us.

The same can be said of Psalm 119:137-144. The psalmist praises God's righteousness and laments the fact that his foes "have forgotten what [God has] said." Yet he does not forget God's precepts, despite the fact that he is "insignificant and unpopular" (v. 141). Even when "stress and strain" (v. 143) come over him, God's commandments are his delight. His focus is on a vision of God's righteousness (justice).

"Paul" in 2 Thessalonians praises God for growing the faith of the church. He prays that God will "fulfill by his power every good resolve and work of faith, so the name of our Lord Jesus may be glorified" (2 Thess 1:11-12, NRSV). The author keeps before him a twin vision of the Thessalonians' steadfastness in present afflictions and the future glory they will share with Christ. He gives thanks for their persistence in the context of God's faithfulness, which is another way of saying God's persistence.

As for Zacchaeus, it took some persistence, perhaps, to climb that tree. But we don't really know how the story came out. We don't really know if Zacchaeus followed through on his dramatic promise of Luke 19:8.

The ethical challenge to us is "Will we?"

GOSPEL IMPLICATIONS

The psalm promises that God's promises have been tried and tested (119:140) and that God's righteousness lasts forever (119:142). Clearly this is the case when we look at the Old Testament. God makes many promises—to stand by God's people, to forgive, to bless—that God fulfills.

When we think about the connections we discern between this text and our Christian hope in Christ, we affirm that God's promises come to us in Jesus Christ, God's eternal Son who embodied righteousness and justice while on earth and faced the bitter consequences. By the resurrecting power of God, through the person of the Holy Spirit, he is here to embolden us to do the same. As Christians we affirm that Jesus embodies God's vision for our future. There will be a great reversal, and for that time we need to prepare. Zacchaeus was on the right track. In preparation for the accounting to come, we can join the author of 2 Thessalonians in asking that our God will make us worthy of God's call and will fulfill by God's power every good resolve and work of faith, so that the name of our Lord Jesus may be glorified . . . according to the grace of our God and the Lord Jesus Christ (2 Thess 1:12).

ALYCE M. MCKENZIE

JOERG RIEGER

Proper 27 [32]

The Lessons in Précis

Haggai 1:15b-2:9 God speaks a word of encouragement to the people of Judah through the prophet Haggai. Even in the ruins of the temple, God reaffirms the covenant of God's unending presence and promises to rebuild the temple to its previous glory.

Psalm 145:1-5, 17-21 The Psalmist praises the works of God that are witnessed throughout the generations and gives thanks for God's continuing presence.

2 Thessalonians 2:1-5, 13-17 In the midst of persecution the people are reminded of God's continuing presence through Jesus Christ. Comfort comes in the presence of God.

Luke 20:27-38 Jesus' answer to the Sadducees' questioning of the resurrection moves beyond their limited understanding of the resurrection as just another state of life that mirrors this age. In the resurrection, death is destroyed. Therefore God is the God of the living and not of the dead.

Theme Sentence
The triune God sustains God's people. The biblical texts focus on God's edifying and sustaining presence with God's people even in the midst of ruin in Haggai and the psalm, and persecution in Thessalonians. Jesus proclaims that through the resurrection even death cannot separate the people from God's sustaining presence.

A KEY THEOLOGICAL QUESTION
The Triune God

The lections for this week invite us to reflect on God's sustaining presence and the depth of being that is God in God's own self. Who is this God, who is ever-present, sustaining, and strong to save? This is the Trinity, the fullness of God's own inner life. From the richness of God's inwardness of mutuality and joy, the love and power and presence of the One-in-Three overflow and are poured out toward all creation and humankind. We see signs of this in the created order and in human history. God's sustaining presence is thus an ongoing gift, given and attested across the generations, in Israel's history, in sacred scripture, in the person and ministry of Jesus Christ, and in the continuing work of the Holy Spirit in and through the church.

In Haggai, the prophet communicates the eager concern of God for God's people in a time of trouble. "Be strong," the people are told—even as they stand among the rubble of their temple, the ruins of their memories and identities. "Be strong," and "work, *for I am with you*" (emphasis added). God calls to mind the unbreakable promises of the covenant, the depth of commitment God shows generation after generation. The exodus is remembered (Hag 2:5), the great determinative moment of liberation in Hebrew history. In the same way that eucharistic prayers, in Christian worship, recall salvation history in part to assure us that God will be with us now and in the future (just as God has been with us in the past), so too God, through Haggai, recalls the covenant and renews the promise: "my Spirit stands in your midst. Don't fear." Peace and restoration and—especially—a sense of place and home are promised. The home that is the fullness of God's life, the triune life, is filled with the power that can make right even that which has gone badly wrong. Even the exile and the post-exilic return to rubble cannot thwart God's covenantal purpose to draw God's people into reconciliation, hope, and participation in the life of God.

In the Luke passage, Jesus points back to the exodus as well, evoking now the memory of Moses before the burning bush (Luke 20:37). Here God the Father calls to Moses, commissioning him to undertake a ministry of prophetic leadership that will serve God's purposes of liberation. In Moses' work we see the power of the Holy Spirit, enacting God's will and purposes that always lead to life. The God of the covenant heard Israel's suffering in Egypt and saved them (Exod 2:24). So also, this God of the living reaches into the suffering situations of all people and seeks to redeem them.

In the overarching scheme of history, the salvific work of Jesus Christ, by the power of the Holy Spirit, is eternally at work to save, heal, redeem, and transform. The occasion of the encounter with the Sadducees provides Jesus with an opportunity not to debate a fine point of marriage laws or eschatological speculation (or doctrine, or ethical codes) but to point backward to salvation history (via the evocation of Moses) and forward to the fulfillment of God's purposes (for to God "they are all alive"). The abundant life that God desires for humankind and all creation (John 10:10) is the very life of the triune God. It is into this life that we are invited, a life characterized by mutuality, freedom, justice, joy, and overflowing love for all around. This is the fullness of life, the consummation of God's desire, which the sustaining presence of God always seeks and enables.

The latter portion of the 2 Thessalonians passage celebrates this gift of life. Thanks are due to God who "from the beginning" has chosen and called God's people "through the sanctifying work of the Spirit" (2:13 NIV). This sanctifying and vivifying work of the Holy Spirit binds us to Christ, whose glory we may share. That glory is not a matter, however, of elevation to an exalted throne: it is the glory of self-giving love, the glory of witnessing to the truth about God's love in Jesus, the glory of joy in seeing others thrive and delight in God's presence, the glory of being free from fear and compulsion. This glory, which we find through intimacy with Christ, will "encourage [our] hearts" and give strength. Again, the fullness of the triune life overflows towards us, enfolds us, and invites us in.

How does this make sense for the church of today? We may not be arguing about multiple marriage partners (as in Luke) or struggling with a return from exile (as in Haggai). We are, however, living through an age of overwhelming change in our cultural contexts and in what it means to be Christian communities. Survival and transformation are watchwords. If the old days of the church are over, what will be next? In many places, there is real fear about such issues.

Thus we need all the more to proclaim that God's covenantal promises and enduring presence remain in the church today. These are gifts that are given each new day to sustain (and embolden) us for Christ's mission. The fullness of God's own inner triune life is the sign and the pattern for us of the life God desires: joyful, free, mutual, self-giving, loving, reconciling. God desires that we seek this same fullness of life and love among and for our neighbours and, yes, even our enemies. Across the generations, God does not give up on us and does not abandon us.

Ever-present, faithful, trustworthy, and true, the triune God's overflowing love toward the world draws us in and sends us out, in the power of the Holy Spirit and in the name of Jesus.

A PASTORAL NEED

Although God sustains God's people through every intersection of life, during times of hardship it can feel like God is absent and unconcerned with humanity. In order to reclaim the sustaining presence of the triune God in the midst of loneliness, suffering, disease and even death, the preacher must remind the congregation of two things. First, pain and suffering are not signs of God's punishment. Second, being a disciple does not mean that God will make life free from trouble. Instead, God sustains God's people in the midst of tragedy, pain and death. Through it all God does not leave us alone.

"I am with you," is the most announced theological promise of God in the Bible. From the time of Adam and Eve to the Hebrew people's journey in the wilderness, to the exile, to the birth of Jesus Christ, Emmanuel—God is with us. God's sustaining presence is not a trite saying but a real promise that should be proclaimed concretely throughout the sermon. The teenager who feels like no one understands her needs to hear that God knows her heartache of isolation and loneliness. The man facing disease needs to hear that God through Jesus Christ knows his suffering and pain. The anxious mother-to-be needs to know that the Holy Spirit will sustain her in her uncertain future. In times of loneliness, uncertainty and tragedy, we must proclaim that the triune God does not leave us alone.

ETHICAL IMPLICATIONS

God's sustaining presence means that we can live a life of determined hopefulness even in the midst of difficulty and pain. God's goodness and mercy endure even in the darkest of hours. When my father was facing the end of his life, he reminded the physicians and his family that God was not going to leave him alone in his final days. When the doctor told him that there was nothing that could be done for him, my father responded by saying, "The Lord is my shepherd and Jesus Christ is my savior." In the dark valley of the shadow of death, my father spoke those words over and over to himself and to those of us who listened. My father was a witness to the promise of God as spoken through the prophet, "my spirit stands in your midst, don't fear" (Haggai 2:5b). The knowledge and remembrance of God's sustaining presence can carry us through the most difficult of days.

God's sustaining presence also serves as a model for our own ministry with others in pain and distress. Because the triune God is with us, we can be present with others. In difficult situations we might retreat to the use of trite phrases and clichés. Instead of speaking unhelpful words that offer little comfort, it would be better simply to be present with the person in need. There are no words that can console someone in distress more than the unspoken presence of a loving friend. The sermon can remind hearers that trite phrases do not help, and that being present to others in their times of need is often greater than any words spoken.

GOSPEL IMPLICATIONS

We can often think of the distress and worry of life as signs of God's absence. We can preach about God's salvation that leads to the goodness of life and neglect the very presence of God in suffering and pain. Matt Maher's song, "You Were On the Cross," asks God, "Where were You when all that I've hoped // Where were you when all I've dreamed // Came crashing in shambles around me" (Maher, Butler, Assad, 2010). The answer comes in that Jesus was on the cross. The good news is that God does not avoid our sufferings but goes through them with us. The passion, suffering and death of Jesus on the cross remind us that God through the Holy Spirit is intimately located within the very places of our own suffering and pain. Through the cross we can believe in God's connectivity to our sorrows.

Conversely through the resurrection we can believe God's promise of new life. In the resurrection of Christ, God destroyed the power of sin and death. God may not take away hardships, but God will sustain us through them. In the resurrection God makes a way through suffering and death that leads to new life.

Notes

Matt Maher, Audry Assad and Kenny Butler. "You were on the Cross." EMI Christian Music Publishing, 2009.

ROBERT W. BREWER

ROBERT C. FENNELL

PROPER 28 [33]

THE LESSONS IN PRÉCIS

Isaiah 65:17-25 God creates new heavens and a new earth where there is joyful and abundant life for God's faithful servants. This alternate reality is a future and yet present promise.

Isaiah 12 Isaiah's song of praise anticipates God's redemption. This is a future-oriented and hopeful declaration of God's promised salvation within the present situation of distress and destruction.

2 Thessalonians 3:6-13 Paul exhorts believers to follow his example of hard work and self-sufficient living. Paul encourages the believer not to grow weary in the midst of persecution while waiting for the day of the Lord.

Luke 21:5-19 Jesus warns the hearers not to be led astray by false prophets proclaiming the arrival of the end of time. Wars, famines and trials are inevitable but Jesus exhorts the hearers not to be afraid, because God will not abandon them to this destruction.

THEME SENTENCE

God gives hope in the midst of distress. The promised future of God's salvation offers hope to those who live in places of calamity, turmoil, and destruction. The biblical texts this week speak to the hope that comes from the certainty of God's redeeming future that is being revealed in the present.

A Key Theological Question
Christian Hope

We live in an age and a cultural milieu in which hope is dearly needed. There is trouble at every turn: nationally and globally, in towns and cities, on farms and in homes, and within ourselves. There is so much suffering, so much pain; we continually see and hear people despairing and giving up—or wanting to find something to hold on to. We all need hope—in this life and for the next. We need hope to believe that relationships can be mended, that jobs will be found, that wars will cease and abuse will stop. But the hopes raised by political systems and cultural panaceas are continually dashed. Where, then, can substantial and empowering Christian hope truly arise?

Hope, when it is grounded in the gospel of Jesus Christ, *is the persistent, enduring, and trusting expectation that God's will shall be done.* It is not hope for a somewhat better life. It is not even hope for the best possible outcome that we can imagine. Christian hope is far more daring, far more vulnerable, and far more faith-filled, for it relinquishes control and turns final outcomes over to God. Christian hope arises not through our own power, which disappoints and is always inadequate. Rather, hope emerges through the combination of God's promises and their fulfillment. God, who has been true to us in the past, will surely be good to us in the days ahead.

God's promises and their fulfillments are seen throughout Scripture. The promise contained in the rainbow (Gen 9:12-17) finds consummation in God's voice through Isaiah, announcing "a new heaven and a new earth." There, no one will ever again hear the sound of weeping (65:17, 19). God's profound care will endure and become all the more obvious: "Before they call, I will answer," God says, and "while they are still speaking I will hear" (65:24). In John's Revelation there is yet another vision of this new and consummated creation. God's faithfulness, in promise and fulfillment, is the foundation of our hope.

For this reason, our trust in God to deliver is reassurance and joy to us. Thus Isaiah can say, "God is indeed my salvation; I will trust and won't be afraid" (12:2). Fear can be set aside—together with anxiety and restlessness about the future. This is especially pertinent in times of chaos, destruction, loss, and grief. In congregations today there is no shortage of these. Jesus addresses such realities, both personal and communal, in the reading from Luke. Amid natural disaster, apocalyptic upheavals, and persecution, Jesus announces this incredible promise: "not a hair on your heads will be lost" (Luke 21:18). God is attentive and loving toward us. Above, beneath, and beyond our troubles is the God of all ages, Creator of all that is, in whose hands are time and eternity. God is trustworthy and sure. Jesus elsewhere tells us that even the smallest birds are fed day by day, and God works to make the flowers beautiful, even though they do not last and are destined to be burnt (Matt 6:26-29).

In communities of faith, the articulation of hope is key. On a personal level and in our social arrangements, hope is elusive but profoundly longed for. The culturally-captive, shallow hope we find in television, films, pop songs, and common conversation is a sugary, thin hope that makes promises it cannot keep. It is "bad medicine." The words of hope we share with one another as people of faith, however, are rooted in thousands of years of God's loving action, even in the midst of much trouble and suffering. We also are written into salvation history, and rightfully take our place as heirs of God's purposes. We have good reason to hope for the fulfillment of God's promises, for eternal life, for redemption, for the renewal of the whole creation, and for final overcoming of all powers and forces that deal in destruction and opposition to life.

God's life and work in and through Jesus Christ signal the best of all the reasons for our hope: God loved the world (the whole cosmos) so much, that God was not prepared to leave it in sin and sadness, alienated from God's purposes (John 3:16). The healing and liberating work of Jesus announces the inbreaking realm of God, where all harms shall one day be healed. The resurrection is the first fruits of that realm, the sign of eternal life promised to all persons.

In many cases, the fulfillment of God's promises will mean disruption for us. The resurrection is the ultimate disruption—infusing meaning into a situation of confusion, unseating sin and death, defeating the final power of evil. Disruption is often, perhaps even normatively, the nature of God's fulfilled promises. God's goodness and love disrupt history in order to bring the fullness of God's plans to completion. Beyond what we can imagine or construct ourselves, mature Christian hope is founded here: upon God's good and loving plans.

Our persistent trust and hopeful expectation are therefore oriented toward God's will for justice, peace, reconciliation, and joy. In the fullness of time, all that is broken in the relationships among God, the earth, and persons will be restored and transformed. This fulfillment of God's purposes will surely be consummated in the power of God and in God's time. Christian hope is the confident expectation that God's will shall prevail; for God, nothing is impossible. So, "Let's hold on to the confession of our hope without wavering, because the one who made the promises is reliable" (Heb 10:23).

A Pastoral Need

There are many situations in life where people want to give up: a mother trying to raise a teenager who seems to never listen to her advice, a father seeking a job without any hint of an interview, a family losing their home in the middle of a terrible economy, a boy bullied at school because he does not fit in with the rest of his classmates. Even if we are not aware of it, there are people in the congregation who are going through something that makes them want to give up. They need to know that there is hope; that God has not abandoned them to languish in the uncertainty and distress of their lives.

People need to know that the present trials will not last. In the midst of exile and persecution, Isaiah proclaimed a future founded on the faithfulness of God to bring salvation and redemption to God's world and God's people. Jesus told his disciples of a time of tragedy and destruction yet exhorted them to endure until his return. People need to know that there is a future beyond the present hopelessness and that the future belongs to God.

The promise of God's redemption does not belong only to the future. In order for hope to be real for those who are at life's edge, the sermon must proclaim the future promise as a present reality. Hope is not just a forward looking expectation of God's redemptive salvation, but a present power that enables people to endure.

Ethical Implications

As followers of Christ we are called to live lives undergirded by hope. But in order for hope to be viable, it must include a healthy understanding of life's messier conditions. The biblical texts do not shy away from naming the ills and sorrows of life. Hope does not negate or ignore injustice and pain. Hope does not negate sin. Instead hope, based on the faithfulness of God in Jesus Christ, has greater power and longevity. Hope outlasts sin. Hope outlasts despair. Hope never fails. Therefore, the sermon should name the personal and structural injustices of the world and proclaim with confidence and certainty that nonetheless God's will shall prevail. This hope is not an optimistic outlook that everything will be all right, but a theological certitude that God's promise of life has the final say.

This hope that undergirds the Christian life motivates us not to be satisfied with the current situations and injustices of the world. You might remember in October 2010 when 33 miners in Chile were rescued from a collapsed mine after spending more than two months underground. Rescuing the men from almost half a mile underground seemed nearly impossible. Yet what motivated the rescuers to search and the miners to survive was hope. The makeshift rescue site was transformed into, "Camp Hope," and the families, rescuers and miners never gave up. Hope empowers us to rescue the lost, feed the hungry, shelter the homeless, visit the sick, and love the unlovable. Hope motivates us to work for a better tomorrow. The aim of a sermon about Christian hope should empower the listeners to seek justice, do mercy and walk humbly with God (Mic 6:8).

GOSPEL IMPLICATIONS

Each of the biblical texts is heavily weighted by the underlying reality of difficult and tumultuous conditions in the world. The promise of a better future is always countered by the present reality that we are not there yet. Because of this, the sermon can easily dwell too long in the difficult realities of our world without an equal and compelling proclamation of the gospel. In the sermon a significant amount of time should be spent on the proclamation of hope that is rooted in the faithfulness of God as shown throughout the Old Testament and in the life of Jesus Christ. God's promises and their fulfillment can be recounted in the sermon through remembrances of the covenant, the wilderness journey, the exile and the good news of Christ's life, death and resurrection.

Hope is also rooted in the promise of Christ to come again. The return of Christ is not just a future oriented event but a present reality. As Jesus told in a parable, if we care for those around us, then without even knowing it we tend to Christ in our presence (Matt 25:31-36). The present hope is that the Christ who will come again is already in our midst.

ROBERT W. BREWER

ROBERT C. FENNELL

Proper 29 [34]
[Reign of Christ]

The Lessons in Précis

The Reign of Christ celebrates Jesus as the ruler of all. Jesus' reign brings salvation and peace.

> *Jeremiah 23:1-6* Jeremiah relays the judgment of God on the shepherds (i.e. rulers) who have led God's people astray. The blame of the exile is placed on these leaders. God will tend faithfully to the flock by raising up a new righteous Davidic king.

> *Luke 1:68-79* The song of Zechariah proclaims the coming of a Davidic ruler who will lead the people in the ways of peace.

> *Colossians 1:11-20* Paul proclaims the supreme authority of Christ. Through his life and death, God reconciles and makes peace with all things in heaven and earth.

> *Luke 23:33-43* Jesus, who is labeled and mocked as a king, hangs on a cross flanked by criminals. In this crucifixion, Jesus gives a place in paradise to one hanging beside him.

Theme Sentence

Jesus, the crucified and sovereign King, brings salvation. Jeremiah and Zechariah prophesy about a godly ruler who will bring salvation and peace to God's people. Paul preaches that through the dominion of Christ, God makes reconciliation and peace possible. Upon the cross, the crucified King extends salvation to a criminal at his side.

A KEY THEOLOGICAL QUESTION

Jesus Christ as Sovereign

Here at the end of the liturgical cycle, we stand poised to enter the new season and new church year. We celebrate this "other" new year's eve not with champagne but by honoring Jesus Christ as sovereign.

On one level this is a strange and counter-intuitive moment in the ebb and flow of time, even church time. Our attention is already becoming seduced by the commercial festivities and demands of the early twinges of the Christmas rush. Full parking lots, parades, decorations, twinkly lights are all cresting the horizon of our cultural landscape.

So what sense does it make to speak of Jesus at this moment in our very worldly lives, let alone to speak of him as a "king"? The massive secular machinery of advertising, buying, and selling kicks into high gear this time of year. We are distracted. Furthermore, we struggle with the very concept of kingship, especially in nations with no recent or positive history of monarchs, and in all the ways we resist hierarchies and unjust power. Stretched even more, we are asked by scripture to understand this defeated man, crucified at the place called "Skull" (Luke 23:33) as *the* king, the Lord of the ages. It is truly a spiritual challenge to let this enter our hearts. Then, the Luke passage recounts the mockery and rejection Jesus received at the time of his death. Only a convicted criminal seems to respect him. Is this really our king?

Perhaps we find it easier simply to set this aside, to let that claim about Jesus' sovereignty just wash over us. After all, who of us could stand before such a king as this, shamefully taunted and rejected as he is? He does not look the part: he does not lord it over anyone; he does not hand out goodies to sycophantic subjects; he does not lead an army to rout the oppressor. He does not triumph, or tax, or oppress, or insist on his prerogative. When he dies, as Michelangelo's *Pieta* depicts him, he lies limp, splayed out in his mother's arms, helpless, unhelpful.

Our Christology is always challenged by this scene. This is hardly a triumphant Christ, resplendent in glory. This does not seem to be, by any human standard, the Lord of the Ages, Creator of all, Alpha and Omega. The Christology we need to take seriously in the crucifixion is that of the Servant King. This is the God of vulnerable, self-giving love. The very life of the Son of God is here crushed by sin, apparently defeated by evil. Here we see that God's agape love is poured out in weakness, not in irresistible power. No wonder we find such a Messiah to be disorienting, even a stumbling block. To call him "Savior" counters not only the logic of the world but even our own hopes for a mighty deliverer.

On Reign of Christ Sunday, to proclaim this Jesus as the sovereign of heaven and earth is to proclaim a different kind of power: that of self-emptying for the sake of others' flourishing. It is power marked not by pride but by humility, and by love that "does not insist on its own way" (1 Cor 13:5, NRSV).

Jesus' kind of kingship is in fact servanthood: he bends to wash the filthy feet of his followers, rises to serve at the table so that others might eat, heals sickness and casts out demons, raises up the lame, and gives sight to blindness—all for the sake of the abundant life he came to bring. Jesus will not let us forget that we are beloved in the sight of God: in the heart of God, you and I are beloved. We may be conflicted, ambivalent, impious, and spiritually adrift—full of hope and ambition and sin and grace—but in all this we are altogether delightful in the heart of God, who loves us with an undying love.

In the suffering, death and resurrection of Jesus Christ, the work and presence of God lie hidden. Paul writes, "God was reconciling the world to himself through Christ" (2 Cor 5:19), but on the cross this is not immediately evident by human standards. Indeed, the mystery and the abyss of the cross "silently [suggest] that God is most hidden at the moment of fullest disclosure" (Dillenberger 1953, xiv). Perhaps, strangely, it is only through the revealed/concealed presence of God in Christ that we may grasp God at all—or indeed that God may grasp us. It is only through faith in Christ (not logical conclusion or the weight of evidence) that we begin to perceive God's intent and to receive our salvation. Only in discerning God in Christ, even in the horror of torture and execution, can we set aside the human desire for victory and vengeance, and learn mercy and forgiveness.

Through the Holy Spirit's gifts to us, as we align ourselves with the self-giving love of Jesus Christ the sovereign of the cosmos, the smallness of our concerns is taken into the greater mission of God. God desires nothing less than the redemption of the whole world, the righting of every wrong, the overcoming of every war by peace, the renewal of the face of this scarred and beautiful earth. Therefore our discipleship and our tribute to the Servant King become a matter not of unavoidable subservience, but of conformity to a joyful way of self-giving love.

A PASTORAL NEED

The imagery of Christ as a king who sits in glory can seem far removed from our struggling world and busy lives. On this day, we need to know that God does in fact rule. We often portray a bright and victorious image of Christ sitting on a throne in royal regalia. We decorate the church with white and gold and sing hymns that crown Jesus with many crowns. All of these images might be appropriate, but they miss the underlying irony of Jesus' form of kingship. Therefore as we preach we need to remember the kind of king Jesus embodied. We remember that this king did not come to sit on a throne but to hang on a cross. This king treated the outcast and poor as part of his royal family. This king invited the lame, the lost and the least to his banquet table. This king welcomed a criminal into his kingdom while dying beside him.

Our congregations need to know that Jesus is not a far removed king on high, but a king who humbly bends himself into our brokenness so that we might be saved. We cannot relegate Christ's kingship to a throne in heaven. As our scriptures indicate, Christ displays his kingship in his service to others and in his death on a cross. In this servanthood and life-giving love, Christ reigns. In the sermon, we can proclaim the presence of Christ our King in the difficult, struggling, and painful places of our world.

ETHICAL IMPLICATIONS

When we proclaim Jesus to be King and Sovereign Lord of all, we are making not only a theological statement but a political one. Politically, we are proclaiming that any allegiances we might have, whether to family, community, country, or creed, are secondary to our allegiance to God. We proclaim that the way of Christ takes precedence in our lives. Theologically, we are pledging our allegiance to a God who comes as a servant who gives himself away so that we might be saved. Christ is not like the tyrannical and oppressive rulers of our world. Jesus does not hoard power for himself. Instead Jesus gives away his power so that those who are powerless, lowest, and lost might be lifted up as heirs in his kingdom.

A sermon about the Reign of Christ can remind our congregations that the Christ to whom we pledge our allegiance is not like a tyrannical worldly ruler. Jesus did not come to control but to save. And if we vow to follow this Christ as our King, we also vow to live in the ways of his kingship. This means that we do not need to seek power for ourselves but seek to empower those around us. This means that the greatest power we have is to give ourselves to the service of our neighbors in need. This means that we do not seek to dominate or oppress or force others to be like us, but instead, through love and graciousness, invite others to share in the mercy and compassion of God. The ways of Christ's kingship are humble, gracious, loving, self-giving, merciful, and invitational. When we encourage our congregations to follow in the ways of this king, then we are leading our people into the realm of God.

GOSPEL IMPLICATIONS

A sermon about the Reign of Christ cannot avoid the fact that this king was killed on a cross. In the Gospel reading Jesus is crucified with a sign above his head that mocks him as a king (Luke 23:38). Ironically, a criminal is the only one aware of the truth behind this mockery, and Jesus offers him a place in paradise (Luke 23:40-43). When we recognize the reign of Christ in his death on a cross, then we re-envision the meaning of authority that comes in selfless love.

Although the crucifixion stands as the primary symbol of Christianity, the cross cannot be separated from the resurrection. In rising from death, Christ reigns victorious over the powers of sin and death. Yet this victory is not about domination but about the power of love. Not even death can overcome the love of God in Christ. Because of the resurrection Paul can proclaim, "I'm convinced that nothing can separate us from God's love in Christ Jesus our Lord: not death or life, not angels or rulers, not present things or future things, not powers or height or depth, or any other thing that is created" (Rom 8:38-39).

Notes

John Dillenberger, *God Hidden and Revealed: The interpretation of Luther's deus absconditus and its significance for religious thought*, 1953.

ROBERT W. BREWER

ROBERT C. FENNELL

ALL SAINTS DAY

THE LESSONS IN PRÉCIS

Although we remember and give thanks for the saints, we should focus our attention upon the God of Jesus Christ who empowers us all to live saintly lives.

> *Daniel 7:1-3, 15-18* Daniel's vision of four terrifying beasts allegorically points to conquering kingdoms that rise and fall around Israel. Daniel foretells that the holy ones will prevail and inherit the kingdom of God.

> *Psalm 149* With new songs of praise in their throats, the faithful execute the judgment of God upon the kings and nobles of unfaithful nations.

> *Ephesians 1:11-23* Through the power of Christ the faithful believers have obtained an inheritance of salvation and redemption, sealed by the Holy Spirit.

> *Luke 6:20-31* Jesus tells his disciples that the heirs of the kingdom of God are the poor, the hungry, the mournful and rejected. Being rich and full does not mean one is blessed or faithful.

THEME SENTENCE

God empowers the faithful. The faithful saints are portrayed throughout the Bible as those who are oppressed (as in Daniel) or those who are meek and hungry (as in Luke). It is through the power of Christ, that people are called to the rightful place as saints of the kingdom.

A KEY THEOLOGICAL QUESTION
God's Communal and Personal Call

The lives and work of the saints, their courage, faith, and sense of vocation, all inspire and evoke gratitude in us. Each of us, whether or not we readily suppose ourselves to be "saints," has a place in God's designs, a vocation to fulfill. Part of the Christian Way is to discern, in community, our life's purposes and our communal and personal calling. Whether it is church ministry or a secular vocation, particular acts of bold justice and reconciliation, or a life of quiet, prayerful giving, the deep meaning of life emerges in the encounter of God's call, the world's needs, our community's charism, and our own gifts and abilities.

So whom does God call and empower? We have many stories and memories of charismatic and remarkably gifted persons through whom God has worked dramatically. But God also calls the unlikely and unnoticed. God has much in store for those who are not the front-and-center, obvious choices for contributing to the purposes of Christ's mission in the world. God does a great deal through the faithful service and willing hearts and lives of the "quiet saints"—ordinary people whose love and goodness make a real difference in the world. Those on the margins are also especially welcome in God's economy of salvation—the "poor, hungry, weeping, and reviled" in Luke's account—whereas the "rich, full, and well spoken of" inherit only woe. We may hasten past the poor, but Jesus won't let us do that if we truly listen to him. In his Kingdom, the least are deeply loved; the last are first.

Among the unlikely people God called in the past, Israel comes quickly to mind. In their long history, the Hebrew people were rarely at the top of the heap. Surrounded by hostile foes, compromised within by ineffective and sinful leaders, plagued by unfaithfulness, and frequently overrun by invading armies, they were (are) nevertheless God's chosen people. It was the depth of God's covenant with the people that saw them through: God made them, loved them, called them, and sustained them. Their own power was never enough on its own. In the passage from Daniel, the "holy ones of the Most High" are to "receive" and "hold . . . securely forever" the kingdom, even though they were at that moment captive to a foreign power. The evocative, even hallucinatory character of the visions throughout this part of Daniel elicits incredulous responses from readers and hearers today. (Indeed, they even terrified Daniel, see 7:15, 19.) In the midst of a massive national disaster, these visions pressed God's people again and again to see and understand that God had not abandoned them and was in fact calling them to be part of

God's purposes. So too the Holy Spirit calls, empowers, and emboldens us, even when things look very bad (7:25). Every follower of Jesus, every "saint," is chosen, equipped and beloved. Every heart given to God's purposes has a special place in the work of Christ.

Later, the stories of the first Christians show us again that God chooses unlikely people. Without substantial financial or political power, with at best marginal social status, and facing the hostility of other religious groups, the Christian movement had to rely on the grace of God simply to survive. Again, God made them, loved them, called them, and sustained them. We think of the many women in the early Church who became public leaders despite social barriers. Even Saul/Paul, the persecutor, became Christ's special emissary.

God's mercy and power worked through such persons, empowering their witness and filling them with a Spirit of joy to persevere. In Ephesians, we overhear the kind of encouragement that early Christian leaders offered to those facing their troubles: the author reminds them that they have been "destined according to the purpose of [the One] who accomplishes all things" (1:11). Their role (and ours) in God's work is strengthened by "the hope of God's call . . . and the overwhelming greatness of God's power that is working among us believers" (1:18-19). In all we do for God's sake, we are not alone, nor dependent merely on our own abilities. The Holy Spirit makes it all possible, guiding, inspiring, nourishing, renewing.

We can bring to mind the saints of today—ordinary people of all races and classes, in circumstances of struggle or of ease, in "successful" churches or those that seem to be declining, people with many resources or none. Most of their names will never be known beyond their own community. Yet it is God who calls and empowers all, with a variety of gifts, and enables all to serve God's greater good: thus together we "were given one Spirit to drink" (1 Cor 12:13), the Spirit who both challenges and liberates us to serve with love.

Looking to scripture, to the Church's past, and to our companions on the Way reminds us that God is at work in countless ways. Our own individual calling, whatever it may be, is also part of God's plan and purposes, interlocking with the calling of our communities. There is peace in knowing that through all expressions of vocation, God's designs are fulfilled. We have much to offer, by the power of the Holy Spirit, and every small or large contribution we make flows into a larger purpose. As John Bell of the Iona Community in Scotland said, "it is not principally in the mighty [that] God puts his faith. It is you whom God encourages, trusts, enables, relies on: you in whose hearts God has kindled the fire of love and the yearning for a better tomorrow" (Bell, 2009).

A Pastoral Need

One this day when we speak of "saints," we often think of those who have gone before us who have had great courage and strength. We think of the venerated like St. Augustine and St. Francis, or we think of modern leaders like Dietrich Bonhoeffer, Rosa Parks and Martin Luther King Jr. Although we rightly remember those who have had a significant effect upon the world, the individualization of heroic and saintly accomplishments can lead our congregants to believe that they have to be extraordinary individuals to be called by God.

Many in our congregations do not feel worthy or qualified to be considered among the great saints that God has called to action. On this day, the sermon can remind the hearers that God often calls the poor, the hungry, the weak, and the lost to fulfill God's purposes. Most saints were not powerful or exceptional people. They were the poor, the weak and the hungry who faithfully responded to God's call. If the sermon envisions saints as those whom God calls to fulfill God's purposes in this world, then being a saint has less to do with the person than it does with the God who calls and empowers all people. The sermon can therefore focus on God's empowerment of all the saints. Those who might feel unworthy need to be reminded of the scriptural promises that say, "I can endure all these things through the power of the one who gives me strength" (Phil 4:13) and "all things are possible for God" (Matt 19:26).

Ethical Implications

The call of God does not always have to be an individual call, but a call that manifests within a community of people, particularly the church, the body of Christ. Remembering the saints should not relegate God's call to the few, but should remind us that God calls everyone to respond to the needs of the world. Paul's imagery of the body of Christ (1 Cor 12) is not about individuals working independently but about each part working with another to form the whole. God calls people to particular tasks so that will complement and benefit the work of another. The sermon can encourage the hearers to respond to the call of God as a church for the greater good of the community and world.

Blake Mycoskie felt called to begin a shoe company in 2006 after seeing children go without shoes while on a mission trip in Argentina. Blake's vision was to give one pair of shoes away to children in need for every pair of shoes sold by the company. The first few years were difficult and the company did not make a profit, but the call to serve children compelled Blake to continue this compassionate model of business. Today the business is a success not only in profitability but in the fact that it has given over a million pairs of shoes away to children in need. Blake's call to give shoes to those in need formed this business, but Blake was not alone. Blake had a team of people working with him and thousands who bought shoes from his business because they followed the same call to help children in need.

GOSPEL IMPLICATIONS

The sermon can rightly celebrate people who have lived faithful and saintly lives, but it is important to remember that it is through the power of God in Jesus Christ that people are lifted into saintly lives. Jesus lifted up the poor and the lowly so that they might live fully. Jesus called tax collectors and sinners so that they might live into holiness. Jesus breathed the Holy Spirit onto his followers so they might forgive the sins of others. Jesus empowered his disciples so that they might make disciples throughout the world. Through his life and ministry Jesus called, encouraged, enlivened, liberated and sustained his followers to live into the life of faithful discipleship.

Jesus still empowers his followers today. The Apostle Paul prayed that those who believe might know the power of God as exerted in the resurrection of Christ (Eph 1:19-20). Through the life, death and resurrection of Christ, sin and death are overcome and all things are placed under the power and authority of Christ. The resurrected Christ continues to empower his followers to confront the ways of sin and death in this world, and in so doing live lives worthy of the saints.

Notes

John Bell, "The Fiscal & Military Impact of Advent: Sermon preached in St Salvator's Chapel, St Andrews on 13th December 2009," http://www.st-andrews.ac.uk/about/UniversityChapels/Preachers/2009-2010/JohnBell/ (Accessed 22 October 2010).

ROBERT W. BREWER

ROBERT C. FENNELL

THANKSGIVING DAY

THE LESSONS IN PRÉCIS
Remembering to be thankful for God's faithfulness and guidance is a central theme on this day.

Deuteronomy 26:1-11 This passage instructs the Hebrew people to give their first fruits to God as a sign of thankfulness for being brought out of slavery and into the land of milk and honey. Giving of the first fruits is to remember that all we have comes from God.

Psalm 100 The psalmist reminds us that a significant aspect of worshipping God is giving thanks for God's steadfast love and faithfulness.

Philippians 4:4-9 Paul believes that because of God's faithfulness and presence, the people of God can always rejoice and be thankful.

John 6:25-35 Jesus reveals to the crowd that he is the bread of life sent by God to sustain the world. The true life-giving source for the world is God's own self-giving love.

THEME SENTENCE
God faithfully provides all we need. Thankfulness is the main theme of the scripture passages this week. Thankfulness arises out of God's faithfulness as seen in the exodus account in Deuteronomy, God's steadfast love in Psalm 100, God's continuing presence in Philippians, and God's life sustaining provision in John.

A KEY THEOLOGICAL QUESTION
The Nature and Will of God

From the earliest ages, God's people have come together in worship to give thanks. Often those moments have been tied to seasons of plenty—harvest, for example. Those who today live closest to the land and sea are still cued to notice the seasons, the times of abundance, and the times of drought or unfruitfulness. When times come in which there is enough and more than enough, it is natural for us to want to give thanks to God. God has laid it upon our hearts that we are not alone and not the source of the grace that has come our way. That awareness is part of God's gift to us, drawing us into community with the triune God, with the earth, and with our companions along the way. We see in the harvest, but also in the ordinary times of goodness and sufficiency, that God's hand is guiding, blessing, providing.

As we uncover the layers of ritual and routine in our Thanksgiving celebrations, looking beyond decorations and favorite menus, we discover a deep truth about the nature and will of God: God regards human beings and all creation with care, compassion, faithfulness, and love. Noticing the fullness of God's love for the world, and God's provision for our needs, engenders trust and a generous response from us, especially in giving to those who go without.

The very acts of creation and redemption are invitations to trust in this ever-gracious God, who desires to bless us in every way. The lengthening days in spring, the growing crops in summer, the fruitfulness of autumn, and rest for the land in winter are gentle, annual markers of God's loving provision in creation. The miraculous structures of the molecular and sub-atomic universes give us ample pause to wonder at the mystery of God's love, expressed in the finest of details. The Psalms are full of delight in God's presence in nature (e.g. Psalm 104). The fullness of God's love expressed in the life, death, and resurrection of Jesus Christ, and the redemption and reconciliation he brings, are the most radical and wondrous signs of God's care and love for us. While we are still far off, even strangers, God runs out to meet us and embrace us. In Christ we are welcomed, embraced, set free, and sent forth with God's blessing of the Holy Spirit. We need do nothing to earn or deserve this love. It is the free gift of grace.

God's love is unfailing, and is seen in depth and across the breadth of salvation history and within our own life stories. In the passage from Deuteronomy, there is a description of a ritual returning of thanks. Core to that moment is the recounting of the Hebrew people's journey to Egypt to find bread, their enslavement there, and God's power that set them free. All who hear and read are invited in their spiritual imaginations to become that ancestor, that "starving Aramean." When God delivers Israel into the promised land "with a strong hand and an outstretched arm," they are struck by the sheer gift of their freedom. The returning of harvest's first fruits points, then, to something deeper than an annual ritual: it is a profound moment of gratitude, almost speechless gratitude, at what God has done for us. The basket of fruit (or whatever we give) is a token of that gratitude. It is a pledge that our labors and their results will be dedicated to God all throughout the year.

Looking beyond that ancient past and its pattern of storytelling and making an offering, we notice for ourselves the marks of freedom and bounty that God places all along the pathway of our personal journeys. It may not be literal manna from the sky as in the exodus, but for many there is great thankfulness in simply having bread on the table and a roof that doesn't leak. And Jesus, the bread of life, gives himself freely to us, always. At no point are we left all alone; at no moment does God abandon us.

As we receive these gifts and reminders of God's love and grace, our attention shifts to our human response. There is nothing we must do to earn God's love, but in the dynamic relationship of a family of faith, with God as our parent, we are called to respond with trust in God and generosity toward others. Every gift given with a good heart is welcome—from a widow's mite to a multibillionaire's endowment of a foundation for health care in a struggling nation. Thanksgiving moves us from passive reception of grace to active sharing of it with all around us. We celebrate God's goodness by learning to love those whom God loves.

One popular worship song describes the great love of God this way: "your love is amazing, steady and unchanging/your love is a mountain, firm beneath my feet" (Brown and Doerksen, 2000). From everlasting to everlasting, this God of care, compassion, faithfulness, and love is forever *pro nobis* ("for us"), shown most fully in the person and work of Christ. Thanksgiving provides us with a dedicated time to count our blessings, to give our first fruits to God, and to return thanks by seeking to share with and to bless others. God's desire is to see all flourish. Through our giving of thanks, of our prayers and songs, and of our material goods to bless others, God is glorified and all life is able to thrive.

A PASTORAL NEED

Thanksgiving is a time to pause and remember the gracious plenty that surrounds and sustains our lives, yet for many people giving thanks can be difficult. Although the sermon can remind the congregation that there is a lot for which we can be thankful, it must also address the real difficulties that undermine our ability to give thanks. It can be difficult to be thankful on the first holiday after a loved one is no longer alive. It can be difficult to be thankful when jobs are lost and prospects are few. It can be difficult to say thanks when families are fractured and holidays are no longer joyful. It can be difficult when someone is alone on a day when people are supposed to be together. Being thankful is not always an automatic or easy action, particularly when life does not produce opportunities that generate gratitude. Sometimes giving thanks to God must be an act of faith.

The sermon therefore should remind the congregation that being thankful does not arise out of our abundance or our condition. Being thankful arises out of an awareness of God's gracious love towards us. Being thankful is not about how we feel in the moment, but remembering that our lives are sustained by Christ who feeds us daily (John 6:35). Thankfulness comes from the very fact that God has made us and we are God's people and God's love for us endures forever (Ps 100).

ETHICAL IMPLICATIONS

When we remember the care, compassion, faithfulness and love that God has for us, then we can, like the Hebrew people, respond by giving to God a portion of what God has given to us. Thanksgiving reminds us that everything we have is a gift from God. Our world, our lives, our food, our homes, our material possessions and our money are all gifts that God offers to us. We are given the opportunity and responsibility in choosing how we might use these gifts.

I grew up in a home where my parents regularly and faithfully tithed a portion of their income to their church. They gave not out of obligation or fear, but out of a deep gratitude to God for all they had. Their gratitude compelled them not to cling to their possessions but to share them with the ministries of the church and with those in need. Jesus often spoke about giving away possessions and sharing the abundance with those who have nothing. A sermon on this day of Thanksgiving might speak to our relationship with the things for which we are thankful. Giving away a part of what we have is easier to accomplish when we remember that everything we posses is a gift from God.

Giving thanks on this day should also remind us to be thankful every day. A life of gratitude that grows out of the awareness of God's compassion and love for us can move us to be generous, gracious and forgiving. Being thankful can lead us to share our abundance with those in need. Being thankful can soften hearts hardened by disappointment. Being thankful can thwart bitterness and resentment. Being thankful can focus our lives upon the mercy and love of God in Jesus Christ, which then leads us to share that love and mercy with the world.

Gospel Implications
Thanksgiving celebrations arise from the bounty of harvest. This day is often commemorated by a feast of plenty with family gathered around the table. In a very similar way, we gather as the family of Christ each Sunday around a table to give thanks for the love and grace of God in our lives. Whether we celebrate weekly communion or not, the altar table stands as a central reminder of God's abundant and bountiful mercy towards us. A sermon about Thanksgiving might point to the feast that we celebrate in the Eucharistic meal.

When celebrating communion we repeat "The Great Thanksgiving" as we remember the faithfulness of God through history, particularly in the life, death and resurrection of Christ. At this table we give thanks for God's very own life that is given for our salvation and sustenance. At this table we are fed. A piece of bread and a sip of wine may not seem like a lot, but in this meal we remember the one who said, "I am the bread of life. Whoever comes to me will never be hungry, and whoever believes in me will never be thirsty" (John 6:35). In this meal it is right to give our thanks and praise.

Notes
Brenton Brown and Brian Doerksen, "Hallelujah (Your Love is Amazing)." Brea, CA: Mercy/Vineyard Publishing, 2000.

Robert W. Brewer
Robert C. Fennell

CONTRIBUTORS

Robert W. Brewer, Campus Chaplain and Instructor of Religion, Greensboro College, Greensboro, North Carolina

Stephen Farris, Dean, St. Andrew's Hall, and Professor of Homiletics, Vancouver School of Theology, Vancouver, British Columbia

Robert C. Fennell, Associate Professor of Historical and Systematic Theology, Atlantic School of Theology Halifax, Nova Scotia

Daniel E. Harris, C.M., Associate Professor of Homiletics, Aquinas Institute of Theology, St. Louis, Missouri

Scott Hoezee, Director of the Center for Excellence in Preaching, Calvin Theological Seminary, Grand Rapids, Michigan

Lucy Lind Hogan, Hugh Latimer Elderdice Professor of Preaching and Worship, Wesley Theological Seminary, Washington, D.C.

Duane Larson, Systematic Theologian and President (Retired), Wartburg Theological Seminary, Dubuque, Iowa

Jennifer L. Lord, Dorothy B. Vickery Associate Professor of Homiletics and Liturgical Studies, Austin Presbyterian Theological Seminary, Austin, Texas

David J. Lose, Marbury E. Anderson Chair in Biblical Preaching, Luther Seminary, Saint Paul, Minnesota

Colleen Mary Mallon, O.P., Associate Professor of Systematic Theology, Aquinas Institute of Theology, St. Louis, Missouri

Alyce M. McKenzie, Levan Professor of Preaching and Worship, Altshuler Distinguished Teaching Professor, Perkins School of Theology, Southern Methodist University, Dallas, Texas

Beverly Mitchell, Professor of Historical Theology, Wesley Theological Seminary, Washington, D.C.

Kevin J. O'Neil, C.Ss.R., Associate Professor of Moral Theology, Washington Theological Union, Washington, D.C.

Robert Stephen Reid, Director of the MA in Communication, University of Dubuque, Dubuque, Iowa

Joerg Rieger, Wendland-Cook Endowed Professor of Constructive Theology, Perkins School of Theology, Southern Methodist University, Dallas, Texas

Cynthia L. Rigby, W.C. Brown Professor of Theology, Austin Presbyterian Theological Seminary, Austin, Texas

Deanna Thompson, Professor of Religion, Hamline University, Saint Paul, Minnesota

Richard Topping, Professor of Studies in the Reformed Tradition, St Andrew's Hall, Vancouver, British Columbia

Mary Vanden Berg, Associate Professor of Systematic Theology, Calvin Theological Seminary, Grand Rapids, Michigan

James A. Wallace, C.Ss.R., Professor of Homiletics, Washington Theological Union, Washington, D.C.

Paul Scott Wilson, Professor of Homiletics, Emmanuel College, University of Toronto, Toronto, Ontario.

Scripture Index